TESTIMONIALS

Stop Justice Abuse should be read by all who are interested in preserving and improving our legal system. Many professionals working within the system wonder whether our justice system can survive if it continues in its current direction. The authors not only address major court problems from a consumer viewpoint, but offer unique solutions to strengthen our legal and correctional systems. Many suggestions in *Stop Justice Abuse* are worthy of the legal community's consideration as we attempt to implement changes and resolve the issues not only identified in this book but by our most eminent jurists and legal scholars.

Dale E. Hanst,
President, State Bar of California
1983-1984

Stop Justice Abuse is the best book I've ever read on the shortcomings of the justice system. It offers solutions that the common man can undertake. *Stop Justice Abuse* is a book people need to read. I would like to see a million copies in circulation. Better than good—it's great!

Paul Gann
People's Advocate

Stop Justice Abuse is a hard hitting fact laden excellent effort that points out how our complex legal system often fails to accomplish its intended purposes. As a police and public administrator I daily see examples where routine decisions of government hinge on the advice of attorneys, a process that needlessly escalates the cost of government. I recommend this book to law enforcement officers and the public at large.

Robert Owens
Police Chief

As a long time correctional professional, I understand the need to question and re-examine the justice system. The system must change to meet the needs of those served by it as times change. The justice system is too important for the public to ignore. It's time that we all get involved. This book provides an opportunity for criminal justice practitioners and the public to examine the complex issues facing the justice system. *Stop Justice Abuse* proposes logical and common sense recommendations for changing and improving the system. It is a **must read** book for all.

Cal Remington
Correctional Facility Manager

APRES LE JUGEMENT.

Drawings are by French artist Honoré Daumier.

STOP JUSTICE ABUSE

Exposes The Unfair System and
Proposes Action You Can Take

Eugene D. Wheeler

&

Robert E. Kallman

Pathfinder Publishing
Ventura, California

1986

STOP JUSTICE ABUSE

Exposes The Unfair System and Proposes Action You Can Take

Eugene D. Wheeler

&

Robert E. Kallman

cop. 2

Published By:

Pathfinder Publishing
458 Dorothy Avenue
Ventura, CA 93003, U.S.A.
1986

WE

DEDICATION

This book is dedicated to the public spirited citizens who have organized and raised their voices against justice abuses and worked to improve the American legal system.

ACKNOWLEDGMENTS

The authors wish to thank the many people and organizations who have helped them to gather information, graciously answered their questions, and explained the workings of the police, legal, and correctional systems.

Within the legal system we especially thank the following: lawyers Dale Hanst, Gerald Rose, Duane Lyders, Kris Kallman and Robert Stone; trial judges Lawrence Storch, William Peck, Bruce Thompson, Joseph Lodge, and Stephen Stone (later appellate justice); appellate court justices Herbert Ashby and Macklin Fleming; court administrators James Fox and Hank Rodgers; correctional manager Calvin Remington; and court clerk Robert Hamm.

Within the police system we thank Chief Robert Owens, Sheriff John Carpenter, and Assistant Sheriff Robert A. Edmonds.

From Victim/Witness Programs and Victim Organizations we thank Candy Lightner (MADD), Sandy Smith, Sterling W. O'Ran, III, Gary Longholm, and Richard Godegast.

Dr. H. Peter Metzger of the Public Service Company of Colorado, Dr. James S. Kakalik of the Institute of Civil Justice (Rand Corporation), public leader Paul Gann, State Farm Insurance Company (All-Industry Research Advisory Committee) James F. Perry, and the Defense Research Institute, Inc. were all helpful.

Of great help in reviewing concepts and editing the book were Eugenie Wheeler and Grant Heil. Kathleen Wheeler, Faith O'Leary, and many others kindly listened to our concepts and offered helpful suggestions.

Eugene D. Wheeler & Robert E. Kallman

TABLE OF CONTENTS

DISCLAIMER

This book is written to provide information about the subject matter covered. It is offered for sale with the understanding that the publisher and authors are not engaged in providing legal advice. No legal advice is offered or suggested. If legal or other expert advise is needed, the services of specialists in that particular field should be sought.

Stop Justice Abuse was written for the purpose of making the public more knowledgable about the workings of the legal and justice system. It does not attempt to offer readers advice on how to conduct their businesses or to handle their legal problems. The authors are not lawyers and are not attempting to practice law.

Despite all attempts to be as accurate as possible, mistakes in content and mechanical reproduction may have been made. No attempt was made to cover all issues or problems of the courts, but only the major ones as seen by the non-lawyer authors.

Pathfinder Publishing or the authors shall have neither liability nor responsibility to any entity or person with respect to any loss or damage caused or alleged to be caused directly or indirectly by the information contained in this book.

INTRODUCTION

Victims of Courts

We are all victims of the criminal and civil court system. If we have not been robbed, assaulted, raped, burglarized, or sued by someone, we have suffered by paying higher taxes for unnecessarily long, public-supported criminal trials, higher insurance payments due to excessive punitive court awards to civil plaintiffs, and a slow moving justice system musclebound by rules and procedures.

The American court system is basically a good one. Unfortunately, due to meddling by appellate jurists and abuses by a variety of interest groups, the court has become a legal Frankenstein. The court is abused by too many frivolous suits; litigants suing to find a 'deep pocket;' legislators passing too many poorly conceived, unnecessary, and complicated laws; irresponsible prosecutors, public defenders, and civil lawyers; jurists seeking social reform and the perfect trial; special interest groups using the court to achieve their goals; and the correction system releasing dangerous criminals prematurely without seeking restitution for victims.

We need an efficient system of justice that tries defendants swiftly, fairly, and protects the rights of offenders and victims equally. Instead, we have a slow moving system that seems to over-protect criminals at the expense of victims and the public. Civil litigants must wait three to five years to have their day in court. Most trials in state and federal courts take much longer today than they did ten years ago.

The costs of this ponderous, inefficient system are astronomical. Everyone pays. Monies that could be used for other needed services (including just plain keeping it in our own pockets) are squandered by a complex interrelationship among legislators, judges, lawyers, and correctional personnel. Many of the expensive so-called solutions to the logjam in our justice system do nothing but cause further complications.

There are sincere attempts by judges to improve conditions. Responsible and conscientious trial judges do try to speed up cases, but often have their decisions over-turned by appellate court judges searching for error and the perfect trial. The sophist attitude on the part of some jurists prevents the public and the offenders from receiving prompt justice. How long should the public continue to pay for inefficient courts?

The public suffers when convicted rapists, child molesters, and murderers are released prematurely into society by appellate judges because of minor legal technicalities. Is this fair to the victim, their families, and the public who suffer again at the hands of a paroled offender?

Why can the British impanel a jury for a major criminal case in an hour, while it may take us a month or more? In a recent case in Lancaster, California it took nine months to select the jury; and it cost the public a half million dollars before the trial even started.

Visit any law library or bookstore that specializes in legal literature. You will find books by judges and lawyers giving their versions of the problems of the system, but you will have difficulty discovering a title suggesting solutions. To bring effective changes to the justice system the drive must come from outside the system by non-lawyers. This book is addressed to identifying the major problems and constraints to better justice and offering achievable solutions to them.

To gain knowledge of the over-complicated justice system, the authors have studied and researched court problems for several years. They interviewed victims, witnesses, jurors, judges, prosecutors, public defenders, criminal and civil lawyers, public-interest lawyers, legislators, policemen, and correctional personnel to obtain their ideas for a better system. Solutions to court problems exist; but only the public, in cooperation with dedicated legal professionals, can put them into practice and improve the delivery of justice to all people.

CHAPTER ONE

A REFORM TOO FAR

Major changes were made in the court system as a result of the reform movements of the 1960's and the decisions handed down by the United States Supreme Court headed by Chief Justice Earl Warren. Before 1960 an inequity of justice did exist for a large percentage of the minority and low income population. Legislation and court decisions concerned with civil, minority, and economic rights made major changes in the court system.

For example, in an attempt to prevent the police from abusing the rights of accused offenders, the Supreme Court brought the exclusionary rule into practice. At first the police didn't believe that the court was serious about its new rules on obtaining evidence. To insure compliance the court said first that police shall collect evidence according to the rules; and second if they don't, the evidence will not be admitted in court. After many convicted criminals were released from prison because of evidence rule violations, the police became better trained and more careful. Other rules pertaining to an offender's decision to remain silent after arrest, access to an attorney, right to a law library, and many more were written. A number of reform-minded lawyers of the 1960's and 1970's became judges and used their positions to achieve social reform goals.

The use of the death penalty came under attack during this period. Rules were written on when and how the death penalty could be used. To insure that minorities and low income offenders were not imprisoned in violations of their civil rights, state convicts could ap-

MEN OF JUSTICE—Not a very satisfied client.

peal to federal courts. The number of suits escalated as a result. Previously, a convict had to exhaust his appeals in state courts before he could turn to the United States Supreme Court. Now a convict could look to a lower federal court after a conviction in a state court.

In some states, reform-minded jurists took federal court decisions and gave them an even broader application. For example, in California it is almost impossible to execute a person convicted of murder (no convicted murderer has been executed from 1967 to date). With built-in automatic appeals it costs about one million dollars to try a person for murder with the death penalty provision. A study in the State of New York found that it is cheaper to send a person to prison for life or for 40 years (cost $660,000) than to execute him (cost $1.8 million) because of the elaborate legal procedures in effect.

Public Revulsion

The public is impatient with the court system because the court reform movement of the 1960's and 1970's went too far. Anger over lenient court actions, including sentencing, has caused riots and even the beating of judges. In Hawaii, citizens enraged over a judge who gave a light sentence to a criminal beat the judge so badly that he was hospitalized and lucky to have survived. After a San Francisco court gave former County Supervisor Dan White a seven year sentence for shooting to death (involuntary manslaughter) the mayor and another supervisor, huge crowds rioted and caused over a million dollars in damage. The fact that White was paroled in less than five years and freed a year after that caused additional protests and unrest.

The trend in the courts to help the accused find someone else to blame for his criminal acts has brought about a public uproar. The New Jersey Supreme Court ruled that when you serve someone an alcoholic beverage, you become responsible for their actions, even to the extent that your guest can sue you for whatever crimes he may have committed.

For years the public, and even people associated with the courts including police, victims, litigants, prosecutors, and judges, complained about the slowness of the chaotic court system. Litigants and victims alike, after surviving a case in court, say they would never go through the process again. Many claim they will take the law into their own hands before trying to get justice in court. Currently, in ever-increasing numbers, citizens are seeking justice outside the present system. To obtain quicker decisions, many civil litigants are hiring their own judges and bypassing civil courts.

Employees of a large supermarket chain in Los Angeles were indicted recently for physically abusing and punishing shoplifters. A 68-year old plumber in Chicago fatally shot a young robber who stuck a gun in his ear in an attempted armed robbery. A man shot four youths who accosted him in a New York subway, and a motorist in the same city was beaten by a crowd after he ran down and killed a woman with his automobile. A Georgia man shot a burglar in the head; and a 78-year old Michigan woman shot and killed a youth who tried to enter her home. On the same day in Georgia, a man shot one of two burglars he surprised in his apartment. In Texas a woman saw two men forcing an elderly woman into the back of a car. She pursued the men, honking her horn for attention in a wild ride through suburban streets. A policeman finally stopped the fleeing auto and the kidnappers.

Are citizens taking the law into their own hands as an expression of frustration with the courts? Many signs indicate that they are. What would occur if no meaningful changes were made to improve the system in the immediate future? Let us look into the future at what could happen if businessmen, corporations, victims, police, and the public revolted against the court system.

Rebellion Scenario of the Future

Picture this scenario: Only big corporations, government agencies, the rich, and the penniless—who receive free legal aid—can obtain lawyers for their criminal and civil court work. Landlords and businessmen cannot afford to take nonpaying renters or customers to court. Court rules make it too expensive and almost impossible to convict shoplifters. In civil actions lawyer fees exceed the amount their clients receive. Bitterness toward the courts and lawyers grows rapidly among the public, property owners, businessmen, and professionals. Not trusting the courts any longer, companies and citizens take the law into their own hands as follows:

HIT AND RUN– BUTTE, MONTANA

Victor Edgar looks out his living room window to see a blue sedan side-swipe his parked pick-up. Remembering the television show he'd seen the night before on the lengthy delays of the justice system, Victor picks up his son's baseball bat, jumps into his wife's car and chases after the hit-and-run driver.

He catches the fleeing auto at a stop light. Like a bull, Victor leaps out of his car. He manages to break every window in the other auto and hit the offender several times before the terror-stricken driver can gun his engine and escape the revengeful hit-and-run victim.

PROSTITUTE ATTACK–
ALBANY, NEW YORK

It is evening. Barbara Jones watches through the window as a tight-skirted prostitute parades about on the corner in front of her husband's drug store. When two women friends join her, they converse tensely and go outside. Armed with a golf club, hockey stick, and jack handle, the three confront the prostitute. They order her to get out of their neighborhood. After an angry exchange of hostile comments, the prostitute refuses to budge. The three enraged women attack the stubborn 'shady lady,' beating her severely.

When the police arrive later, investigating officers ignore the woman's mutterings that "three housewives did it." The three women believe the prostitute will not ply her trade in their neighborhood again. Witnesses to the assault tell the police they didn't see a thing.

FURNITURE REPROCESSING–
SAVANNAH, GEORGIA

In Savannah, Georgia Bill Boyd, the credit manager at Southern Department Store, storms out of the store manager's office. He is tired of being blamed for deadbeats who repeatedly renege on merchandise payments. Most are not penniless or unemployed. The last straw is the arrogant Mrs. Oliver. She bought an expensive stereo set and would not make her payments. She was three months in arrears and thumbing her nose at him. Bill knew she had money from her credit references. Mrs. Oliver knew, as he did, that it would take reams of paperwork and months of effort to recover the merchandise through the courts.

From previous experience, Bill estimates the legal costs will run about four times the value of the stereo equipment.

Fed up with the cumbersome legal system, he orders a van with a driver and heads for Mrs. Oliver's showy house. The fact that no one is home does not bother the credit manager. He is not wasting any more money on extra trips or legal fees.

Bill breaks a window pane, releases the lock, opens the window and climbs into the house. An alarm startles the driver, but Bill pays no heed to it. He disconnects the stereo equipment and hands it to the driver through the window. After loading the van, Bill tells the driver, "that deadbeat won't steal from the Southern Department Store again."

SHOPLIFTERS PUNISHED–BOSTON

Tired of losing goods to shoplifters and of prosecuting them at great expense only to see them released again and again, the Great Wigwam chain of supermarkets takes direct action. One boy caught stealing $30 worth of candy is taken to a back room and forced scrub the entire store floor. Other juveniles caught repeatedly are roughed up.

The store takes pictures of men and women apprehended and places large photographs of them on a wall in front of the checkers and customers with a sign reading, "These are store thieves caught in the act."

DEFENSE AGAINST BURGLARS– WASHINGTON, D.C.

Court penalties against burglars become lighter and lighter. More and more people buy guns to defend themselves. In Washington, D.C. Alex Clark awakes with a start in his tenth floor hotel room. Someone is in his room. Thinking of the things he had heard about the rash of crimes and the court's softness on criminals, Alex takes his old army '45' automatic on trips. He quietly pulls the pistol from the holster beside the bed. His heart pounding, Alex reaches for the light switch and turns it on. Revealed in the sudden brightness is a man in a ski mask holding a flashlight.

The man swiftly pulls out a switchblade knife and rushes at Alex. With little time to think, Alex aims the pistol and pulls the trigger. The force of the bullet knocks the man back away from the bed. Alex thinks, "That burglar sure won't get probation."

POLICE INACTION–NATIONALLY

The police become more and more tolerant of the public's shooting of thieves, robbers, and burglars. They have no desire to start accused offenders through the legal process only to see them free on bail or out on a technicality a few days later. When police think a shooting or beating is justified, they give little aid to the district attorney's office in obtaining evidence for a prosecution. After a known rapist or offender is hurt, they are slow in calling for medical assistance. Shopkeepers receive free training from police on use of guns and defending themselves against robberies and assaults.

BUILDING PERMIT AVOIDANCE– EUGENE, OREGON

The legal process for obtaining a building permit for a fence or simple addition to a house becomes so complex and expensive that many citizens ignore the regulations. Sometimes trouble occurs as a result. George Watt's neighbor decides to build a tall redwood fence—without a zoning clearance—that cuts off his ocean view. George tries to stop his neighbor, but has no success. George knows it will take years and cost him several thousand dollars in legal fees to get the court to force his neighbor to remove or cut the fence down to the proper height.

When it is midnight, George checks over his chain saw and lugs it close to the fence. A neighbor's dog barks as he pulls on the starter cord for the first time. He quickly pulls again. This time the chainsaw roars into action. He starts cutting the top three feet off the fence. The noise is tremendous in the still of the night. Lights of adjoining houses flash on. Windows and doors open as people try to see who is making the noise. George continues to cut, determined to finish the job.

By the time his neighbor reaches the fence, George has restored his view and is retreating back to the house.

George is accompanied by loud oaths of vengeance, but he doesn't care. He has done it!

COURT REVOLT AND REFORM START– SACRAMENTO, CALIFORNIA

Finally, an incident in Sacramento triggers a nationwide revolt against the courts. The California Supreme Court, not believing in the death penalty, reverses a lower court on a murder conviction for the umpteenth time. The accused sadistically raped and murdered three young girls at a slumber party. One of the girls is a popular television actress. By now the rules of the judiciary have driven the average costs of a capital offense trial to over $3 million. This trial costs $6 million. The court rules that the police had not read the accused his arrest or Miranda rights correctly. Because the police questioned the murderer first and didn't tell him within ten minutes of his arrest that he had a right to remain silent, the State is ordered to retry him. The public, incensed at the court's action and another expensive trial, start a media writing campaign to reverse the court action.

Matters become worse when the Supervisors in the county where the murders took place, tell the court that they cannot afford to pay for another trial and are recommending that their district attorney release the murderer. The Court orders the Supervisors to pay for the new trial or go to jail for contempt of court. The Supervisors hold firm and disobey the order. The Court sends marshals to jail the Board of Supervisors. The public can't believe the arrogance of the high court.

Then the Court orders the State to pay for the new trial. The Governor, with support from his cabinet and a large group of legislators, refuses to pay. The state budget is depleted from paying out vast emergency funds to storm and earthquake victims, as well as other expensive trials. Many politicians recognize that the public is really angry this time and will not tolerate support of a vicious criminal by the courts.

The State Supreme Court orders the Governor and legislature to pay for the new trial or join the County Supervisors in jail. After great haggling and arguing among themselves, a slim majority of legislators refuse to pay. Most of the rebellious legislators are not lawyers. The Court, angry at the rebuff, orders the marshals to arrest the governor, his cabinet, and the legislators voting against the court order. The media comes from every part of the country to cover the crisis. Victim groups, police organization representatives, and citizens rush to the capitol by car, plane, and bus to support the Governor and rebellious legislators. As the armed marshals move toward the capitol entrance, the huge crowd surges around them yelling obscenities and telling them to "leave before its too late."

The two dozen marshals, frightened by the surging mass, draw their service revolvers. What happens next is not clear. Security police, massed at the capitol steps, charge toward the crowd swing their long clubs at the nearest heads. Several of the marshals fire their guns–some say into the air, some say into the crowd. Men and women scream in fear and pain as they are hit with the heavy clubs and bullets. More shooting occurs. Several people in the crowd fall, severely wounded.

The already aroused crowd becomes a hysterical mob. Some turning to run, knock down and trample those behind them. Some attack the marshals and police with their fists, feet, and any handy stick or stone. The assault is terrifying to witness.

By the time capitol police and highway patrolmen and local police can stop the crowd, two of the marshals are dead and more than twelve are badly injured. Eleven citizens die from gunshot wounds and beatings. Over forty citizens are hospitalized—some for weeks.

The press and television coverage of the tragedy is broadcast to every state and most foreign countries. Letters to newspapers, television stations, and legislators flood in, demanding that the medieval and uncaring court system be dismantled and replaced with something more responsive to the people. Those federal and state legislators with a legal background appear on public platforms to warn that there should be no hasty changes in the court system. This only angers the public more.

Successful recall movements spring up all over the country removing those who resisted improving the court system. New political parties form outside the traditional Democrat and Republican organizations. Usually, the anti-court groups put forth non-lawyers as legislative candidates for office. The new lawmakers, after holding hearings throughout their states and reviewing task force reports, pass legislation that changes the court system radically.

COURTS DECENTRALIZED–NATIONALLY

The public takes great interest in the legal and court process. Courts for lesser crimes and issues are decentralized into neighborhoods. Non-lawyers are appointed as judges for the lower courts. Legal specialists advise them on points of law as is done for city councils and legislatures. Courts are open at night for the benefit of participants and the public. Local residents take great interest in the cases and pack the hearing rooms.

SEPARATE CIVIL AND CRIMINAL COURTS ESTABLISHED–STATES

Municipal and superior courts are disbanded. Traffic offenses are handled by transportation departments in cities and counties. Separate civil and criminal court systems are established. The nation's judiciary responds with stunned disbelief at the public's strong action.

Prophecy

The citizen rebellion in the above scenario could take place if needed reforms do not occur. Many of the actions prophesied in this chapter have already taken place in various parts of the country. In the following chapters, the authors summarize the major abuses of the legal system and suggest solutions that could put the courts back on track and avoid a harmful public rebellion.

CHAPTER TWO

STOPPING
LITIGANT ABUSE OF COURT

A heavy backlog exists in most courts of the United States. The reason? Private citizens sue more and appeal decisions more. Criminals litigate and appeal more. People sue business associates, relatives, the police, cities, state, and federal governments. As criminal cases have priority, civil cases are delayed. Legislators and activist judges helped make it possible. Rulings by the judiciary to protect the legal rights of the accused in the 1960s and 1970s resulted in an increase in prisoner suits and appeals. Legislators and courts gave civil litigants greater access to the courts, increasing suits and the need for more lawyers.

This chapter addresses the problems generated by the increased litigation and offers action to stop frivolous and unnecessary suits that clog our court system.

The Court Workload

In most states it takes three to five years to bring a civil case to trial. State court civil lawsuits increased at twice the rate of the national population growth rate and appeals increased at a rate eight times faster than the general population growth. An estimated five million lawsuits are filed nationally or about one person in ten either sues or is sued every year. Over 220,000 civil cases are filed each year in California alone. The average civil jury trial takes five days.

Civil litigants file and wait an equally long time to reach settlement in United States District Courts. The number of civil cases filed increased from 59,284 in 1960 to 261,485 in 1982, a 340%

MEN OF JUSTICE—"Sue, Sue... Taking the case to court will be a good trick on your neighbor. We will consume a lot of his money."

"Yes, but you will eat up mine and I don't relish that."

increase. The number of appeals filed in the United States Court of Appeals increased from 3,899 in 1960 to 28,000 in 1982, a 618% increase. The employment in the federal judiciary increased rapidly to keep pace with the case growth.

The Rand Corporation, in a study covering a 19-year period in Cook County, Illinois, found that about 95% of the civil suits filed settled out of court or were dropped before reaching trial. About 19,000 civil cases were heard by juries over the 19-year period, rejecting 49% of the claims and awarding $398 million in damages. When awards were granted by juries, they were high, averaging $275,000 in product liability cases, $203,000 in malpractice cases, $160,000 in contract and business disputes, and $150,000 in worker-injury cases.[1]

In the same study by Rand's Institute for Civil Justice in 1983 in Cook County, Illinois, they found that the average award to plaintiffs for product liability cases jumped from $143,000 in the late 1960s to $377,000 in 1979. The awards for worker injuries increased by more than 250%, street and sidewalk hazard cases jumped 830%, and medical malpractice awards increased 700% in the same period.

A similar study of the courts in San Francisco County revealed almost the same statistics. Medical malpractice awards in San Francisco averaged $457,000 in 1979, up from the $89,000 average ten years earlier.

Punitive Damage Procedure In Court

People suing in civil court can claim not only direct damages but punitive damages. This can amount to huge sums of money, well in excess of that needed to compensate the plaintiff for the actual harm sustained. In the case of Richard Grimshaw's suit against the Ford Motor Company, the badly burned boy (injured while in a Pinto car) was awarded $2.5 million in compensatory damages and $125 million in punitive damages by the jury. At a later time the judge lowered the punitive award to $3.5 million, still a large amount. Similarly high awards have a direct impact on the cost of goods and services we buy. Insurance companies claim that punitive damages in product-liability cases, like the Ford (Pinto car) case, increase the cost of automobiles 2% to 3% and 10%, or $10,000 to the cost of a $100,000 light plane.

Theoretically, these high awards are granted when a defendant acted with intent to harm the plaintiff or acted with conscious disregard of the substantial possibility that harm might result from his conduct. In actuality, this means that punitive damages are a windfall to plaintiffs because they are awarded for the purpose of punishment and not for the purpose of compensation.

Punitive awards of over a million dollars are granted by juries, in addition to the actual damages, to punish an insurance company or an offender for permitting the manufacture of a defective product. Civil cases could be administered more rapidly and fairly if the recovery for punitive damages was removed from the civil system and put back into the criminal system. Wrongful conduct on the part of an individual in a dispute should be settled under criminal law rather than civil law. Individuals in the civil system are subjected to both criminal and civil punishment, when punitive damages are awarded, for the same act without the safe-guards available under criminal law. On this issue the trial lawyers's Defense Research Institute (DRI) states:

> While criminal penalties are, for the most part, limited by statutes, the amount of punitive damages which may be imposed upon a civil defendant are limited only by the discretion of the jury that awards them. In fact, the civil punishment of punitive damages may be more severe because of exercise of a jury's discretion than the criminal penalty for the same act which has been established by the legislature. In fact, a person may be punished twice for the same wrongful conduct—once through criminal law and the second time through the imposition of punitive damages in a civil lawsuit.[2]

A civil defendant facing possible punitive damages does not receive the same substantive and procedural safeguards guaranteed by the Constitution under a criminal law situation.

The imposition of punitive damages can be unfair and uneven in its application. In cases where the actual offender has disappeared or has no money, under the rules of vicarious liability the plaintiff may sue the employer or manufacturer or another party, even though "that person or corporate entity in no way directed, participated in or approved the wrongful conduct of its employee or other agent." The purpose of punishment and deterrents falls by the wayside in the quest of a 'deep pocket.' For obvious economic reasons, lawyers for plaintiffs seek a party who can afford to pay the bill.

Stopping Abuse of Courts by Criminal Offenders

The court reform movement of the 1960s and 1970s made it possible for convicts to file more appeals and habeas corpus suits. Judiciary decisions permitted a variety of appeals and tactics by offenders that slowed and disrupted justice. Of the 261,485 civil lawsuits filed in federal courts in 1984, one eighth were filed by prisoners. Roughly 90% of them were considered frivolous and dismissed by judges. For example:

- In Salt Lake City, convicted murderer Walter J. Wood, sued the Utah State Prison for letting him escape in August 1984 and putting his life in jeopardy. Wood was condemned to death in 1979 for killing a Minnesota minister, but the sentence was vacated by the Utah Supreme Court. He was free six months before being captured. Wood sought $2 million in damages from the prison for allowing inmates to escape. He wrote in his 1985 suit that "Because of extreme fear of being shot to death, I was forced to swim several irrigation canals, attempt to swim a 'raging' Jordan River and expose myself to innumerable bites by many insects."
- Group of Wisconsin inmates, claiming "mental distress," sued a local radio station. Reportedly they found that the station played only 57 minutes of music in an hour, not 58 minutes as advertised.
- Some New Orleans prisoners, upset that a scheduled movie had been canceled, sued the local television station for $75,000. The men claimed that they had told other inmates of the film and were "embarrassed" by the late cancellation.
- In the California prison system, inmates file an estimated four suits a day. Former head of the Federal Litigation Team, John Murphy, said "One insistent fellow filed 36,000 pages in one year. When he was transferred to another prison, they had to rent a van to move all his legal materials. When he arrived at the new facility, he had to carry the boxes filled with his documents to his cell—and sued the state for back injuries. He lost."[3] While some suits appear

PETITIONS FILED BY STATE AND FEDERAL PRISONERS

12 MONTHS ENDED JUNE 30, 1962–1980

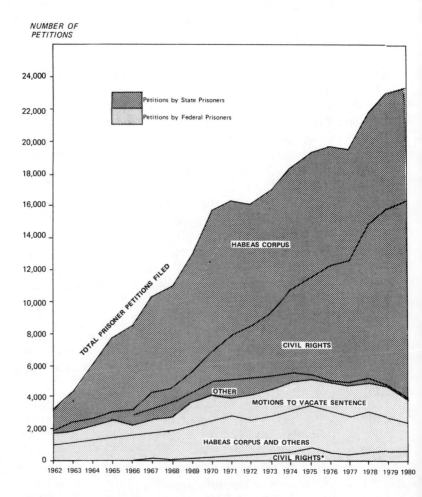

NUMBER OF
PETITIONS

24,000
22,000
20,000
18,000
16,000
14,000
12,000
10,000
8,000
6,000
4,000
2,000
0

Petitions by State Prisoners
Petitions by Federal Prisoners

TOTAL PRISONER PETITIONS FILED

HABEAS CORPUS

CIVIL RIGHTS

OTHER

MOTIONS TO VACATE SENTENCE

HABEAS CORPUS AND OTHERS

CIVIL RIGHTS*

1962 1963 1964 1965 1966 1967 1968 1969 1970 1971 1972 1973 1974 1975 1976 1977 1978 1979 1980

* "Civil Rights" prior to 1966 are included in "Other Prisoner Petitions".

silly, defendant lawyers must prepare documents and file them in court to prevent losing.

Two Court System Problem

By the 1950s two distinct court systems existed in the United States with a strict demarcation line between them. In his book, *The Price of Perfect Justice*, Justice Macklin Fleming analyzed that:

> In our federal scheme of government, the American judicial system is comprised of two sets of courts, one maintained by the national government as a form of limited jurisdiction for the enforcement of federal rights, the other by the state governments as a form of general jurisdiction for the determination of all other rights. Within this system, the United States Supreme Court performs two functions. It is the court of last resort for the federal courts and the ultimate authority on the division of power among the branches of the federal government; and it is the final arbiter of the federal constitutional system and the resolver of conflict between federal and state authority.[4]

The concept of two separate legal systems changed in 1953 in a decision of the Supreme Court in Brown v. Allen. The court's decision, in essence, ruled that "a state court defendant can obtain two sets of reviews of his conviction, for should he fail to overturn his conviction in the state courts on direct appeal, he may apply for relief in the federal courts under the banner of habeas corpus."[5] Justice Fleming noted that, "Dual review in the garb of constitutional right has become such a commonplace, it is now routine."[6]

Other decisions followed the 1953 case, broadening the ability of defendants to appeal. In states like Oregon, Pennsylvania, and Georgia five to six reviews were granted for issues involving admissibility of state courts, federal courts of appeals, and the United States Supreme Court. These cases are often appealed by special interest and lobbying groups.

Appeals by Convicted Offenders

George Cochran Doub, former Assistant Attorney General of the United States, found convicts gained little in their endless appeals. He wrote:

Conviction in the state courts now has become merely the starting point of interminable litigation. State appeals are followed by successive petitions for federal habeas corpus and successive federal appeals. What is involved is a repetitious, indefinite, costly process of judicial screening, re-screening, sifting, re-sifting, examining and re-examining of state criminal judgments for possible constitutional error. ...No other nation in the world has so little confidence in its judicial system as to tolerate these collateral attacks on criminal court judgments.... This comparatively new concept of federal habeas corpus has dangerously prejudiced the delicate balance of federal-state relations and has seriously degraded the authority of the states and their judicial tribunals.[7]

As a result of the court entertaining dual and additional reviews, petitions from state and federal prisoners seeking habeas corpus, civil rights and other relief in the federal courts increased from 2,177 in 1960 to 23,287 in 1980. Judge J. Edward Lumbard of the Federal Court of Appeals in New York voiced the uselessness of these endless appeals:

For all of our work on thousands of state prisoner cases, I have yet to hear of one where an innocent man had been convicted. The net result of our fruitless meddling in search of the non-existent needle in the ever-larger haystack has been a serious detriment to the administration of criminal justice by the states.[8]

The costs of criminal appeals are paid for by the public except in a few cases.

Changing the State/Federal Dual Court System

The existence of the dual state/federal court system gives an imaginative lawyer almost endless opportunities to prolong and delay a case or retry it for years to benefit a client. Our "court conglomerate" should be simplified if the nation is to achieve an efficient justice system.

To change the basic structure of our courts, we must either develop one system of courts or carefully define what is to take place in state courts and federal courts and reduce overlapping between them. The change of responsibility within the two-court systems in the last 20 years has created many problems; and the American public has been victimized by unnecessary criminal appeals permitted under the dual system.

The judiciary, bar associations, and the public must understand how expensive the present dual system is in terms of inefficiency, injustice, and costs of operation. The public and the judiciary must also comprehend what a unified system, with responsibilities clearly defined, could be like and how it could operate in relation to what we have now.

Abuse of The Court System by Civil Litigants

The civil justice system is designed to handle disputes between people, businesses and government which do not involve criminal action. Because criminal cases get priority, civil cases are put on the back burner. The lengthy legal process is especially painful and expensive to individuals in conflict with an insurance company, a big corporation, or a government agency. Frivolous suits, or suits without merit, have slowed the court process and prevented worthy suits from reaching trial stage. Special interest and environmental groups have stopped or delayed thousands of private and public housing, water, and energy developments, sometimes partially constructed. As a result, taxpayers paid millions of dollars more for their electricity, gasoline, heating fuel, water, roads, houses, and food without knowing why.

Proliferation of Frivolous Suits

Frivolous suits are a special problem to the courts. The American Bar Association Commission on Court Costs and Delays reported recently that personal issues have increasingly turned into lawsuits. The Commission found that people have unrealistic expectations and believe that a legal remedy exists for every wrong. More commonly, emotional anguish is a reason for filing a lawsuit.

A disgruntled Chicago Bears fan sued the owners for fraud when they had a losing streak. He claimed that they falsely billed themselves as a professional football team.

The *Wall Street Journal* reported an interesting case that occurred in 1980. General Motors was sued by a woman who claimed job-discrimination. In the following months she filed 150 appendixes, named over 90 defendants, including friends and her daughter. She also claimed that the then attorney general had promised to give her (1) $1 billion dollars; (2) the City of Anderson, Ind.; and (3) the Presidency of the United States.

The U. S. Magistrate processing the case claimed a legal assistant worked half-time on the case for three months and spent a month of his non-court time on the case. Another six weeks was required to write an opinion and a week to mull over it. The case was finally dismissed in October 1982; but it had cost the public considerable time and money.

Loss of Love Suits

A tourist sued a motel in Texas for $200,000 for a neck injury. He claimed he had injured his neck running into a nude female in a room he entered because the motel clerk gave him the wrong key. The injury occurred when he made a quick about-face after encountering the woman. His wife claimed also that she lost the use of her husband's service after the injury.

Another loss of love suit was filed in California by a man against the Los Angeles County Fair for depriving him of sexual relations with his live-in girl friend. While at the fair, she fell off a mechanical bucking bull and broke her neck. She sued the fair for medical bills, lost earnings, and other damages. He also sought damages for "loss of love, companionship, affection ...sexual relations and solace." He stated in his lawsuit that he suffered "severe emotional shock" when he was a witness to his girl friend's spill. While it is very unfortunate that his girl friend was injured in the fall and had become paralyzed, he suffered no damages from her fall.

Because of the suit, the fair authorities were forced, at taxpayers' expense, to hire an attorney and prepare an expensive legal defense. Often people file suits, knowing they have no case, in hopes that the defendant will pay them off to avoid costly legal expenses.

King Tut's Curse

While guarding King Tutankhamon's golden funeral mask in 1979, Police Lieut. George E. La Brash suffered a stroke. He later filed a suit, claiming $18,400 in disability pay for his eight months of recuperation. It was reported in the *Los Angeles Times* that the attorney for La Brash, said, "Egyptians believed in a curse pronounced by Osiris, god of the dead, on all who disturb the dead." As a result, he claimed, "La

Brash suffered a stroke after having positioned himself, as his employment required, directly in front of the golden mask. . .which for 3,300 years covered the head and shoulders of the mummified remains of the god-King Tutankhamon."

Others guarding the King Tut exhibit in San Francisco were not affected by the curse. La Brash's lawyer responded to this by indicating that La Brash may have been more susceptible to psychic phenomena by the ..."stressful employment of guarding the most precious of the world's greatest archeological finds."

The court found at a later time that the guard was not entitled to disability pay as a result of King Tut's curse. However taxpayers were victimized because more worthy cases were displaced, and they subsidized the processing of the suit through the court system.

Other Frivolous Suits

Examples of frivolous suits filed in the United States could fill volumes of books. A few are summarized below:

- While in the process of burglarizing a school, one of the four men involved fell through a skylight into a gymnasium 25 feet below. As a result he became a quadriplegic. He sued the school district, however, won, and received a settlement of $260,000 plus $1,200 per month for the rest of his life.
- A man stole a motorcycle and went riding on the ranch of the man who owned the vehicle without the owner's permission. He hit a hole, flipped over, and injured himself. The thief sued the property owner and collected $500,000 for his injuries.
- Kimerli Pring, the former Miss Wyoming, sued *Penthouse* magazine for defaming her in a story alluding to her sexual exploits during the Miss America pageant. She won $26.5 million for her libel suit in the United States District Court in Wyoming in 1981. A judge later reduced it to $14 million.

Who wouldn't like to be defamed for that amount? Unfortunately for Miss Wyoming, in 1982, a federal appeals court overtuned the libel award saying the magazine was protected by the First Amendment's guarantee of free speech.

Preventing and Reducing
the Filing of Frivolous Suits

Chief Justice Berger, speaking at the American Bar Association convention in February of 1984, indicated that lawyers must "move away from total reliance on the adversary contest for resolving all disputes." To stop frivolous suits Berger urged federal judges to take advantage of their recently broadened court power and impose fines against lawyers who abuse the courts, and curb delaying tactics used before and during trials. He said, "A few carefully considered, well-placed penalities of $5,000, $10,000 or $15,000 will help focus attention on the subject of abuses by lawyers."

Burger wanted more disputes handled by negotiations and arbitration. He said, "Trials by the adversarial contest must in time go the way of the ancient trial by battle and blood."

The Chief Justice admonished the convention members saying, "The criticism of our profession is not always casual or irresponsible." To control frivolous suits, Berger thought trial court judges should take a greater interest and role in overseeing pretrial proceedings. He said, "the day has long since past when we can simply let the lawyers-run-a-case." Under amendments to the Federal Rules of Civil Procedures, August 1, 1983, judges have greater authority to limit the frequency and extent of pretrial discovery, and impose sanctions against lawyers causing needless delays or aggravation to the opposing party. Berger reported that in one case a state judge found that a plaintiff's case was based on "totally frivolous allegations" and ordered the plaintiff to pay almost $2.0 million in fees and expenses.

To encourage settlements, Berger said that the United States Judicial conference was seeking ways to allow either party in a lawsuit to offer the other side a pretrial settlement. Under a change in Rule 68 of the Civil Rules of Procedure, if the offer was refused and judgement at the trial was less favorable to the "refusing party" than the earlier offer, then the "refusing party" would be liable for payment of all costs the opposing party incurred after rejection of the pretrial offer including attorney's fees.

Counter-Attacking
With a Malicious Prosecution Suit

An effective but seldom used method of responding to a frivolous suit is to take an action called a "malicious prosecution."

Under this action, a litigant can recover damages from a person who previously and unsuccessfully sued them in a civil or criminal proceeding without probable cause and with malice. A person, property, or reputation can be an issue.

Harvey Krieger, a lawyer specializing in business and corporate law, indicated in an article in *Silver Circle,* that each state has fairly uniform laws governing such actions, but six elements must be satisfied to take the action:

1. The commencement of prosecution of an original civil proceeding;
2. The causing or instituting of such original lawsuit by the present defendant or defendants;
3. The termination of the original lawsuit in favor of the plaintiff in the malicious prosecution action;
4. The absence of probable cause for bringing the original action in the first place;
5. The malicious institution or prosecution of the original action; and
6. Damages suffered in the original action.

The injured party can be entitled to recover compensation for all injuries suffered as a result of the action by the original suing party. Recoverable damages include loss of time, injury to reputation or character, mental suffering, general impairment of social and credit standing, and business losses. Legal and defense costs involved in the original lawsuit can be recovered also. In some cases punitive damages are allowed.[9]

A Doctor Fights Back

A southern California doctor did use the malicious prosecution approach in recouping legal costs in a frivolous malpractice lawsuit. In 1974, Dr. Sarah Kaiman of Thousand Oaks, was sued by a former patient, Marion Myers, for medical malpractice. Myers was being treated for diabetes. The lawsuit was dropped two years later in 1976.

The following year, 1977, Dr. Kaiman filed a lawsuit for malicious prosecution against Myers and her lawyer. In 1983, when the case went to trial, Dr. Kaiman won and was awarded $100,000 by the jury. The verdict was appealed and is pending.

Citizen Action To Stop Frivolous Suits and Unnecessary Suing

Citizens should contact their state legislators and request that legislation be passed that assesses litigation costs against the losing parties in civil disputes. As mentioned before, British courts use this system effectively. Many frivolous suits would be discouraged, if not stopped, by this action as an aggrieved person would be faced with paying out thousands of dollars in legal fees for the opposing party if the case was lost.

Public groups should insist that their legislators pass laws to eliminate the liability of an individual or public entity property owner when a person is injured on their property while committing or attempting to commit a felony. California Assemblyman Alister McAlister and Senate GOP Leader Jim Nielsen introduced just such a bill to protect property owners. Bills should be adopted to prevent car owners from being sued when someone steals their vehicle and harms himself or someone else with it.

Citizens should request that state legislators pass legislation requiring judges to fine plaintiffs for filing frivolous cases. State courts should review civil cases, sort out frivolous type cases, inform litigants of alternative methods of settling cases, and warn them of possible fines if they proceed with their cases.

Organizations should write television sponsors and the print media, criticizing programs that show cases in court that give a false impression of the court's role.

Citizens should write and put pressure on congressmen to refrain from passing laws giving victorious lawyers court and legal fees for winning cases against government agencies. The laws permitting lawyers to receive such fees should be identified; and congressmen asked to amend those laws. Citizen groups should identify the congressmen who drafted and voted for such legislation and put pressure on them to change the laws.

United States Supreme Court Takes Action

In June of 1983, the United States Supreme Court, for the first time, invoked a three year-old rule ordering a Lincoln, Nebraska black man to pay $500 in damages to the University of Nebraska for filing a frivolous race discrimination lawsuit. The rule known as Rule 49.2 of the Supreme Court's rules of procedure permits the court to assess "appropriate damages" when an appeal is determined to be "frivolous."

Elmo C. Tatum, a retired minister, filed a suit against the University of Nebraska in 1981 when he claimed that they would not allow him to enroll for the fall semester. The university refused to permit him to register until he paid $350.39 in unpaid school fees. Tatum filed a second suit claiming discrimination because the university refused to provide him housing in a dormitory for the fall semester. He had lived in the dormitory during the summer session.

A federal judge dismissed the suit when a university representative explained that they would not allow anyone to register or live in their dormitory when money was owed them. Many court watchers hailed the action of the high court as a sign that they intended to take action against people who filed frivolous suits, and took up the court's time with petty cases.

'Deep-Pocket' Suits

An example of a search by a 'victim' for someone to sue for money who was not at fault occurred in the case of Jose Clemente's suit v. the California Highway Patrol. It took six years for the case to go to trial. A previously brain-damaged pedestrian, Jose Clemente, while walking across a pedestrian walk, was hit by a motorcyclist on a City of Los Angeles street in 1975. An off-duty highway patrolman, driving by the area, saw the accident and stopped to help. Not having jurisdiction in Los Angeles City, the officer called an ambulance and the Los Angeles Police Department for assistance. By the time the Los Angeles Police Department members arrived, the motorcyclist and possible witnesses to the accident had left the scene.

Clemente had suffered brain damage in a fall from a roof eight months earlier. The fall required removal of the left side of his skull. It was brought out in the trial that Clemente had contributed to his own injury in the street because he had ignored his doctor's advice to wear a protective helmet. The California Highway Patrolman, testified that he offered Clemente first aid, but Clemente refused any medical aid.

Because of the missing motorcyclist, Clemente's lawyer decided to sue the State of California. His reason: the CHP officer had failed to take the cyclist's name, which prevented Clemente at a later time from having someone to sue. Normally, in a case such as this, the injured party would sue the insurance company of the person who injured him. The State, in its argument, pointed out that Clemente did not seem to be seriously hurt at the time. Clemente then claimed that Patrolman Loxsom had failed to fulfill his duty as a reasonable and prudent traffic officer, even though he had no jurisdiction in that area.

Clemente sued for $137,863 for past medical expenses, $147,700 for future estimated medical costs, and $2,249,400 in costs for future attendant care. The jury, in a 9 to 3 vote—the minimum required in civil type verdicts—awarded Clemente a $2.2 million liability verdict.

It was not clear that the damages suffered by Clemente were actually caused by the accident. A strong possibility existed that his injuries were caused by his previous accident. The taxpayers were held responsible, however, even though the state had nothing to do with the accident.

Woman Sues Rescuers

In Gillette, Wyoming on Dec. 20, 1983, Dale Chamberlain went to the home of Doug Olsen, a close friend, shot him, Olsen's girlfriend, Pam Houle, and her two children, and blew up their house. He then held Mary Alice Beatty hostage in her home. Police believed that Chamberlain held Beatty because of a sexual harassment complaint she filed while working with him at a local utility plant.

During the time Chamberlain held Beatty hostage, he shot and killed a Gillette policeman, Jon Hardy, and seriously wounded another officer, Del Wright, before he killed himself with a homemade bomb. In the explosion of the bomb Beatty was injured.

A year latter Beatty filed a claim with the City of Gillette and Campbell County, claiming that the law enforcement officers acted negligently when they rescued her from Chamberlain. She stated that a shot from a policeman caused the loss of the use of her right hand. Beatty sought $975,000 from the city and the same amount from the county in compensation for her injuries.

Law enforcement personnel could hardly believe that she would sue them for rescuing her from almost sure death. County Attorney Hilderbrand said, "She's alive today and I think she can thank the sheriff's office and police for it. I don't know why you'd sue someone for saving your life."

Officer Marty Wozniak, Hardy's roommate and fellow officer, said, "When you have one of your best friends murdered... you think about that every day. I think about Jon every single day."[10]

Suits Against Police

The 40,000 police agencies in the United States have become fertile targets for lawsuits in recent years. The organization, Americans for Effective Law Enforcement, Inc., found that lawsuits against police departments increased from about 2,170 in 1967 to 13,410 in 1976 and have escalated in the years since. Police litigant consultants claim that suits against police have increased 50% from 1978 to 1984 and that the awards are bigger. Lawyers have discovered that suits against police is a new field of malpractice and a potential growth area due to an amendment of the Civil Rights Act in 1976. For example in Riverside, California a jury awarded a plaintiff $30,000 for damages, but gave his attorney $230,000 for legal fees. In North Carolina a man was awarded $600 because a policeman slapped his face, but his lawyer was granted $6,000 for a half-day trial.

In 1983 a federal jury in Detroit ordered the City of Troy to pay the Prior family $5.75 million for accidentally shooting David Prior. The accident occurred while Prior was staked out one night in front of his house to catch the vandals who had burglarized his expensive van. Two Troy police officers, thinking Prior was an armed burglar, shot and killed him. Prior had armed himself with a pellet handgun. While the shooting was a tragedy, should the award have been nearly $6.0 million? Assuming the case was handled on a contingency basis, the lawyer would have received about $1.9 million. The interest alone on the remaining $3.8 million would amount to about $450,000 per year to the family.

Multi-million-dollar suits are filed alleging false arrest, excessive use of force, unwarranted shootings, and injuries caused by police chases. The major reason for the increased litigation includes court rulings that have removed obstacles to suing police; congressional legislation making it practically routine for lawyers to obtain large fees; and some huge jury awards granted plaintiffs in the cases.

Suits Against Local Government

Suits gainst local government have escalated in recent years. Litigants have sued California communities and collected big awards for injuries received while swimming and surfing in the Pacific Ocean. In 1961, only 270 civil rights suits were filed against local governments. By 1981, the number had risen to 13,534 suits.[11] Some accident suits filed against communities have received high awards from juries. In December of 1984, the City of Newport Beach, California was ordered by Superior Court to pay John Taylor $6 million. He had been paralyzed two years previously after diving into the surf and hitting his head on the bottom.

Many cities had trouble raising funds to pay off the suit awards. South Tucson, Arizona was faced with bankruptcy because it did not have sufficient funds to pay for a $3.6 million award a jury granted policeman Roy Garcia. He became paralyzed after being shot accidently by a fellow officer. Garcia had already received $200,000 for medical bills from the city of Tucson and was getting $840 a month in worker's compensation payments. Many in the city were angry at the additional high award knowing that Garcia's lawyer was to receive 45% or $1,620,000 of it. The public pays for the high jury awards in higher taxes and higher insurance premiums to protect the community from possible future losses.

Product Liability Suit Abuses

Over 110,000 product-liability suits are filed annually. Every year plaintiffs are awarded millions of dollars due to injuries resulting from a company's defective product. Because of the manner in which laws are written, plaintiff attorneys know that they have a better chance than a product manufacturer of winning a settlement for their client and a big fee for themselves.

Many states permit people injured by a defective product to receive large awards even when the manufacturer was not negligent. In recent years, several companies, faced with court awards greater than the value of the company, have declared bankruptcy and gone out of business. Johns Mansville, for example, filed for bankruptcy in 1982 because of the number of asbestos damage claims and the potential financial threat to the company. By 1985, 9,500 property damage suits totaling $69 billion in claims had been filed against them. Just the health damage claims against the company totaled $12.5 billion.

Ford Motor Co. Suit

An example of an unusually high award for a product liability case that effected consumers, was the case against the Ford Motor

Co. in Corpus Christi, Texas by Jeanette Henrichson and her daughter, Chastity Marie. In 1976, while Mr. Henrichson was making a right turn, his Ford car was struck from the rear by a man under the influence of alcohol. The drivers of both cars died, and Mrs. Henrichson and her daughter suffered severe burns.

In 1984, the Ford Motor Co. agreed to purchase an annuity worth more than $47 million to the two surviving women. The settlement reportedly provided the daughter with $850,000 in cash and $9,000 per month for the rest of her life. Mrs. Henrichson, who received an unknown amount, stated that she was pleased with the settlement. Even though the car that hit the Henrichson's car was driven by a man under the influence, Mrs. Henrichson's lawyer claimed that a poorly designed and unsafe fuel system caused the damage.

Legislation to Prevent Product Liability Suit Abuses

Some Congressmen, such as Senator Bob Kasten (R-Wis), are taking notice of the unfair product liability laws and introducing legislation to give more equitable treatment to businesses in such suits. Kasten introduced a bill in 1984 to establish a uniform federal statute on product liability in the 50 states. Unlike most laws, the bill would prevent compensation until an injured consumer proved that a company was at fault, had failed to act reasonably in designing the product that caused an injury, or had not warned the user of potential hazards.

Punitive damages would be restricted to the first suit only, and not any following suits as is the case presently. Damages could be paid, but not punitive damages in later suits. Consumers have an interest in a fair product liability law as they pay more for a product if unreasonable awards are made to litigants.

Betts v. Allstate Insurance Company
Personal Injury Case

A good example of legal gymnastics in a personal injury case that leaves a layman bewildered, is Deborah Betts' case against Allstate Insurance Company (Sears). She won a $3,850,000 suit against the insurance company and her former lawyers on the grounds that they failed to negotiate a settlement in an accident case in which she was ordered to pay $450,000. The case goes back to 1975 when Betts, who was then 17 years old, allegedly ran a red light

31

and crushed another vehicle, severely injuring and paralyzing the driver, a 32-year-old woman. Allstate insured both Betts and the other driver, Ann Galucci. The family of Galucci sued Betts for negligence and won a $450,000 judgment. Ann Galucci was brain-damaged, a quadraplegic, and blind as a result of the accident. She will continue to suffer the rest of her life as a result of the accident.

The jury trial took place in 1977, two years after the accident. Allstate Insurance paid $100,000 to Galucci under the terms of the auto insurance policy. Miss Betts was left with a debt of $350,000 to pay to Miss Galucci. As she had no assets, she was unable to pay her. Miss Betts decided after the trial to sue her insurance company and her lawyers for "bad faith" in representing her in the accident case. It was alleged that Allstate was unwilling to consider an out-of-court settlement proposal by the victim's lawyers and also failed to inform Miss Betts that an offer had been made.

Under California State Supreme Court's decisions, a client has the right to sue for punitive damages when "good faith" is lacking by an insurance company. Betts sued and was awarded $3,850,000. She then paid Miss Galucci $350,000, the remainder of her $450,000 judgment awarded six years previously. Betts made $3,500,000 minus an assumed one-third contingency fee to her lawyers.

Should a person causing an accident be awarded eight and a half times more than the accident victim received and become a millionaire in the process? Insurance rates were impacted adversely by the high award. Other insurance companies charged higher fees and put funds in reserve to cover possible future court awards. The accident victim, unfortunately, suffers in agony every day as a result of the accident. The $450,000 will have to last a life-time for Miss Galucci. Only under the American court system could a person become a millionaire as a result of causing an accident and damaging someone else.

'Bad-Faith' Award

Because a Hollywood, California couple did not get a prompt settlement of their insurance claim of $17,000 for 'run-of-the-mill' neck and back sprains from a minor auto accident, they were awarded $7.4 million in May of 1985. For acting in 'bad faith' with their clients, Alex Rhonis and his wife Mary, Liberty Mutual Insurance Co. was ordered to pay them $375,000 in compensatory damages for humiliation and mental anguish and $7 million in punitive damages. The couple's lawyer indicated that the Rhonis' would have accepted the $17,000, but the insurance company did not offer them $7,500 until four years after the accident and the case was going to trial. The 'bad-faith' suit was filed because of the delays in receiving payment from the company.

Lloyd's of London Hurt by Legal System

The chairman of Lloyd's of London, Peter North Miller, stated in a speech in June of 1985 that "Without reform of tort law in the United States, there will not be a market to cover the liabilities Americans want to see covered." In the most recent audit the three centuries old insurance firm paid out more in claims than it received in premiums in 1981. Miller indicated that the company had been hurt by liability litigation and extravagant court awards in this country.

Innocent Boat Captain Sued in Hawaii

An example of an innocent party being sued for damages caused by another person, occurred in Hawaii. On March 30, 1981, a crewman on the 90 foot cruise boat, *Spirit of Adventure,* became angry at the owner of a nearby boat, the *Oz.* Several days earlier, Benjamin Ko had asked Monroe, owner of the *Oz,* to take him to Tahiti. When Monroe refused, Ko went beserk.

Ko took over the *Spirit* and commenced to ram the *Oz* while Monroe and Katherine Garside were sleeping on board. Ko reportedly screamed that "If I can't go to Tahiti, nobody can," and rammed the *Oz* three times. He then attempted to run down Monroe and Garside in the water after they were knocked overboard. The irate crewman rammed the big 90 foot craft into two other boats before he was subdued. Twenty-three passengers were on board the *Spirit* during the rampage.

Ko was charged with 49 counts of attempted murder, terroristic threatening, kidnapping and other offenses. He was found mentally incompetent and confined for treatment at the state hospital. Ko was not expected to pay for any of the damages.

The owner of the *Spirit* paid Monroe $54,000 for the loss of his boat. Apparently not satisfied, Monroe and Garside sued in Maui court for additional damages. Judge Harold Fong ruled that the captain of the *Spirit* was negligent in permitting Ko to remain on board after he acted "erratically." He awarded Monroe $40,000 in general damages, $25,000 to Garside in general damages, and $8,000 to both of them for medical expenses. The owner of the *Spirit,* or its insurance company, paid a total of $125,000 for something another person had done.

Fraud Suit Abuses

An unusually high punitive judgement was awarded the plaintiff, Julie Titchbourne, in her fraud suit against the Church of Scientology in Portland, Oregon. In May of 1985, the jury found the church guilty of fraud because of their failure to provide the goods and services that they claimed they would give Titchbourne in courses that she needed for self-improvement. The jury awarded her $3,203.20 for general damages and $39 million for punitive damages.

Several thousand church members traveled to the Multnomah County Courthouse to picket, chant, and sing religious and freedom songs. The church indicated that it would appeal this "...wholly unreasonable and blatantly excessive monetary award." In a letter to the Governor, the church said that "The case strikes at the very heart of the dearly held American concept of free religious practice." Later in July of 1985, Judge Donald H. Londer voided the $39 million fraud verdict and declared a mistrial.

Medical Malpractice Suits: A New Epidemic

In 1985 several states, primarily Florida and New York, faced an epidemic of medical malpractice suits. In the two states neurosurgeons were paying annual insurance premiums as high as $100,000 and obstetricians up to $75,000 for protection from patient suits. The crisis was not limited to the two east coast states, but was spreading across the country.

The fear of malpractice suits was preventing doctors from providing needed service to thousands of patients in the two states. One neurosurgeon in St. Petersburg, Florida said:

> I now refuse to see patients referred by attorneys, insurance companies, other patients or self-referrals. I only see new patients who are bona fide emergencies in the emergency room and patients who are referred by other physicians.[12]

Four obstetricians operating from Tampa's Women's Hospital said that they paid $15,000 a month for their malpractice insurance that covered the delivery of about 30 babies a month plus their gynecological work.

The chairman of the American Medical Association's board of trustees, Dr. John Coury, said:

> There will be opposition from the legal profession, but people must be told it is as much their problem as the doctors; problem because the public will have to pay for it in dollars or in quality of care. It is the highly specialized doctors who will stop what they are doing.[13]

Medical malpractice liability claims began to increase rapidly in the country in the early 1970s and grew at an accelerating rate every year. Malpractice insurance rates escalated as much as 300% in one year in California. Many doctors gave up their practice or stopped carrying insurance.

A decade ago California doctors faced a similar problem until the state legislature under great pressure passed legislation limiting the amount patients could sue for medical malpractice. The legislation California passed in 1975 was found to be constitutional in 1984. The medical act provides a $250,000 limit on non-economic loss such as pain and suffering, periodic rather than lump-sum payments for judgments over $50,000, a sliding scale of fees for plaintiff attorneys, and a provision allowing defendants to introduce evidence that the injured party had received other benefits such as medical insurance or disability payments.

But the situation is changing in California despite protective legislation. In a 1983 report by the Medical Underwriters of California, it was found that of the 66 court awards of $50,000 or more, 17 were for birth injuries and totaled $20.6 million, 40% of the amount for the 66 cases. From a total of $68.7 million granted in 1980, malpractice awards and settlements reached $117.1 million during 1983.

Murderer Sues Mental Hospital for Malpractice

In Cambridge, Massachusetts a convicted murderer filed a malpractice suit against the McLean Hospital of Belmont claiming that the mental hospital ignored his homicidal tendencies and negligently released him a few months before he killed his former girlfriend. The former patient, Bradford Prendergast, was convicted and sentenced to a life term in 1980 for stabbing Patricia Gilmore to death in 1979.

In the 1982 suit the killer claimed that his release caused him "serious injury" and "great pain of body and mind." Gilmore's family had already filed a $20 million suit against the state for releasing Prendergast from jail without warning the family.

Preventing Product Liability and other Questionable Suits

Product liability, 'deep pocket,' and other questionable lawsuits have escalated. There is a trend toward the abandonment of the fault principle used in traditional court law which seems to encourage litigants to seek and find a 'deep pocket' somewhere which can be held liable for injuries.

The legal Defense Research Institute, an arm of the trial lawyers of the country, does not believe any reduction of product liability and medical malpractice suits will occur:

> Unless the trends toward comprehensive governmental regulation of all phases of life, increased judicial activism, and abandonment of the fault principle in tort law are curtailed, it is difficult to expect our citizens to become less claims-conscious and less litigious. It may be reasonably expected, however, that widespread litigiousness will decrease when judges and other governmental officials take affirmative steps to remove the persuasive incentives to the litigiousness. Part of any attorney's ethical obligation, irrespective of his own financial interest is to discourage litigation of doubtful benefit to clients as well as discouraging litigation of doubtful merit. Similarly, we must try to dissuade contentious clients from "proving a principle" where the "principle" is disadvantageous to the client.[14]

Legislators have generated an environment encouraging law suits at the federal and state level and subjected more spheres of activities to government regulation. Small businesses have been subjected to regulation by the federal or state government for a range of activities including employment practices, labor relations, wage policies, fringe benefit programs, plant conditions, product packaging, and competition. Potential legal problems and opportunities for lawyers open up with each new area of regulation.

Jurists have invited more legal work through judicial activism, the process of changing the law through court decision rather than legislation. The Defense Research Institute found that:

> Many judges are willing to use the lawsuit as a vehicle to right every perceived wrong. Disputes that not too long ago would have been considered purely political or social or familial have become legal, and thus grist for judicial mills. This fact is attributable only in part to legislative and administrative activism. And part is due also to the readiness of our courts to accept jurisdiction over every kind of dispute. As defenses and immunities are diminished constantly by court decisions, the incentive to sue increases.[15]

Public Cost of Excessive Litigation

Taking a civil dispute to trial by an individual is expensive. For instance, to sue the federal or state government and go to court over a land condemnation case, one must be wealthy or hire an attorney on a contingency basis. Contingency fees vary from one-third to one-half of a final award. Court battles can be long and expensive. Lawyers cost from $60 to $250 per hour and more to move cases and clients through court procedures. A government agency or a large corporation can delay and procrastinate for years in disputes.

The Rand Corporation's Institute for Civil Justice completed a comprehensive study in 1982 of the processing of civil suits related to personal injury, death, and property damage, called a tort in legal language. The study indicated that during the year of 1982 alone, an estimated $320 million of public funds were used to process tort cases through the civil justice system.[16]

The study found that a jury trial usually costs more than a case tried before a judge only. In 75% of the trials studied, the average cost of a jury trial, about $8,000, cost more than the amount at issue by the litigants. The Rand researchers indicated that in California excluding Los Angeles, jury trials occurred in only 4.3 percent of the tort cases filed but absorbed 58% of the public's funds.[17]

Amount of Compensation Awards

The amount and number of civil litigation awards are growing annually. The independent analysis company, Jury Verdict Research, found that the number of million-dollar verdicts awarded each year in the United States zoomed up from one in 1962 to 251 in 1982.

The public is the victim in the end, and pays more for its services and goods as companies increase their insurance coverage and set aside funds for legal costs. Health care costs have rocketed upward as doctors and hospitals protected themselves with expensive malpractice insurance. The costs of automobiles, insurance, water, electricity, and hundreds of products and services cost more because of our litigious society, aggressive lawyers, and permissive judiciary. While judicial activism in tort and insurance law cases receives less immediate attention than criminal cases, its impact on the justice administration and the cost to the public is significant.

Why Are Americans So Litigious?

Because more people with different ethnic and cultural values now live in the same communities, more conflicts arise. Americans, taught for decades to respect independence and individualism, are running afoul of the need for collective cooperativeness in high density urban societies.

Disputes, once prevented or settled within a family, church, or by neighborhood pressure, are taken to court. People in divorced or one-parent families and under stress often react to conflicts with more hostility and go to court for resolution. The American society is more transient. People will say or do more hostile things to others because 'social pressure' does not bother them. They care little about what the neighbors think because they do not know them or plan to move away soon.

The court system itself encourages litigation. A person can hire a lawyer on a contingency basis and pay only when the plantiff's lawyer wins. If the case is lost, the plantiff pays nothing. What has a plantiff to lose? Only their time and their lawyer's time and expenses.

The courts are used to administer and regulate too many social, economic, medical, and environmental problems, public or private, that are normally processed outside the courts in most countries. It seems quicker and easier to right a wrong by filing a suit than getting a government agency or legislature to address the issue.

A Lawyer's View On The Proliferation of Suits

An outstanding lawyer and legal author, Bernard E. Witkin, believes the legal system is overburdened because the viewpoint in the United States is that, "the legal system exists in great measure for the protection of private rights—rights against the government, rights against other individuals and that anyone has access to the courts...." He explained in an interview with Kay Mills of the *Los Angeles Times* that the public gets its knowledge of the law from the media which stresses:

> ...human interest and sensational events instead of substance. A broad understanding of the law and its operation would enable people to realize that in a great many instances—perhaps the majority—the legal remedy is not very rewarding.
>
> The winner frequently doesn't get the fruits of his judgment, the loser is always very unhappy and an embittered person and there is a great feeling that they wasted precious time in a complicated forum that isn't really the place to handle normal kinds of disputes. More realistic reporting about the law and its actual operation and meaning might help intelligent people avoid rushing into litigation.

Preventing Excessive Civil Jury Awards

Excessive civil jury awards could be reduced for personal injury type cases if a national accident insurance program covered such situations. When damaging accidents occur in which no one is really to blame, the nation should share in financing needed insurance to care for the victims. By cases being processed like workman compensation cases, the injured could be cared for more promptly and less money would be paid out for legal services. To seek a person or agency to sue, not necessarily involved with an actual accident, only because he happens to have a 'deep pocket' is not the way a justice system should operate.

If legislative action is taken to eliminate or reduce the possibility of huge punitive damage awards, less liability cases would go to court, injured parties would spend less for legal fees, and the public would pay less for products and for private and public insurance.

CHAPTER THREE

PREVENTING LEGISLATOR ABUSE OF THE COURT SYSTEM

When a new problem or issue surfaces in the United States and the media generates public interest, state and federal legislators show their concern by passing innumerable new laws. Legislators, thinking more of the votes than of the impact of legislation, generate new problems and new costs by passing poorly conceived laws. On other occasions, legislators avoid facing important issues by not passing any legislation or adopting vague laws. The courts are later forced to resolve the tough issues dodged by elected representatives, thereby moving into areas of responsibility that constitutionally belong to the legislative branch of government.

Often resources are not available to pay for the staffing and administrative costs generated by new legislation. But the legislator has made political points and built a track record among constituents that will aid him in his reelection. More work is generated for the legal profession and the judiciary, but the unwary public picks up the tab.

Since many legislators are lawyers, they have little interest in reducing the complexities of the justice system. Instead of focusing on the needless, costly, and time-consuming procedural aspects, they pass additional laws that add to the cumbersome layers that already exist. The legal profession is protected and the taxpayer is subjected to increased costs.

In California some 6,000 new bills are introduced every year in the legislature. In one year for example, approximately 1,800 new

41

THE LEGISLATIVE BODY—View of the ministerial benches of the virtuous Chamber of 1834.

laws went into effect on January 1, 1985. All enacted by the legislature and approved by the governor, the laws were scarcely entered into the books when the legislature returned to the capital to start making new laws.

An example of a poorly written bill that has been misused and applied in different areas than originally intended is the Racketeer Influences and Corruption Organization Act (RICO). Passed to fight organized crime, it has been used in the civil courts on product liability and other types of cases.

Citizens have resorted to passing difficult and costly public initiatives because too many legislators have refused to pass needed laws or correct existing bad laws. This form of voter rebellion has caused resentment among elected officials. Attempts have been made by some legislators to limit the number and scope of initiative petitions from the public.

Art Buchwald and Masterman
On Impact of New Legislation

Art Buchwald, in his humorous column entitled "D.C. Lawyers Losing in Red Tape Game," commented that lawyers benefit greatly from the new laws that Congress passes. Washington, D.C., with an estimated 20,500 lawyers, has the greatest number of attorneys per capita of any American city. Buchwald says, "For every law that Congress puts on the books, 20 government lawyers were needed to write the rules interpreting what the legislators really had on their minds." Continuing, "Then, once the regulations were passed, thousands of lawyers in the private sector had to be hired to figure out ways of getting around them."

Commenting on the Washington legal profession's concern that President Reagan would really reduce the number of laws and regulations: "Masterman, a lawyer who makes $250,000 a year, was bitter. Most of the lawyers in Washington worked for Reagan's election, and now he's trying to eliminate every federal regulation agency that kept us alive." Buchwald quotes imaginary Masterman who, angry that Reagan will abolish government regulations, do away with regulatory agencies, and cut back on bureaucracies, says, "I have cases with regulatory agencies that have been dragging on for years. One with the Environmental Protection Agency paid for my rent, three lawyers, and five secretaries, and we still had two years to go before we were going to get a decision. The other day, I got a call from the client who told me to forget the case. No one is afraid of the EPA these days." Buchwald said to Masterman, "I guess all your white-collar crime business is shot to hell, too." Masterman answered, "It's non-existent. I don't know one corporate executive who even talks about staying out of jail anymore."[1]

Problems With Too Much Legislation

Responding to a newspaper editorial criticizing lawyers as having "a built-in affinity for more laws," Ventura County Superior Court Judge Bruce A. Thompson, reacted strongly. Thompson believed responsible judges and lawyers do not want more complicated laws, even though it might mean more business for them. The Judge stated:

> As a result of the spate of new laws these days, it is almost impossible for a legal practitioner to keep abreast. This makes it difficult to predict what a court's ruling might be and, more important, it makes it almost impossible for a private practitioner to advise his client what conduct is legal or permissible.
>
> Stability and continuity in the law are vital to an effective justice system, and nobody realizes this more than somebody who practices in the field of law.[2]

Thompson indicated that much of the caseload in court results from legislators passing too many laws while reacting to pressure from their constituency. Judge Thompson said: "...You know as well as I do who generally demands more laws—the people do. Legislators are subjected to tremendous pressure from lobbyists and citizens pleading for laws to 'cure' our various problems."[3]

Need for New Law Impact Studies

Chief Justice Warren Burger, equally concerned, has written and made many speeches on the problem of too much legislation and its impact on the courts. As far back as 1972, he referred to the need for a "court impact statement on all new federal legislation that creates work for the federal courts." A "court impact statement" would show how many additional judges, auxiliary personnel, and services would be needed to support new federal legislation.

Environmental Impact Statements or Reports were first required by the federal government under the 1969 National Environmental Policy Act. The states soon followed, requiring Environmental Impact Reports on all projects that would significantly affect the quality of the environment or would have a possible adverse impact on the environment. The Environmental Impact Report process has been abused in many parts of the country, but, with care, legal impact analysis could reduce unnecessary legislation and shed light on its cost. The ardor of legislators to pass new legislation should be cooled.

In the opinion of the former Dean of Stanford University Law School, Bayliss Manning, an impact analysis of proposed legislation is needed. He stated:

> Each new legislative or regulatory proposal should be required to be accompanied by an "actual cost" impact statement that brings before the legislature at least a gross estimate of the true cost and implementation burdens of the program, direct and indirect. It is tempting to argue for a rule that requires one old program to be repealed for each new one enacted, but in the absence of that Quixotic principle, legislators can at least establish procedures that will require them to weigh the true cost and burdens of a legal program when they consider whether to adopt it, and no legislative bill should be allowed to pass without appropriations to provide administrative, judicial, and other legal agency resources required to give it effect.[4]

The Judicial Council in California has been interested for some time in the concept of preparing impact reports on proposed legislation. In a report proposed for the council in 1984, it suggested that three major areas be reviewed: caseload, case disposition, and fiscal impacts.

There is a growing interest nationally in preparing legislative impact statements. At a recent national conference held by the National Center for State Courts, a monograph on "The Implementation of Court Improvements" was discussed. The monograph included a recommendation that judicial impact statements be prepared on legislation affecting courts. The conference representatives endorsed a recommendation supporting the concept of judicial impact statements, including an analysis of the impact of legislation, executive, and administrative policies in the state.[5]

Various state courts are preparing reports on the impact of legislation within their boundaries. They address the consequences to the courts themselves, but not the impact on the tax-paying public.

Problems Obtaining Justice Reforms Through Legislatures

Justice Richard Neely, a member of the West Virginia Supreme Court of Appeals, indicated in his book *Why Courts Don't Work* that "criticism of the total structure of the court system structure is usually left to lay, popular writers, or else to lawyers who have never practiced..."[6] These critics are easily dismissed by the legal profession. Since political rewards go to those who oppose court reform, the lawyer dominated legislatures show little interest in reforming the courts. Reform is often the subject of political campaigns, but no one really expects the politician to change the system after election. The machinery of most elected bodies can almost guarantee the maintenance of the status quo except when great pressure is put on it.

Many believe that legislative procedures are designed to kill, as silently as possible, any unwanted legislation without anyone having to be on record as opposing it. The most common technique to accomplish this is to devote as much time as possible to exhaustive hearings so that the final work on bills must be done in a few days at the end of the session. From the public's viewpoint, the sheer numbers of bills to be considered makes each one fade into insignificance.

At times when both houses of the legislature are feeling heavy constituent pressure to pass specific legislation, it is not uncommon for each to pass a different version of a bill. Then the clock is allowed to run out as committees of each house deadlock on bringing out a compromise. This way, every member can face his constituents with a record of supporting the bill without having to worry about it ever becoming law.

Legislative Ties With Legal Profession

Unfortunately, court reform has no active lobby. But plenty of interests are against it. Attorneys are traditionally the backbone of political campaigns and organizations. Politically active lawyers regularly tell their legislators that they are opposed to certain bills and they know the result will be a do-nothing approach to the legislation. Over the years, political rewards are granted to those elected officials who oppose court reform not sanctioned by the legal profession.

Public Politician Action

Our court legal and legislative system is dominated and controlled by one profession: lawyers. The judges are lawyers. More lawyers than any other profession are in the state and federal legislatures. Until recently, the legal profession dominated both houses of Congress, in spite of the fact that no necessity exists for a state or federal legislator to be a lawyer.

National political parties should recognize that in order to bring about real changes in the justice system it will be necessary to elect legislators with a broader representation and a more balanced perspective on issues affecting the population. Legislation should be enacted that is more considerate of court users, consumers, and the public and still achieve an efficient and effective court system. Each individual can make a contribution toward curbing the trend toward more laws and complex legislation that is taking place in our state capitols.

The United States is a nation of laws. It must have laws to regulate society. Without laws, there would be no safety, no standards—there would be chaos. The nation is faced, however, with a need to take action to keep our legal system within a safe dimension. Legislators have imposed a layer of legal mazes, barricades, obstacles, and entanglements upon us. It has become almost impossible for citizens to manage their own lives and businesses without legal conflicts. This nation of laws has become ensnarled in a tangled confusion of duplicating laws that has caused an horrendous diversion of energy from productive pursuits to unnecessary lawsuits with attendant costs to the country. The massive litigation explosion must be controlled. That control can only be exercised by the voters.

Federal and State Legislative Action Needed

Crime victims, organizations, court watchers, bar associations, city councils, boards of supervisors, district attorney associations, and others should present their views strongly to state and federal legislators on action needed to simplify and improve the court system.

47

Legal Bills Soaring

In the decade of the 1970s, Congress enacted more than 100 laws authorizing judges to award attorneys' fees to victorious plaintiffs in suits against government agencies. Although the purpose of these so-called "fee shifting" laws was to encourage private citizens to file suits to protect their rights, the results have come under increasing attack as state governments are forced to take monies from other programs to pay millions of dollars in attorneys' fee claims.

The fee shifting process has resulted in a massive windfall for lawyers. Some fee awards made by judges exceed the amounts won by plaintiffs themselves in successful lawsuits. A recent fee shifting law generated nearly 3,000 federal and state court decisions nationwide over a three-year period. Up to 1985 in Massachusetts, about 2,000 fee claims totaling several million dollars were pending. In the State of Washington more than $8 million in fee claims were pending.

The Reagan administration has supported bills in the House and the Senate that would limit substantially the awards that attorneys have been receiving in cases against federal, state and local government defendants. Michael J. Horowitz, Special Council in the federal Office of Management and Budget, said that the "fee shifting" laws are "...another entitlement program...and I can't imagine anyone less 'entitled' than the legal industry."

What Can The Public Do?

It is easier to shoot holes in a structure than to repair it or build a new one. It will be up to the voters to decide what direction they wish their legislators to take in handling the justice system.

The public can act to elect responsible legislators, more non-lawyers and persons who will correct the imbalances in our justice system. The present trend to introduce legislation that results in a "band aid" approach to problems only causes new ones. Legislation that is poorly conceived and thought out forces the judiciary to interpret the laws, thereby bringing the judicial branch of government into areas that should be the responsibility of the legislative branch.

Voters should establish goals and standards for legislation. New legislation should require that each new law contain a goal that is measurable. The agency administering the law should report annually on the progress made toward that goal. "Sunset clauses" should be added to legislation so that the results can be assessed at some definite time in the future. A review of the impact of legislation should be made on a periodic basis, for example every two years, to permit the alteration or elimination of laws without a legislative fight when bills do not meet expectations.

The evidence is overwhelming that Americans are disenchanted with the confusion of laws that pour out of the legislative halls. At local, state and federal elections, political parties should search for candidates that do not carry an affinity for the legal profession and can write legislation that considers public and taxpayer impact more and the legal profession less.

MEN OF JUSTICE—"He invariably defends the orphans and widows; unless he has been retained to attack them."

CHAPTER FOUR

PREVENTING ABUSE OF THE COURT SYSTEM BY PROSECUTORS, AND CRIMINAL AND CIVIL LAWYERS

This chapter illustrates how the legal and court system is abused by prosecutors, and criminal and civil lawyers; and the impact it has on the public, their rights and taxes.

Abuse of Court System by Lawyers

At the annual American Bar Association Convention in August 1981, Supreme Court Justice Byron White criticized lawyers, their attitudes, and their behavior in the courtroom. He said that they were deliberately dragging out cases so that they could increase their fees to excessive levels. Finding that the financial reward for inefficient work was hurting efforts to reduce overloaded court dockets, already suffering from a greatly increased number of lawsuits, Justice White said,

> A great many thoughtful people are now convinced that there are other sources of delay for which judges and lawyers are wholly or partially at fault. Procedures are too complex and time-consuming. Lawyers and judges are too slow and argumentative. And cases simply take too long.[1]

White said litigation had increased enormously during the 1960s and 1970s. He believed lawyers were not enthusiastic about reducing the time it takes to process a case because "reducing the time involved in achieving a particular result for a particular client may reduce the fee for that case. Hopefully, the lawyer will have

51

other cases and overall will not suffer financially."

White encouraged lawyers to rely more on the expertise of economists and public administrators to reform the process. He found that the cost of lawsuits to the public had reached a point where it discouraged a large percentage of citizens from seeking legal help because of its cost. White stated:

> The other people who obviously suffer are the clients. They pay the bills and those bills, consisting mostly of lawyers' fees, are too high! Not only is it true that delays and expense in the resolution of lawsuits have increased and are increasing at an alarming rate, but there is also a widespread conviction that most of the current delay and expense is unjustified, as well as avoidable.[2]

Appellate Court Justice Richard Neely indicated in his book *Why Court's Don't Work* that the legal profession has found that the best way to stop change is not to attack it, but rather to talk it to death. Bar committees, research reports, and endless nit-picking can lead to delays that discourage the proponents of positive change. Law is a profession that is usually picked for its financial rewards. Lawyers are therefore not thinking about reforms if it is not financially or academically rewarding.[3]

Competence of Lawyers

Chief Justice Warren E. Burger holds views similar to those of Justice White about lawyers and the legal system, stating publicly that between one-third and one-half of the nation's trial lawyers are incompetent.[4] Former President of the American Bar Association Chesterfield Smith, believed that between 20% and 25% of the legal profession were incompetent.[5] Judges interviewed by the authors said that it pained them to watch incompetent lawyers perform in their courtrooms—they hurt their clients and prevented them from obtaining a fair judgement. Unfortunately, judges are limited in how much they can intervene to help a person receiving incompetent counsel.

Harvard University's President On Lawyer's Role

In Harvard University President Derek Bok's annual report to the Board of Overseers in 1983, he severely criticized, in fact made a sweeping indictment of the legal profession and its education and training in the nation. Bok wrote that: "The blunt, inexcusable fact is that this nation, which prides itself on efficiency and justice, has developed a legal system that is the most expensive in the world, yet cannot manage to protect the rights of most of its citizens."[6] Before becoming President of Harvard, Bok was a Professor of Law at Harvard Law School for several years.

Bok wrote that the United States legal system had become too complicated and expensive and overcrowded with lawyers and had failed to provide access to the middle class as well as the poor and disadvantaged. He found that much of the present inefficient and chaotic court system stemmed from the country's law schools' policies and curriculum, charging that they emphasized the advocacy or conflict approach to settling disputes in court rather than the "arts of reconciliation and accommodation." Such schools taught that lawyers look after the interests of their individual clients rather than those of society as a whole. Bok urged that law schools throughout the nation review their educational approach and change it as Harvard's law school is presently attempting to do.

Bok questioned why the United States has so many lawyers and highly developed countries like Sweden, England, and Japan have so few. He said the Japanese have a saying that "engineers make the pie [economic] grow larger; lawyers only decide how to carve it up." On a per capita basis, the U.S. has "three times as many (lawyers) as in Germany, ten times the number in Sweden, and a whopping twenty times the figure in Japan."[7]

Procrastination Of Lawyers

Lawyers for defendants in many criminal cases try every ploy to procrastinate and delay the start of a trial. Professor Delmar Karlen explains why delays aid a defendant:

> Why should the accused in a criminal prosecution plead guilty? More than likely he is free on bail or on his own recognizance, for this is becoming more and more the practice in the United States; he is probably well advised by counsel, supplied at public expense; he knows that the case will not reach trial for six months or a year, possibly longer. The prosecution witness may forget or disappear, and the victim of the crime may become so disgusted with delays

and adjournments that he will drop the charges if he can or fail to appear at the trial when it is finally reached... Because delay yields such rich dividends, it pays to demand a trial quite apart from the chance of winning the case either at the trial or the appellate level.[8]

It's not only the defendants who procrastinate; it's the whole court system. Former Appellate Court Justice Fleming found that trial judges, court clerks, and court reporters procrastinate; lawyers procrastinate; and appellate judges procrastinate. No incentive exists for judges to put pressure on lawyers to move faster in court.

Delaying Tactics In Court

Once a case is underway in a court, a variety of attacks can be used by a criminal defendant's lawyer to delay a trial and aid their clients. Justice Fleming described in *The Price of Perfect Justice* at least 26 different delaying tactics that can be used by an attorney to defend his client. By combining different delaying approaches to seek judicial review, the justice found about 50 opportunities available.[9]

Attacks on Court

Fleming also found that lawyers try to divert the judge and jury's attention away from the main issues in a case. They may attack the court's administration of the case, the conduct of investigators, police and jailers, the prosecutor's control of data and information, the constitutionality of the death penalty, the media, or an unfavorable court ruling.

Incentives To Stop Procrastination

Under the present management of most courts, incentives to speed up the trial process are difficult to implement. Legal counsels for plaintiffs and defendants continue to be paid. Prosecutors, defense attorneys, judges, marshalls, bailiffs, clerks, and stenographers all continue to receive their salaries, no matter how long a case takes. The beneficiaries of the criminal court system are the operators of the system. A lower case-load, more efficient procedures, and shorter trials could be perceived as a threat to their jobs.

Improving Trial Lawyer Efficiency

With competent and responsible trial lawyers, trials can move quite rapidly. A special committee appointed in 1974 by Chief Judge Irving Kaufman of the Second Circuit and chaired by Anthony Robert Clare proposed that "only lawyers who had taken courses in evidence, civil and criminal procedures, federal jurisdiction, professional responsibility, and trial advocacy be admitted to the Federal District Courts of the Second Circuit."[10]   Other committees have suggested similar minimum educational experience and requirements for lawyers before admittance to practice in federal courts. Unfortunately, a large percentage of law school educators have had little experience in a law practice or as trial attorneys and little concern for efficiency in court.

A variety of actions by lawyers permitted by judges, especially appellate court judges, has given our court process legal constipation. When the different delaying tactics, pretrial motions, evidence rules, and criminal rights' rulings are fully utilized by an imaginative attorney, it is a wonder that an offender is actually sent to prison and serves the term originally set by the trial judge.

Once a lawyer has passed the bar examination, it is assumed he is competent to practice law in a courtroom. As Judge Burger stated previously, this is not true. In England lawyers specially trained to appear in court are referred to as "barristers." "Solicitors" are lawyers who prepare cases, do research, and handle other non-trial work. Barristers are highly skilled in the techniques of conducting a case in court. As a result, trials are conducted efficiently.

Abuse By Prosecutors in Federal Courts

Federal and state government prosecutors are sometimes guilty of abusing the court system by taking poorly prepared or ill-conceived cases to trial. When this occurs courtrooms are not available for more worthy cases and the public's tax money is wasted. The United States Attorney General's case against the Hell's Angels is an example of an ill-conceived case.

Hell's Angels v. U.S. Attorney General

After two mistrials and costs running to about $10 million, the federal government finally threw in the towel and gave up trying to convict the Hell's Angels motorcycle gang on conspiracy and racketeering charges. They asked the San Francisco Federal Court to dismiss indictments against 11 gang members and their associates.

The federal prosecutors attempted to prove that the motorcycle gang was engaged in full-time criminal activity during the 1960's and was deeply involved in extensive drug and narcotics operations in northern California and elsewhere. They were accused of using illegal firearms, murder, threats, and assault in their operations.

The first trial which began in 1979 continued until July of 1980 and ended in a hung jury. The second trial which started in October of 1980 ended in February 1981 when the jury advised Judge Orrick that it was hopelessly deadlocked.

One of the jurors, William Aylward, told reporters, after the jury was dismissed, that the vote of the jury was 9 to 3 for acquittal. He described the government's case as "pretty inept." He told the reporters that the government's key witness, a former Hell's Angel, who had admitted being paid $30,000 in exchange for his testimony, was "despicable and beneath contempt."

A total of 214 witnesses and more than 100 exhibits were put before the jury in the second trial. The total testimony filled 62 volumes and 13,500 pages.

The federal government brought charges against the Hell's Angels two years previous to the trial under the federal Racketeer-Influenced and Corrupt Organization Act (RICO) that was passed under the Nixon administration. The Act was originally intended to be used against Mafia-like operations. Because of the broadly worded statutes, prosecutors were able to charge anyone with having undertaken a pattern of racketeering if, within a ten-year period, they had participated in any two of 32 crimes ranging from extortion to murder.

Eighteen defendants were charged in the initial trial. Several of these were convicted on charges such as possession of drugs or possession or use of firearms; but only one was found guilty on the important conspiracy and racketeering counts that prosecutors considered the major thrust of the case.

While the indictments against 11 Angels were dismissed, only two of the 11 were able to leave the courtroom free. The remainder continued to serve sentences from previous convictions or awaited trial on other charges.

United States Attorney G. William Hunter admitted that

some of the government witnesses were a "despicable set of characters," but said that the Hell's Angels should have been prosecuted. He believed the case failed because of its complex nature. Hunter estimated that the government spent $4 to $7 million on the two trials and a total of 14 months in the courtroom. The defense attorneys believed the costs were greater and ranged between $10 and $20 million.

During the two trials five members were found guilty of firearms and narcotics violations. In April of 1983, however, the United States 9th Circuit Court of Appeals reversed their conviction by the lower court. The court held that the men had been convicted on evidence seized from invalid search warrants. On the night the search warrants were executed, June 13, 1979, evidence of criminal activity was found not to be covered by the indictment. This resulted in a new indictment charging firearms and narcotics violations.

Who paid for this $10 million plus legal folly? The American taxpayers, naturally! While the Hell's Angels may be of concern, an attorney general should not start such an expensive trial without having more reliable witnesses and a better prepared case against them. The American taxpayer is not an endless source of money. More appropriate prosecution targets certainly exist in the United States. Not only was the trial unnecessarily expensive, but it prevented other cases from being heard for 14 months or longer. The public, unfortunately, paid for the prosecutor's extravagance and poor judgment.

Federal Government's Creation of a Crime—BRILAB

Worse than initiating a weak case against the Hell's Angels, is the FBI's part in "creating" a crime in order to prosecute someone who was originally innocent. The FBI hired convicted felons in the BRILAB case and sent them into the field to create a crime. The FBI's normal duty is to investigate, apprehend, and prosecute those engaged in criminal violation of federal laws. In the case of BRILAB (Bribery/Labor), the FBI started its "investigations" without a specific suspect in mind. The BRILAB trial, concluded in federal court in Houston, was a display of injustice and a costly venture for the taxpayers.

In an article in the *Los Angeles Times,* David H. Berg, a criminal attorney from Houston, Texas, described how the BRILAB trial case started:

> Joseph Hauser was an ex-convict who had been found guilty of one multi-million dollar insurance fraud and was awaiting trial on another when he was hired by the FBI to act as undercover agent in BRILAB. His job was to press bribes on public officials through their labor associates. In exchange for "working off his case," the government promised Hauser lenient treatment. He was paid approximately $55,000 to cover both his "fee" and his personal expenses. Hauser operated out of a Beverly Hills office. He was forced to rely on contacts in Texas. He could not have implicated three less likely candidates for "bribes" than the men he chose.[11]

Billy Wayne Clayton, the Speaker of the Texas House of Representatives had plans for becoming governor. Randall "Buck" Wood and his partner, Donald Ray, were well-known lawyers in the state capital. In August, Wood, who was chief lobbyist for Common Cause, worked successfully to reform state campaign-financing laws. Ray had served as Chief Counsel to the Texas Attorney General and to a previous Speaker of the House.

Hauser posed as an agent for Prudential Insurance Company seeking state employee insurance business. When he finished with Wood and Ray, each was indicted for allegedly facilitating a bribe to Clayton. Clayton was indicted for accepting $5,000 allegedly in return for throwing state insurance business to Hauser. The government produced what one defense lawyer described as "20 miles of tapes" secretly recorded by Hauser. Ostensibly, these tapes were obtained to capture the truth; instead they revealed a scenario of bribes and influence-peddling created entirely by Hauser.

When Hauser spoke to FBI agents, he referred to "bribes;" but when he talked to the attorneys, he spoke of "campaign contributions." Nevertheless, there are instances on the tape in which Hauser's suggestions to spread money around were quite clearly rejected. Wood said to him, "We don't do business like that in Texas."

At the conclusion of the six-week trial, the jury acquitted all three men in one vote. Nevertheless, the FBI hurt the innocent men. Berg indicated that, due to the FBI's innuendos released in newspapers, Clayton will probably never serve as governor, and Wood and Ray will have trouble rebuilding their once-successful law practice. The men are being hurt by the court process they endured. The saying "You can beat the rap, but you can't beat the ride,"[12] may come true, Berg said.

As a result of pressure from the public and Congress to stick to their authorized role, former Attorney General Benjamin R. Civaletti instructed the FBI to stop inducing individuals to commit crimes that they would otherwise not commit.

Congress has the authority to stop the funding of such "sting" operations. BRILAB cost the taxpayers millions of dollars needlessly.

FBI 'Scam' Fails

Sometimes the 'scams' fail. Although the FBI's participation in 'scams' was supposed to stop, they continued into the Reagan administration. After an FBI attempt to bribe the Chief of Police of Bridgeport, Connecticut, went awry, the Mayor of the City, John Mandanici, demanded that United States Attorney General William French Smith stop the federal 'scam' in his city. The mayor asked Smith to suspend the two United States Attorneys who were heading the organized crime task force in Connecticut "for their ineptness and fruitless investigations that have proved nothing."

Apparently this scam was aimed at trapping Police Superintendent Joseph A. Walsh. Unfortunately for the FBI, Walsh was onto the scam. When a hireling of the FBI, Thomas Marra, Jr., offered a $5,000 bribe to Walsh for obtaining a lucrative towing contract, Walsh arrested him on the spot. Anticipating the bribe, Walsh had wired himself prior to the meeting. Walsh claimed that the FBI had threatened Marra with jail terms for multiple car thefts unless he cooperated with the them.[13]

The FBI has used other convicts in attempting to get convictions of people. Joseph S. Hauser, an acknowledged perjurer and swindler who had been convicted of cheating union workers out of $8 million, was used in the BRILAB case and in a case against former Attorney General Richard G. Kleindienst in Phoenix, Arizona and in other places in the United States.

Continuation of 'Stings'

Apparently such operations will continue. After auto maker John Z. DeLorean was acquitted of cocaine-trafficking charges, then Attorney General William French Smith and FBI officials said in August of 1984 that 'sting' operations would continue despite the loss of the case in court. DeLorean had been prosecuted under an FBI investigation in which a government informant, James Hoffman, drew DeLorean into an alleged scheme to sell cocaine.

Smith claimed that the 'sting' technique was the only way in many cases to attack organized crime, drug trafficking, bribery, and public corruption and that the Justice Department would continue to use undercover operations "wherever they may be necessary."[14]

Abuse of System by State Prosecutors

State district attorneys sometimes select and prosecute "special cases" that are easy to win or prosecute politically-rewarding cases to build a record for career advancement. Because the public does not have access to the decision making process of a prosecutor, it is difficult to evaluate district attorneys' actions.

Management of Victim/Witnesses by Police and Court.

For decades prosecutors looked upon crime victims as objects necessary to win their cases in court. A victim's psychological and economic needs were often neglected by both the police and prosecution. Victims usually became important just before cases went to trial. Victims were then hurriedly called in for a review of their testimony. Many witnesses, angry and disillusioned by the callousness with which they were treated, became uncooperative and hostile to prosecuting attorneys. Sympathetic and sensitive prosecutors found witnesses more cooperative.

Changing Pretrial Procedures for Offenders and Victims

In crimes against persons where the victim survives, that person is a potential witness and possibly the only witness against the offender. The police and the prosecutor need that witness to apprehend, prosecute, and convict the offender. It is important that the police, prosecutor, lawyers and the court treat that victim/witness with respect. When witnesses fail to testify, the result is costly to the taxpayers in wasted investigating and legal work, and frustrating to police and prosecutors. The public should insure that state and local governments adopt policies that protect victims.

Police Treatment of Victim/Witnesses

The police have an important and fundamental role in assisting victim/witnesses and generating friendly feelings toward the police and court authorities. The police are usually the first to see a victim. A policeman's attitude and action often determine whether an offender is arrested, prosecuted, and convicted. To insure that victims receive fair treatment and are cooperative witnesses later, the police need to adopt procedures and services that show they care.

After a victim has called the police, the emergency call should be patched through to the responding officers so that they can talk directly with the person on the way to the scene. Officers must make certain that the victim's emergency medical, and emotional needs (if under stress), are taken care of before initiating an interview. Officers should be well-informed and knowledgeable about existing social and psychological services for victims. Interviews need to be conducted in private, without unnecessary interruptions, and with officers explaining to the victim what to expect from police procedures and the prosecutor's office later.

After property needed by police for evidence in court has been photographed and checked with the prosecutor's office, it should be promptly returned to the victim. Police should inform victims of the investigative status of their work. High priority must be given by police in investigating any reports of threats or intimidation by witnesses. The prosecutor should be notified immediately.

Victims should not have to pay for the cost of providing evidence the prosecutor needs from them. If not in existence, legislation must be enacted to insure that the government pay for the cost of physical examinations and materials used to obtain evidence from sexual assault victims.

Need for Victim Representative in Courts

Victim/witness representatives or an ombudsman ought to be available in every jurisdiction to contact victims after an offense has occurred. Soon after an incident a victim should be notified of the availability of medical and social services.

Legislative Action to Protect Public from Dangerous Offenders

At the federal and state levels legislation must be enacted to give intimidation protection to victim/witnesses, and to prevent additional offenses against the public by the premature release of dangerous persons while awaiting trial. To provide greater witness protection in the prosecution process, legislation should be enacted that insures pertinent evidence is admissible and is considered sufficient at the preliminary hearing, so that victims need not testify in person.

Bail laws should be amended to permit judges to deny bail to persons found to be dangerous and a threat to the community. Evidence of the person's danger has to be clear and convincing, however. The prosecutor should be given the right to expedite the appeal of any adverse bail determinations without jeopardizing the rights held by a defendant. Existing case law should define the authority of the court to detain defendants where conditions of release are not adequate to insure appearance at trial.

In the case of a serious crime, legislation should reverse any standard that presumptively favors release of convicted persons awaiting sentence or appealing their convictions. Legislation should require that defendants refrain from criminal activity as a mandatory condition of release, and provide penalties for failing to appear in court while released on bond or personal recognizance.

Improving the Treatment of Police Witnesses by Judiciary

For police to be more efficient in court and to aid the prosecution of offenders, management changes need to be made within the criminal court system. With the establishment of efficient victim/witness programs and better court organization, prosecution, and court procedures, police officers would spend less time waiting outside courtrooms to testify. Saving an officer's time keeps him on the job and saves the taxpayers money. With good court management, police officers can spend more time in the field where they are needed.

The present rulings on collection of evidence under the exclusionary rule and the Miranda decisions, need to be clarified to give the police more opportunity not only to apprehend an offender, but also to foresee a conviction.

Making Prosecutors Efficient and Accountable

Prosecutors have tremendous power in deciding who should and who should not be prosecuted. The public is not always aware of a prosecutor's occasional misuse of it. While this should not be taken from them, state and federal prosecutors should be held more accountable for their actions. The public should insist that they be better informed about their prosecuting goals, policies, and priorities.

Judges, bar associations, and victim organizations should initiate procedures to evaluate the quality and quantity of actions by state prosecutors. Perhaps annual reports should be made available concerning the reasons for prosecuting or not prosecuting sensitive cases.

Prosecutors must be efficient, prosecute offenders, but yet be considerate of the cost to the public. They should not prosecute an already convicted person if it is not necessary. Evaluations should be regarded as a process to improve prosecutors and not a vehicle to harass or embarrass them.

To gain greater court efficiency, reduce court costs, and to ensure proper treatment of victim/witnesses, prosecutors should incorporate the following procedures into their programs:

- Victims should be kept informed of the status of cases from the arrest of an offender to the time a parole decision is made.
- When bail decisions, continuances, plea bargains, dismissals, sentencing, and restitution are discussed, the views of victims of violent crime should be assertively presented in court.
- If any accused offenders threaten, harass, injure or attempt to intimidate a victim or witness, the prosecutor should aggressively charge that person to the fullest extent of the law.
- Prosecutors are often as guilty as defense lawyers in asking for

continuances. The practice should be strongly discouraged.
- Victims and witnesses should be contacted early for their availability to prevent any need for a continuance.
- Police officers and civilian witnesses should be on call and not brought into court until time to testify.
- If a prosecutor's office does not have a victim/witness unit or program, one should be established, and the police, prosecutors, and victim organizations should be kept in close contact.

Indigent Defense Abuse and Costs

As a result of legislation and actions by an activist judiciary, more legal representation and rights were given to criminal defendants at the taxpayer's expense. According to a report by the Bureau of Justice Statistics of the Justice Department released in 1984, indigent defendants had legal representation in 3.2 million cases during 1982. It cost the nation $624.6 million. This was 44% above the estimated $435 million spent during 1980 and 213% above the $200 estimated for 1976.

Law professor Norman Lefstein reported that in 1982 defense services for the poor nation-wide accounted for about 1.5% of state and local criminal justice funding, while six percent was spent on prosecution services. In 1983, the federal government spent $34 million for legal assistance on 47,000 indigent cases. The largest law firm in the country, the Legal Services Corporation, was funded with a $250 million budget. Legal Services provides criminal and civil assistance from a staff of 4,800 full-time lawyers and 6,700 paralegals and support personnel.

Over the years, beginning with President Jimmy Carter's enlargement of the Legal Services Corporation to provide services in civil matters, the public law firm has continually expanded the scope of its operation.

The Bureau indicated that indigent defense grew because of Supreme Court decisions holding that the Constitution's Sixth and 14th Amendments gave indigents the right to counsel in federal and state courts in felony and misdemeanor prosecutions that could lead to prison.

How Is Counsel Provided To indigents?

Indigents are provided legal service by three basic programs:

- The public defender program. Under this plan a county or state selects a lawyer to operate an office that represents indigent criminal defendants. This system is used in 34% of the country's 4,137 counties. Only 19 states have public defender plans. Due to rulings by appeal courts, a public defender's office can be prevented from representing two or more co-defendants, judges have been appointing private attorneys to represent individuals in these cases. Because 25% of felony cases have co-defendants, this system "can have serious cost implications."
- Assigned counsel systems. Under this approach, judges or local administrators appoint private attorneys to represent indigents. Three-forths of the smaller counties in the country operate under this program.
- Contract systems. Under this approach lawyers are appointed by judges to act in the public defender' role for a fixed fee. Only 201 counties used this system in 1984, partly because it is a new approach. Some counties use the contract system to process the conflict of interest cases.

Of the states, California has the largest number of indigent cases, 661,000 in 1982, which cost the taxpayers $166.7 million, a quarter of the cost of the entire nation's indigent costs. County governments paid $150 million of the costs, the state $10.8 million, and local and federal funds covered the remaining $5.1 million. In the rest of the country, eighteen states paid for the total costs of the program.

Per-Capita Costs

The highest per-capita costs for indigent defense were in Washington, D.C. with $13, followed by Alaska, with $8.77, and California with $7.05. Based on the average cost per case, California was number 11 at $252 for its 661,000 cases while the next largest state, New York, had nearly one half the caseload and an average case cost of $211.

Abuse of Indigent Defense Systems

In 1985, the Los Angeles Board of Supervisors, after hearing complaints, authorized a study of the county's method of appointing private attorneys to represent the poor. The county auditor-controller's office found that "significant abuses" by lawyers existed and that the county could save millions of dollars a year with a different system. The study indicated that:

- While courts averaged only six operating hours a day, some lawyers claimed that they spent more than eight hours a day in court. One lawyer charged the county for 25 1/2 hours of court time on one day.
- Duplicate claims for the same services were submitted by some lawyers, or they charged twice for the defendants with more than one case pending when the cases were processed at the same time.

The auditor's office estimated that $3 million could be saved a year by using the Alternate Defense Counsel System—the county hires a firm to supply lawyers at a fixed hourly fee in court referred cases. The Board of Supervisors asked the District Attorney to investigate the irregularities in the county's system in which $25 million was spent for court-appointed criminal defense lawyers. It was reported that three private lawyers collected nearly $1 million in fees to process indigent cases during one 16-month period.

United States Anti-Trust Prosecutors v. IBM

Many anti-trust lawsuits are expensive to the public to conduct and the settlements often leave observers questioning the wisdom of the suits in the first place. An example is the anti-trust lawsuit that the U.S. Justice Department filed against IBM in 1969 that continued for 13 years. In January 1982, the Assistant Attorney General for anti-trust prosecution, William Baxter, made a decision to drop its case after determining that the suit was "without merit" and the government's contentions were "flimsy." Originally, the Justice Department accused IBM of monopolizing the markets for "general purpose" computers and peripheral products that are compatible with IBM equipment. In May of 1975, the trial commenced and continued for six years until January of 1982. The government attempted to prove that IBM had intended to monopolize the market for its products. During the long trial, IBM contended that the suit was without merit. Mr. Baxter apparently came to that conclusion after reviewing the case.

What did this unnecessary case cost the American consumer?

The lead counsel for IBM, Thomas D. Barr of the law firm Cravath, Swaine, and Moore of New York., indicated to the *Wall Street Journal* that during the 13 years the case had been pending, 2,500 depositions were taken and 66 million pages of documents produced. He said, "More than 200—maybe 300—lawyers were involved. The amount of money spent was enormous." Continuing, he said, "All those things are deductible, so that this case has cost the taxpayers hundreds of millions of dollars."[15] IBM's cost of the litigation was borne by consumers in increased costs of their products. Mr. Baxter claimed that the cost to the taxpayer of the IBM case amounted to only $13.6 million from its filing date on January 17, 1969.

IBM indicated to the *Wall Street Journal* in May 1982 that since Judge David Edelstein had ordered them to preserve everything that related to 'electronic data processing,' they had collected an estimated 46,726 tons of disposable documents in 1.9 million storage boxes in overseas locations. IBM claimed it was costing them about $5 million a year in storage fees. In addition over 160 government agencies had warehouses and rooms stuffed with records.

Actually, the anti-trust legislation that Congress passed created a billion-dollar business for lawyers, economists, expert witnesses, and supporting services that consumers subsidized. Consumers might ask what the legislation has done for them? Was the federal government considerate of the American taxpayer and consumer when it initiated this expensive lawsuit in 1969? If Assistant Attorney General Baxter is correct that the government had a weak case, why was it initiated in the first place and why was it continued for so long? The only group that really benefited were the lawyers.

The *Wall Street Journal* reported that "many academics in the lower federal courts already have moved in the same direction as Mr. Baxter—toward a view that some anti-trust precedents have wrongly prevented big companies from competing vigorously and from giving consumers the full benefits of greater efficiency the big companies often can achieve."[16]

The Japanese and European governments file very few antitrust suits. Their reasoning is that corporations and businesses know better than government lawyers and experts how to achieve efficient operations. This must be true, as Japanese firms are obviously very competitive with American companies in several fields.

It seems time for the American consumer to ask more questions about the legal activities of federal government lawyers.

United States Government v. American Telephone & Telegraph

On the same day that the government dropped the IBM case, it also dropped its seven-year-old lawsuit against the American Telephone and Telegraph Company. Settlement was reached between the government and AT&T in which the Company divested itself of 22 of its local operating companies within the following 18 months.

While the preparation for the AT&T case took about six years, the trial took only ten months. The handling of the case by Judge Harold Green was considered by many anti-trust attorneys as being a model management of complex litigation. The Judge regulated normally verbose lawyers by requiring that court presentations be simplified and kept brief. He insisted that, before the case went to trial, both sides define what facts they agreed on and what facts were in dispute. During the trial he set firm deadlines and discouraged redundant evidence.

Just the opposite happened in the IBM case held in the New York Federal Court. As previously mentioned, the trial dragged on for more than six years. Many of the attorneys criticized the IBM case Judge for refusing to limit the issues and evidence both sides brought into the trial.

Undoubtedly, the cost to AT&T and to the United States Government for preparing and trying the case ran into millions of dollars. The consumers, however, will pay for the expensive litigation as they did in the IBM case. Utility analyists and consumers wondered alike, at the confusion that resulted from the division of AT&T. After the breakup the availability of service was impaired, cost of service and equipment increased, and many a consumer wished that they had the old "Ma Bell" back in its monopolistic form. If an analysis had been made of the impact of the government's legal action, and the final impact on the consumer perhaps the lawsuit would never have been filed.

Lawyer Abuse of the Organized Crime Control Act

In 1970, Congress proudly passed the Organized Crime Control Act, and stated that its purpose was "to seek the eradication of organized crime in the United States." But because of the way the legislation was written and the interpretation given it by lawyers and judges, the results are very different from what Congress intended.

Under Title IX of the act, named the Racketeer Influenced and Corrupt Organizations Act or RICO, private civil attorneys found a legal gold mine. The act has not been used to prosecute the Mafia, but rather to sue hundreds of businessmen and corporations without any ties with organized crime. A decade after the act was passed, lawyers realized that the Act could be used in business and commercial disputes.

Large corporations, brokerage houses, banks, accounting firms, law firms, and insurance companies have been sued. Companies such as Rockwell International, Crocker National Bank, IBM, Hitachi Ltd., General Foods, Chase Manhattan Bank, Loeb, Rhoades & Co, and Shearson/American Express have either accused others or been accused of racketeering themselves. The misuse of the RICO Act by lawyers is an example of how a law or statute, enacted for one purpose, is utilized by the legal profession in a manner that the legislators never foresaw, and can be used to generate new litigation never imagined.

The American Bar Association, concerned about the action of lawyers, formed a committee and held a conference to discuss the problem. Some lawyers were angry about the misuse of the legislation while some who intended to use it, were enthusiastic about it.

In 1982, the ABA recommended changes in the criminal RICO provisions that would restrict its use. Several bills were introduced in Congress, but three years later no changes had been made. It seems that once an act like RICO is passed it takes on a life of its own.

Abuse of Personal Injury Suits— The Hyatt Regency Case

In July of 1981, the skywalks in the Hyatt Regency hotel in Kansas City, Missouri collapsed and killed 114 people and injured another 269 people. As a result personal injury lawyers scrambled to Kansas City to seek out victims. Lawsuits rolled in to the courthouse the Monday following the Friday tragedy.

Because of the manner in which the lawyers represented their clients, some were filed in the state court, some in the federal court as a class action suit. The defendants settled for a total cost of about $120 million, but the awards to the individuals varied greatly. John Dixon, who suffered loss of his only leg, died four months after the accident. His widow received $76,00 plus a $1,500 a-year annuity, worth less than 100,000. A woman who was in an elevator when the skywalk collapsed and walked out of the hotel safely, received $172,000—more than Dixon's wife. Sally Firestone, one of four who was seriously injured, did not settle her compensatory-damage claims, and went to trial. She received a verdict of $15 million which was reduced to $12.5 million on appeal. Other appeals followed.

The defense lawyers said that the average compensation paid to wrongful-death claiments was about $150,000 and to the seriously injured, about $300,000. Insurance covered the payments.

The defense lawyers indicated that due to the warfare among the plaintiffs' lawyers, they could negotiate more favorable settlements in most cases.

The *Wall Street Journal* reported that hostility among lawyers jockeying for control of the litigation and for legal fees led the presiding federal Judge Scott Wright to denounce the plaintiffs' lawyers as having an "unethical preoccupation with their own selfish interests."[17] It was estimated that plantiff lawyers received an estimated $30 million in legal fees. Judith Whittaker, Associate General Counsel for the builder of the hotel said, "It was quickly apparent that the trial of the skywalk cases would not be a search for the truth or what caused the collapse, but for the buck."[18]

Accident, Injury and Contingency Fees

What is a fair legal contingency fee? Under a contingency fee arrangement, a lawyer takes a personal injury or a condemnation case for a client with the understanding that the plaintiff will pay him when an award is made or a settlement reached. A lawyer takes the case for a percentage of the award, usually one-third, but sometimes up to 50%. Clients use this approach when they cannot afford to pay the legal fees. Lawyers believe the contingency fee is justified because they stand to lose a lot of money if they do not win. The high award cases also help lawyers pay for the cases they lose.

The public should put pressure on state judicial governing bodies to adopt more stringent rules governing the amount of contingency fees a lawyer can receive on negligence and related cases. After careful study, maximum percentages that lawyers can receive in contingency cases should be established, with a sliding scale that reduces the amount a lawyer receives as the total of an award increases. For example, for a client award up to $25,000, legislation could permit a lawyer to receive 30%, from $25,000 to $100,000, 25%, to $200,000, 24, 23, 22, 21, and 20% by $20,000 increments; from $200,000 to $300,000, 20% to 16% by the same increments, from $300,000 to $400,000, 15%; from $400,000 to $500,000, 14% and anything over $600,000, 12%.

When people are injured in accidents and have insurance, they should be paid promptly. That is not always the case. Because of unmet needs in accident cases a public indemnity compensation program for catastrophic accident situations is needed to compensate victims fairly and quickly. As stated previously, legislation is needed to create a uniform national accident insurance system to cover major accident tragedies where the victim's injuries are not covered adequately. Limits should be set also in states limiting the total amount of personal injury and medical malpractice suits.

It is suggested that review boards, made up of specialists in medicine, law, economics, and psychology, review accident cases that meet their criteria, and make prompt decisions. Based on the progress made by victims of accidents, structured awards could be adjusted and altered as victims respond to medical treatment and therapy.

"No-fault" insurance may or may not be the answer, but a better system than our present one must be found. New Zealand and a few other countries have systems that seem to work well. The Congress or the President should assert leadership and initiate a national task force representing consumers, accident victims, insurance companies, legal profession, medical economists, and others to investigate and recommend a catastrophic accident insurance system for the United States. With a better system for handling accident cases in which technically no one is at fault, victims can be reimbursed promptly for damages, eliminating lengthy, expensive court cases. Lawyers may lose income, but consumers will gain. Too much money now goes to lawyers in negligent cases rather than the deserving victims.

A Lawyer Balks At Charging Excess Legal Fees

A lawyer in Minneapolis became so outraged at the exorbitant fees charged by his own law partners that he sued them. Michael Doshan of the Rerat Law Firm accused his three partners of charging a client "an exorbitant and unreasonable fee" and demanded that the excessive amount be returned to the client. The original case involving Craig Merchant was settled out of court for about a million dollars at the time. The contingency fee charged was $515,000, or a little more than one-half of the settlement award. Due to Doshan's objections and pressure, the fee was reduced first to $375,000 and then to $278,000. Apparently this did not satisfy Doshan. The Minnsota Lawyers' Professional Responsibility Board began investigating the Rerat firm as a result of Doshan's complaints. Responding angrily to the investigation, the partners of the law firm forced Doshan from the board of directors, "locked him out of his office, removed his name from the firm's business cards, and placed him on an indefinite leave of absence."

The firm's normal contingency fee was apparently 25%, but for some reason Merchant's fee was set higher. The client was a switchman who lost both legs and badly injured his arm as a result of an accident in 1976. Merchant was to get a "structured pay-out" over a period of 20 years. Assuming he would live for 20 years, he would get about $2 million. The original amount to be paid him was around $570,000. Doshan became angry when he realized that the client wasn't fully aware that he was paying 50% to the law firm because of the complications of the pay-out procedure. He believed that the nature of the damages warranted the client's getting more of the money. Due to the large fee the law firm received, Doshan claimed the law partners voted themselves a salary raise from $70,000 to $90,000 a year. He objected to this and refused to accept his $20,000 raise.

Cost of Lawyers and Legal Services

Large sums of money are spent on legal services in this country, an estimated $30 billion a year in 1983, more than any other nation. Lawyer fees have increased rapidly in the last few years, even though an abundance of lawyers graduate from law school each year.

When lawyers join a law firm, they do well. In 1981, in a survey made by Altman and Weils of 472 law firms, they found lawyers made an average of $69,709 in 1980 in firms with more than 40 lawyers. In smaller firms of two to six, the average lawyer's salary was $47,145. By 1983, the median yearly income for male lawyers reached $53,000. Wall Street lawyers at the top of their fields made around $300,000 a year.

In 1960, there was one lawyer per 632 people. By 1970 the ratio reached one per 572, by 1980 one per 418, by 1983 one per 375, and it is estimated to be one per 260 persons by mid-1990. About 25% of all lawyers are in two states, California and New York.

In 1983, of the 622,000 lawyers, 68% were in private practice, 10% in private industry, 9% in government, 4% were judges and law clerks, 4% in educational institutions, legal aid and public defender offices and special interest groups, and 5% were inactive. Between 1970 and 1980, the number of state and local government lawyers increased a huge 70%. Federal lawyers increased only 3% during the same period.

Congressional Lobbying by Legal Profession

Lawyers make large financial contributions to candidates for Congress to gain influence for their clients or their causes. The *Wall Street Journal* reported in 1983 that while the medical profession donated $2.1 million during the 1982 campaigns, lawyers provided more than double that amount. During the 1982 House and Senate elections Federal Election Commission records showed that individual lawyers gave $2.9 million, law firm PACs gave $500,000, and the "Attorneys Congressional Campaign Trust" of the Association of Trial Lawyers of America provided another $800,000. One law firm contributed $126,508 to political candidates.

President of Common Cause, Fred Wertheimer, disapproved of lawyers giving so much money stating in 1983 that: "This money holds out no pretense of constituency. This is straight access buying, an extension of the hired gun principle."[19]

Ethics and Overcharging

In an article by Chief Justice Burger in the *Cleveland State University Law Review,* the Supreme Court chief accused lawyers of overcharging clients. Burger believed that bar associations and law schools were neglecting professional ethics. He referred to surveys that found only one person in four believes attorneys have high standards of ethics.[20]

Burger claimed that too many lawyers charge relatively high fees for simple transactions. He said, "In all too many cases—the purchase of a home being a good example—clients are 'ripped off' by fees that are greatly out of proportion to the complexity of the transaction or the time spent by the lawyers."[21]

On teaching ethics, the Chief Justice wrote: "Surely the failures of the law school in teaching legal ethics and professional responsibility are responsible in some measure for the ethical problems in our profession."[22]

Court Transcriber Speaks Out
On Lawyer Efficiency and Ethics

In a letter to the Editor of the *Star-Free Press* of Ventura, California, Phyllis J. Hall, a court transcriber stated:

> I have been a transcriber for court reporters for many years, and I know first hand how the system works, in both criminal and civil courts.
>
> In thousands of civil cases that I have transcribed, I have seen attorneys conduct lengthy, tedious, totally unnecessary depositions of witnesses, asking the same questions over and over, simply to prolong the litigation in order to collect larger fees from their clients. I make a living by transcribing this garbage. but it literally makes me sick to see it happening.
>
> Without a single exception, all of the depositions that I have transcribed could be cut by at least 75 percent in length and still serve their purpose. When you realize that on the average, a deposition runs roughly 100 pages, for which a deposition firm receives anywhere from $350 to $500, the attorneys each receive anywhere from $500 upwards, if all of the redundant and unnecessary questioning was cut out, that would save the clients $750-plus on just one deposition. And there are as many as 30 to 100 depositions taken on one case.[23]

Changing Lawyer Attitudes

As shown previously, the attitudes of lawyers toward court and legal procedures contribute greatly to the courts' problems, inefficiencies, and high cost. The present court system provides no incentive to lawyers or trial judges to be efficient and move cases along rapidly. In fact lawyers make more money by delaying cases. Unfortunately, an efficient trial judge's actions may be overturned by an appellate court if he tries to prohibit frivolous motions and delays in court. He should try, nevertheless.

Changing Law School Education Concepts

Law school deans should make every effort to change the attitudes of instructors in law school toward developing a greater respect for the truth in disputes and for the rights of victims as well as offenders.

Law schools play an important role in educating lawyers technically as well as philosophically. If law school professors advocated to students that they not seek court delays, not file frivolous motions to sidetrack issues, and not endlessly analyze the meaning of every word, the interests of clients and the public would be better served. Law schools should advocate that lawyers become efficient in court, skilled in negotiating settlements, and use court as a last resort.

Victim organizations, the media, and the public should keep pressure on bar associations and law schools to change their present advocacy and technical orientation to one concerned with the intent of laws, rights of all parties in disputes, and to be responsible in court when representing clients.

Harvard Changes The Education of Lawyers

University President Derek Bok, a former law school professor at Harvard, believes that law schools must do as Harvard is doing and draw from actual experience in exploring "problems of professional responsibility, the delivery of legal services to poor and middle-income populations, the adversary system and alternative methods of resolving disputes." Harvard is establishing courses on negotiation and alternative means of dispute resolution, economics and sociology of the legal profession, and providing practical or on-the-job training while in law school. The law school faculty is studying different organizational structures that could better serve the public, such as a prepaid legal services plan. Other projects involve finding ways to reduce the costs and delays of litigation, and the problems of government and public-interest lawyers.

Bok finds that more paralegal people will be needed in the field and could be trained in law schools. He states: "In short, a just and effective legal system will not merely call for a revised curriculum (in law school); it will entail the education of new categories of people. It is time that our law schools began to take the lead in helping devise such training."[24]

Trial Lawyer Training

Bar associations and the judiciary should adopt policies that will permit lawyers to practice in court as trial lawyers only after receiving trial training, or serving in an apprentice program under the supervision of experienced trial attorneys. Inexperienced and incompetent trial attorneys severely slow down trials. The American Bar Association should take leadership in establishing an acceptable criteria and procedure for becoming a trial lawyer. If the associations take no action, the state legislatures should establish minimum educational and training standards before permitting lawyers to try cases.

Judicial Assertiveness

Judges should warn lawyers in court what the court's policy will be on delays, unnecessary motions, and unprofessional behavior and fine or discipline them when out of order. Judge Manuel Real, Chief Judge on the federal bench in Los Angeles did just that to a lawyer in his court.

In 1984, Real dismissed a suit Attorney Stephen Yagman filed against two pathologists for $20 million, ruling that it could not be supported with enough evidence to warrant continuation of the trial. The two pathologists then charged Yagman with filing the action "in bad faith for improper motives."[25]

During the trial in May of 1984 Judge Real, became angry with Yagman's behavior in court and fined him $250,000. Yagman responded later by telling reporters that the judge "suffers from mental disorders." Real received backing from many in the legal profession for his actions.

When lawyers realize judges intend to manage their courts efficiently and will resort to fining tardy, delaying, and disrespectful lawyers, most counsels will respond positively.

CHAPTER FIVE

ABUSE OF COURTS
BY PUBLIC INTEREST LAWYERS

Before the Federal Office of Economic Opportunity was established, courts appointed attorneys to provide services to the poor when a person could not afford legal counsel. With the War on Poverty Program in the 1960s, the Office of Economic Opportunity created thousands of new jobs for lawyers. Numerous legal assistance organizations were formed, such as The Western Center on Law and Poverty, Inc., The California Rural Legal Assistance Program, The West Texas Legal Services, National Consumer Law Center, and many others. Basically, their role was to assist low-income people with their legal problems such as divorce, tenant-landlord disputes, and civil lawsuits in which they would normally be unable to hire an attorney. These are worthy activities and needed. Evidence surfaced, however, that these offices attracted lawyers who were more interested in changing society than in representing the poor.

Legal Services Corporation

In 1974, Congress formed the Legal Services Corporation to distribute funds to local legal aid programs throughout the country. Up to 1982, about 300 local legal assistance programs employed approximately 6,000 attorneys throughout the United States. The federally supported Legal Services Corporation funded the programs. Its budget increased from $71.5 million in 1976 to $321 million in 1980. Every county in the United States was cov-

MEN OF JUSTICE—"What gets me is being accused of twelve robberies." "There were twelve? Good! I'll plead kleptomania."

ered by a Legal Services Program. They provided about two staff attorneys per 10,000 population.

The LSC's program came under attack by critics for: 1) financing "social engineering activities," 2) attacking the establishment, 3) waging class warfare and in general misusing public funds for programs not justified under the Legal Services Corporation Act.

Critics were angry because legal aid societies filed class action lawsuits against the same federal and state governments that funded them originally. A number of large public and private road, dam, and water projects were halted for years by lawsuits filed by publicly funded law offices. The legal service lawyers claimed to "protect the public interest and the welfare of the poor." *The Wall Street Journal* referred to these activists as "the public interest law industry."[1]

Under federal enabling legislation, legal assistance offices were not permitted to take part in organizing groups or lobbying for their own interests. On several occasions government officials became aware that the offices were violating the law under which they operated. While Governor of California in 1970, Ronald Reagan, voted against funding the California Rural Legal Assistance (CRLA) organization. To justify his veto, the Governor's office released the Uhler Report which documented that CRLA had interests other than the poor. The report said that CRLA displayed a "blatant indifference to the needs of the poor. . .(and) a disposition to use their clients as ammunition in their efforts to wage ideological warfare."[2]

Other states had similar views to Governor Reagan's about the activities of legal assistance lawyers in their states. They included Arizona, Connecticut, Florida, Louisiana, Missouri, and North Dakota.[3]

In a publication entitled *Government Activists: How They Rip Off the Poor,* H. Peter Metzger, Ph.D., and Richard A. Westfall wrote that lawyers "involved in legal aid programs often do so not because they want to help the poor as they claim, but because they want to substantially change the fabric of American society."[4] Their view is supported by an article in the journal *Law and Society:*

> Top graduates from elite law schools came from Supreme Court law clerks and wanted to work solely on "test case," law reform, appellate litigation. Young lawyers left

corporate law firms hoping to enjoy direct client contact. 'Radical' lawyers came committed to continue their representation of militant community groups. To 'counterculture' lawyers, Legal Services work bore the least resemblance to "a real job."[5]

Illegal Lobbying by Legal Assistance Centers

Metzger and Westfall reported that: "In June 1978, a congressional investigative staff, directed to conduct an investigation of the Legal Services Corporation, found that California Rural Legal Assistance based in San Francisco maintained a permanent office in Sacramento with five lawyers—all registered lobbyists—for the purpose of lobbying—an activity strictly forbidden to government-paid Legal Services-funded lawyers.[6]

It was discovered also by the investigative staff that the Western Center on Law and Poverty, Inc., a federally funded organization (over $1 million) in Los Angeles, had four registered lobbyists involved in legislative and administrative advocacy. The investigative report stated that "there had been no accounting for their time (the lobbyists)."[7]

The public was paying the salaries of lawyers to lobby for new laws to benefit their movement. This activity was considered illegal under the enabling legislation of the Legal Services Corporation.

The Government Accounting Office stated in a report in 1980 that a LSC-funded lawyer group in one state had made decisions "by themselves, for themselves" that statutory exceptions in their state exempted them from the lobbying prohibitions of the act governing their activities.[8] The same GAO report stated that "corporation officials at the headquarters level advised us that they do not share this opinion..." The regional LSC-funded lawyers apparently interpreted the law in their favor despite the intent of Congress or the wording of the act.

In proposed Legal Services Corporation appropriation legislation, Representative Carlos Moorhead (R-California) attached an amendment that made it even more clear that any type of lobbying activity was forbidden.

Illegal Organizing Activities

Other legal services offices such as the West Texas Legal Services, an LSC grantee, were involved in promoting and distributing manuals and literature advising clients on organizing and how to hold anti-utility company demonstrations.[9] The Legal Services Corporation Act is clear on limiting the organizing activities of legal services organizations. It states:

> No funds made available by the corporation under this subchapter, either by grant or contract may be used. . .to organize or to encourage to organize or to plan for the creation or formation of or structuring of any organization, association, coalition, alliance, federation, confederation, or any similar entity...[10]

The LSC staff reportedly tried to remove the Congressman Moorhead amendment, but were unable to do so. The GAO, concerned with what LSC and its grantees were doing nationally, stated in its report on the corporation: "It has not yet acted to establish procedures for systematically determining if its grantees are, in fact, in compliance with the Act's provisions."[11]

Loss of Support

Conservative columnist, James J. Kilpatrick, who had been a strong supporter of the Legal Services Corporation until he became aware of the act violations, wrote:

> The Legal Services Corporation, through its own failure to heed repeated warnings against its own activism, will have done itself in...The question is whether the corporation, under present law and present leadership, is capable of adhering faithfully to the humble but important duties for which it was created. The Houseman memoranda raise almost insurmountable doubts.[12]

Having studied and analyzed activist activities in government, Metzger and Westfall found that:

> ...an activist tyranny that claims to represent the 'public interest' but doesn't is more than a match for the real public interest. That's because activists are intense full-timers, while ordinary people pay scant attention to politics after election day. Voids thus created are quickly filled by zeal-

ots and, being unscrupulous and dedicated, these modern activists have shown themselves to be highly creative in inventing ways to bypass democratic processes in order to achieve their political goals. Intimidation of elected representatives by staged media events and circumventing Congress entirely in favor of delaying tactics in the courts have been their most effective weapons, but they have never crossed the border into illegality before.[13]

Metzger found that lawyer activists achieve their goals within public agencies by the following mechanisms:

- Using a collusive lawsuit to divert millions in federal anti-poverty funds to activist organizations dedicated to attacking business;
- Suborning Congressional intent so as to misdirect an entire federal program from helping the poor and elderly pay their utility bills, to paying instead the salaries of professional activists and providing massive support for an entire "network" [their word] of anti-business activism;
- Suborning Congressional intent so as to use another federal program, designed to provide legal assistance to the poor, instead to attack business in the courts (all in the name of 'the poor'); and
- Circumventing Congress to distribute, illegally, millions in what the activists fondly call 'Robin Hood money,' fines extracted from oil companies by questionable rules, then diverted to yet even more 'public interest' law firms and activist organizations.[14]

The two analysts consider the actions of activist lawyers as a threat to democracy. They state: "As long as we continue to excuse criminal behavior inside of government with the claim that the intention, however misguided, was to serve the 'public interest,' we will be slowly and inexorably drawn away from representative Democracy and into a government-by-activists, with the taxpayers footing the bill."

The Simer vs Oliverez Case

It seemed on the surface to the judge to be a legitimate suit of eight low-income people against the federal agency, Community

Services Administration. Eight so-called 'poor persons' claimed that the Community Services Administration had mismanaged the fiscal year 1979 Fuel Assistance Program. CSA was the new name for the old agency, Office of Economic Opportunity. The CSA had the responsibility of assisting low-income people pay heating costs during the winter if they did not have enough money to pay the increased cost.

The eight plaintiffs were supported and represented by a group of legal aid lawyers funded by the Legal Services Corporation. It was revealed later that the lawyers actually solicited the lawsuit, not for the poor people, but for their personal 'cause.' *The Wall Street Journal,* analyzing the case, later reported: "Of the claimants named in the suit who could be reached for comment, those who were aware of the suit at all insisted that they had been steered into the lawsuit by public interest law firms."[15]

Upon completing the hearing on the case, the judge found as stated that the CSA did mismanage the assistance program and would have to reach a settlement with the plaintiffs. It was suggested at the hearing that the legal aid lawyers and the lawyers for the Community Services Administration meet privately and work out a settlement. The judge assumed that both parties were adversaries and, because of that, an agreement fair to both sides would be reached. He discovered later the Community Services Administration lawyers and the legal aid lawyers were not adversaries.

The Simer settlement recommended by the lawyers was that the eight named poor-person plaintiffs receive $250 each, for a total of $2,000 out of a total award of $18 million. The Community Services Administration agreed to distribute the rest of the $18 million, totalling $17,998,000 to a number of other "public interest groups and others who were third persons and not party to the case."

Investigating the case, Metzger and Westfall found: On April 25, 1980, the same attorneys appeared once again before the judge. They presented to the judge a "Stipulation and Agreed Order," which they had drafted jointly. Assistant U.S. Attorney Moran said: "So what we did, Your Honor, with the money left over was to try to provide a program whereby people who would meet all the requirements of the 1979 program would gain the benefits of this money...this is...a fair and just way of resolving the matter..."[16]

What they actually did, upon closer reading, was provide mil-

lions of dollars to "energy advocates who were anti-energy company oriented" and would not assist the poor directly.

Division of Money

The remaining $17,998,000, according to Metzger and West-
fall, was divided among such groups as "the completely federal
funded National Consumer Law Center (a $2.3 million beneficia-
ry), the Citizens/Labor Energy Coalition (sponsors of 'Stop Big
Oil' Day), and the Community Services Administration, which,
having 'lost' the suit, awarded itself a $350,000 consolation prize,
specifically to put four more activists on CSA's payroll, a plum simply not available from the Congressional appropriations."[17] Another $4 million was granted to "local groups to fund anti-utility 'ener-
gy advocacy'."

Metzger and Westfall informed the Pacific Legal Foundation
who in turn released a legal opinion on August 18, 1980, which
stated that the Community Services Administration "had indeed
circumvented Congressional intent by allowing price intervention
funds to be used for purposes other than grants to low-income
households as a result of the Stipulation and Agreed Order in
Simer v. Olivarez." The Pacific Legal Foundation is a privately
funded public interest group. The Foundation contacted the federal General Accounting Office and suggested they investigate the
Community Services Administration's actions.

The Wall Street Journal, reviewing the case and the terms of the
Simer agreement, reported on August 20, 1980: "The CSA and
the Public Advocacy and Legal Services groups may have hit upon
a marvelous recipe to render Congress' intentions moot and feather their own nest."[18]

The Capital Legal Foundation, a private group, upon analyzing the situation, filed a complaint representing Senators Laxalt
(R-Nevada), Hatch (R-Utah), and Zorinsky (D-Nevada) on September 29, 1980, saying that the Simer case "appears to have
been a collusive lawsuit" and that "literally everyone except the
plaintiff class members (the poor) received a 'piece of the
action.'"[19] The judge, upon reading and hearing of the actual contents of the settlement, asked all parties to a hearing for an expla-
nation by the lawyers on how the settlement could carry out Congress' intent. The judge stated: "I am not sure just why the court
was drawn into the matter, except possibly from the standpoint of

conferring a legitimacy upon the whole undertaking that might otherwise have been absent."[20]

Metzger and Westfall believe that, "Simer is now widely realized to have been a 'sweetheart' deal, a friendly, collusive lawsuit in which government defendants and government plaintiffs cooperated with each other covertly in order to divert federal fuel assistance funds away from the poor and elderly and pour them instead into the movement."

The author of *Fat City*, Donald Lambro, said that the Simer case: "Was...[the] latest episode in CSA's wasteful saga provides a revealing glimpse into how a coterie of bureaucrats, consultants, advocacy groups, and other poverty professionals have been feeding off the government's poverty program at the expense of the poor."[21]

Three weeks after the judge held the October 6th hearing, he wrote a "blistering memorandum opinion"[22] according to *The Chicago Lawyer*. The lawyers were condemned by Judge Grady as being "opportunistic and manipulative." The Judge reported on how he had been duped:

> At the conclusion of the brief colloquy, I signed a Stipulation and Agreed Order...Lulled by the appearance of an adversarial situation, I assumed, perhaps incorrectly, that the defendants would not have agreed to a settlement which contemplated their spending the funds in an unauthorized manner. To repeat, the parties did not share with me their knowledge that my signature on the order was to be the sole authority for the expenditure of the funds."[23]

Continuing, the Judge said, "I believe that the parties, both by what they said and what they did not say, misled me both as to the facts and to the law."[24]

Protecting Democracy

The Simer case points out the need to be on the alert for government legal service lawyers advocating lofty goals. Justice Brandeis states the issue well:

> Experience should teach us to be most on our guard to protect liberty when the government's purposes are bene-

ficial. Men born to freedom are naturally alert to repel invasion of their liberty by evil-minded rulers. The greater dangers to liberty lurk in insidious encroachments by men of zeal, well-meaning but without understanding.

Legal services should be provided for the poor who cannot afford legal services, but primarily for: 1) family matters—marriage dissolution, 2) housing—landlord and tenant disputes, and 3) child custody and support—paternity and wife beating—cases.

The courts and the public were victimized in the Simer case and many like them by over-zealous lawyers. The public should not have paid for government funded lawyers to advocate society changing programs. Lawyers working for public supported LSC programs should remember its purpose is to provide financial support for competent legal assistance in non-criminal matters and proceedings and for persons who are financially unable to afford it. If lawyers stray from its purpose a public backlash could evolve that could harm the quality of services to the poor.

Attempt to Abolish LSC

President Reagan's staff, concerned about the activities of the LSC Corporation and misuse of funds, recommended in 1980 that the corporation be abolished and that other means be found to give legal assistance to the poor. This action was strongly opposed by the American Civil Liberties Union, and many lawyers and judges in the country. A letter was written by about 578 state and federal judges in June of 1981 opposing the Reagan administration's plan to abolish the program.

The President was not successful in abolishing the LSC, but he did cut its budget from $321 million to $241 million a 25% reduction, for the next two fiscal years. In fiscal 1983-84, Congress increased the budget to $275 million. In 1982, the President appointed new members to the board of directors of LSC who were more sympathetic to his point of view. By 1984 Legal Services had lost more than 1500 of its 6,350 lawyers and shutdown about 400 of its 1,475 neighborhood legal aid offices in the country. LSC lawyers complained bitterly that the program was being ruined by the cutbacks, but grew quiet when it was announced in July of 1982 that a surplus of $41 million existed.

Because of the cutbacks, the Legal Aid Foundation in Los Angeles reduced its staff 40%, including 20 of its 50 lawyers. Four of the foundation's nine offices were closed because of the funding cutback. The California Rural Legal Assistance group lost one third of its 77 lawyers and had trouble keeping its 13 offices open.

To fill the void and need for lawyers to assist low income people, the legal establishment searched for alternative means to provide legal help. Private lawyers were urged to provide free legal work for the poor, known as *pro bono publico* or "for the public good." In El Paso, Texas about 10% of the city's lawyers provided *pro bono* work. In Ventura County, California Judge Lawrence Storch appointed private attorneys to represent indigent people at no charge to the county when the court had run out of volunteers. A small group of the local bar association protested the action. The power of a court to appoint lawyers to represent indigents without compensation is pending appeal before the California Supreme Court.

California Legislature Responds to Problem

To provide consistent funding, the California legislature in 1983 required the state's 80,000 some lawyers to contribute the interest earned on clients' funds held by them that are in interest-bearing accounts to a state fund. Every quarter the banks send the interest from these accounts to the State Bar Association where a panel disburses the funds. The program is called the Interest on Lawyer Trust Account Program, or IOLTA. The association anticipates receiving $4 to $5 million a year for 30 some Legal Services-funded agencies in the state. Because of a controversy over the fund, none of the money was distributed until 1985 when the Bar's Board of Governors voted to release it.

Administrative Law Proliferation

Congress should monitor and review the growth of administrative agencies such as the Environmental Protection Agency, LSC, and others that have latitude to write their own laws and regulations based on enabling legislation given them by congress. There has been a proliferation of regulations and laws passed by state and federal agencies. A new judiciary has evolved to administer these laws and disputes over them. The public pays a high tax bill every year for these extra legislative and judicial branches without knowing much about them.

For example, disability-benefit claim cases, a relatively new field, are attracting lawyers who have found legal opportunities that benefit clients and themselves. In 1981, 733 administrative law judges reviewed 1.6 million applicants in the Social Security agency,. Lawyers found that while only 27% had initial success, if they appealed higher, the applicants had a 70% to 80% chance of winning. The number of lawyers handling Social Security cases (called the 'public service' business) grew in two years from zero to 13,000 members.

The *Wall Street Journal* reported that in 1974 the Social Security Administration paid out only $6 million in fees to lawyers handling 9,000 disability claims. During 1981, however, the agency paid out $65.2 million to 59,000 claimants, a considerable jump.

Stopping Illegal Actions
by Government Activist Lawyers

For a 'cause' some LSC layers violated the public's trust and the law under which their agency was founded. Agencies such as the LSC must not be placed in positions independent of supervision by a federal department. When organizations are removed from direct accountability by Congress, irresponsible persons can abuse their authority for a long time before being detected. Public-funded legal groups must be placed under close supervision and held accountable for their actions. Congress should review the need for having so many agencies doing legal work and consider consolidating, eliminating, or merging them to gain control of their activities.

CHAPTER SIX

CONTROLLING ABUSE OF
COURT SYSTEM BY JUDICIARY

Most of the trial judges in our courts act in a responsible and professional manner and attempt to make the system function well. Despite serious weaknesses in it, much work is accomplished by dedicated jurists. However, ample room exists for major improvements in court management by the judiciary, especially in the higher courts.

Judicial excesses are costly to Americans. Examples of lack of judicial restraints and methods of limiting these excesses are illustrated to show what must be overcome to obtain an efficient, effective, and economical justice system. A number of high court justices especially, have overstepped their judicial bounds and interjected themselves into the legislative process.

Search for Perfect Justice

The Constitution promised Americans fair and speedy trials, not perfect justice. Unfortunately, the public unknowingly pays a high price for the relentless search for perfection by some justices. Chief Justice Burger of the United States Supreme Court believes that the present system is inefficient and a mockery of justice. In his address to the American Bar Association in 1981, Burger said:

> The search for perfect justice has led us on a course found nowhere else in the world. A true mis-carriage of

MEN OF JUSTICE—"Yes, they want to convict this orphan, whom I don't consider young as he is fifty-seven. But he is, nonetheless, still an orphan. I always comfort myself, gentlemen, with knowledge that judges always look with open eyes upon all the circumstances."

justice, whether 20, 30, or 40 years old, (cases) should always be open for review, but the judicial process becomes a mockery of justice if it is forever open to appeal and retrials for errors in the arrests, the search, or the trial.

He asks:

Is a society redeemed if it provides massive safeguards for accused persons—including pretrial freedom for most crimes, defense lawyers at public expense, trials and appeals, retrials and more appeals, almost without end—and yet fails to provide elementary protection for decent, law-abiding citizens?

On the subject of conducting criminal trials, Burger expressed alarm at our system:

Many enlightened countries succeed in holding criminal trials within four to eight weeks after arrest. . . Our criminal process often goes on two, three, four, or more years before the accused runs out of options. Even after sentence and confinement, the warfare continues with endless streams of petitions for writs, suits against parole boards, wardens, and judges. So we see a paradox. Even while we struggle toward correction, education, and rehabilitation, our systems encourages prisoners to continue warfare with society.

For years, a contemporary "Jack, the Ripper" brutally terrorized and killed women in Great Britain. The offender, when caught, was brought to trial and convicted in six weeks. In the United States, selecting a jury alone could take six weeks.

The Impact of Appellate Judges' Search For Perfect Justice

The "relentless search for legal error" by appellate judges and their decisions on some cases seem senseless to non-lawyers and court-watchers. In many trials, the appellate court's rulings put trial judges in a "damned if he does and damned if he doesn't" situation. Even if a defendant enters a guilty plea, the plea can be overturned at a later time by an appellate court because of the manner in which the trial judge instructed him or the jury.

Competent attorneys are virtually coerced into filing motions and appeals of all sorts because of the issue of 'competent counsel.' If an attorney fails to file certain motions or appeals he may later be found to have failed to provide competent defence—a finding which could have a crushing impact on his career.

The United States Supreme Court has made various instructional requirements a matter of constitutional law. These regulations require that a trial judge interrogate at length a defendant who wishes to enter a guilty plea. He must do this, even though the defendant is represented by counsel. The instructions in court to the defendant must show several things: 1) that the plea was intelligent and voluntary; 2) that the defendant had waived his privilege against self-incrimination; 3) the defendant had waived his right to a jury trial; 4) that the defendant had waived his right to confront his accusors; and 5) that the defendant possessed a full understanding of the connotations and consequences of his plea. Some states go beyond these regulations and require that the impact of the guilty plea to the defendant be explained.

The Abuse of Justice
by Exclusionary Rule Interpretation

The exclusionary rule states that no evidence of the guilt of an accused criminal can be used against him if it was obtained in the course of, or as a result of, an illegal arrest or search and seizure. The rule developed out of a decision by the United States Supreme Court in 1961 known as the Mapp v. Ohio case. The court's action made the exclusionary rule part of all constitutional criminal law in the 50 states.

Even though the accused is guilty of an offense, he may be released because of the use of illegal evidence. The rule places a difficult burden on a police officer who, seeing a crime committed, may accidently obtain evidence illegally in pursuing and arresting an offender. Authorities claim hundreds of criminals are freed and many dangerous lawbreakers are not brought to trial because of technical violations of this rule.

As the exclusionary rule now operates, a dangerous offender may be set free, not because the individual was innocent, but because a judge finds that evidence used to establish quilt was taken in violation of the Fourth Amendment reasonableness standard for searches. One should keep in mind that the exclusionary rule is not part of the Constitution, but is a judge-made rule of evidence adopted in 1914 from federal criminal trials. The rule was not used by state courts until 1961.

Braeseke Case—A Classic Misuse of Exclusionary/Miranda Rulings

The rules, procedures, and techniques involved in seeking delays, changing venue, etc., are designed to protect the defendant but delay justice and cost the taxpayers more. The direction of the adversary system in the United States generates an environment in court in which it is the lawyer's goal to 'win.' Knowing a client is guilty, a defense lawyer is considered derelict in his duties by the judiciary or plain crazy to acknowledge as much. He is expected to try every maneuver possible to free his client, whether that client is dangerous or not. This game, played in our courtrooms every day, and in every state, is costly to the public in taxes and in the erosion of justice.

Dangerous offenders freed by technicalities or free on bail are a threat to society. The authors of *Criminal Justice Reform: a Blueprint,* Randall R. Rader and Patrick B. McGuigan, state that 19 studies of current bail policies over a 15 year period, "document the high incidence of crime committed by individuals free on bail."

A classic example of the misuse of court rulings occurred in the Barry Floyd Braeseke case in Dublin, California. Barry Braeseke was in his room an August night in 1976 taking 'angel dust.' For some reason, he decided to shoot his mother, father, and grandfather. Sneaking up behind them, while they were watching television, he shot and killed all three. He was taken into custody shortly after the killing.

According to court records, the police informed Braeseke of his rights before asking him any questions. Braeseke later asked the police if he could talk "off the record." When told that he could, Braeseke reported that he disposed of the rifle "where some kids may find it." He was informed of his rights again. A few hours later, he made two additional separate statements admitting that he had killed his family.

An experienced defense lawyer, James Leonard Crew, was appointed to defend Braeseke. Crew did what was expected of him and aggressively defended his client. During the trial, Crew made a motion that Braeseke's confessions be invalidated because Braeseke did not realize what he was doing when he spoke "off the record." He claimed that the police should have told Braeseke that there was "no such thing" as "an off-the-record" statement.

Even though Crew did an able job, he knew his client was guilty. The trial court found Braeseke guilty and convicted him of murder. The case, as usual, was appealed to the State Supreme Court. The court ignored the findings of the trial court, threw out the confessions, and reversed the conviction of Braeseke. They made their ruling in November 1979. Two of Braeseke's confessions were invalidated as violations of the Miranda Rule, the United States Supreme Court requirement that police tell all suspects of their right to silence and counsel before questioning. Braeseke had been warned several times, but continued to confess. One can't help but form the opinion that the court does not uphold the right to confess a crime.

Because the state Supreme Court invalidated the second confession, the Court also held as inadmissable the use of the rifle as evidence because both were products of the first confession. In 1978, before the California Supreme Court heard the case, Braeseke was interviewed on the CBS program 'Sixty Minutes' by Mike Wallace. The program concerned the effects of 'angel dust.' On that program, Braeseke admitted to Wallace and to the country over television that he had killed his mother, father, and grandfather. In Braeseke's words, "I was in my room and I had a rifle with me...and I came downstairs and walked into the family room. And the family was watching the TV set with their backs to me. Then I started firing the rifle...." The California Supreme Court refused to consider this confession as well.

The case was appealed to the United States Supreme Court in May of 1981. The United States Supreme Court upheld the state Supreme Court's position by refusing to reinstate the conviction. Although he was Braeseke's defense lawyer, Crew could hardly believe that the United States Supreme Court called the confessions inadmissible. It angered him so much, he wrote a letter to the United States Supreme Court and sent copies to the press. His letter stated:

> Your recent decision in the case of People v. Barry Braeseke was predictable. On the other hand, it is difficult

to understand how a system of laws conceived to protect innocent people can become twisted to give freedom to a person who deliberately kills three innocent human beings, thereafter confesses four times to these killings, the last confession being on national television, and with all this somehow finds that freedom awaits him...

I (am) a responsible citizen in my community and shudder to think that my family has now been given less protection by our courts. No wonder the citizens in this country refer to attorneys in a disrespectful fashion and to many of our courts with comparable lack of respect.[1]

Crew in his criticism of the way courts applied the 'exclusionary rule,' the court-issued doctrine that prohibits the use of evidence obtained unlawfully in searches and interrogations, said, "We're losing sight of what the framers of the Constitution intended. The Braeseke decision is a super example of applying the logic of the rule to the point of absurdity."

The prosecuting attorney for the case, Deputy District Attorney Michael Cardoza of Alameda County, commented on James Crew's letter: "When somebody like Jim Crew—who is an excellent and tough defense attorney—criticizes a decision, then you realize just how bad the Braeseke decision was. In effect, he's saying to the court, 'As an attorney, I did what I was supposed to do. But you bought it. Are you crazy?'"

Competent defense lawyers are faced with similar conflicts. If they do not use delaying tactics and file numerous motions to free a client they know is guilty, they could be declared incompetent by an appellant court months or years later on an appeal and the case retried.

Crew said in his interview that he did what he was expected to do as a lawyer for Braeseke. He was speaking out because "as a lawyer and a citizen, I think the decision was dead wrong." In response to Crew's letter to the Supreme Court, the legal community responded in various ways. Some supported his position, and others believed he should have remained quiet. *Time* magazine quoted Los Angeles criminal lawyer Anthony Murray, a member of the State Bar Associations' Board of Governors, as saying, "It is inappropriate for a lawyer to take one position as an advocate and then to publicly decry that position as a private citizen. He's in effect saying, 'I took a position, but I hope to God the courts don't listen to me.' If a lawyer does this, he is prostituting himself."[2]

Unfortunately, the public paid for Braeske's expensive trial, appeals, and retrials. Why have a charade of a costly trial when the man confessed and is obviously guilty?

Crew was soon attacked by a fellow lawyer. Apparently angered at the criticism of the U.S. Supreme Court, he filed a complaint against Crew asking for an investigation of Crew's actions by the Bar Association.

Crew, responding to the complaint, said:

> The basic issue is very, very simple. It's whether I have a right to speak out on matters of community interest. I think I do. Apparently, the State Bar has a different view. But, with all due respect, I think those people are wrong. If you speak out against the higher courts, some people don't like it...but, fortunately, the First Amendment applies to us all.[3]

Hundreds of similar cases occur throughout the country that prevent offenders from being convicted. Frank Carrington, author of *The Victims* and a member of the United States' Attorney General's Task Force on Violent Crime, said:

> ...the exclusionary rule, in addition to suppressing the truth and benefiting the guilty, places an enormous burden on the court system, both at the trial and appellate court level. Our court dockets are so crowded, the backlog of cases so staggering, that in many parts of the country "speedy justice" is a mockery. The exclusionary rule has contributed no end to this situation.[4]

Defenders of the exclusionary rule argue that only a small percentage of offenders are ever released due to error in obtaining evidence. The police and prosecutors, however, think the rule's impact is much deeper. It is not sufficient to look at those cases dismissed or lost in court as the result of the 'exclusionary rule.' The behavior of police officers and the screening mechanisms of their organizations as well as the standards of the prosecutor's offices and the courts are far more critical in determining the acceptance for prosecution of cases. Police officers, their supervisors, and prosecutors are constantly trained and tutored about cases that are 'acceptable' for prosecution. The fear of being in conflict with the rule has changed the operating behavior of the police and prevented them from aggressively investigating and arresting offenders.

In England a search and seizure rule is used to prevent the police from abusing the rights of suspects. The British use more common sense in its application believing that the public should not be punished for the mistake of a police officer. If a violation occurs in a search and seizure, the officer is reprimanded in some form for his misconduct, but the guilty offender is not released on a technicality. In the United States, just the opposite occurs: a guilty person, even a murderer may be released on a technical search and seizure error by a police officer.

Naturally the public should be protected from unlawful seizures and searches. No police officer should be allowed to break open a citizen's door and wander freely through a house looking for possible evidence. However, when a police officer suspects someone and has good cause, he should have the right to investigate; and if he finds evidence, use it. If policemen are involved in obtaining information illegally or withholding evidence, they should be fined, demoted, or fired. In the case of lawyers, they should be fined, denied court privileges, or disbarred. But the public should not be punished for an evidence infraction by the releasing of a criminal.

A strong lobby group exists, however, to keep the exclusionary rule the way it is, and the loudest voice is the American Civil Liberties Union. Conversations with several experienced trial judges, indicate that the exclusionary rule could be made less severe and still be workable.

Changing the Rules of Evidence

To make it easier to find the truth in disputes, a number of procedures should be changed. The rules of evidence should permit available information pertinent to a case to be introduced as evidence in court. Obviously, if a defendant has been beaten by the police to obtain a confession, that forced confession should not be admitted in court. It is recommended that legislation be enacted to change the exclusionary rule as it applies to Fourth Amendment issues. For an analysis of the rule see the *President's Task Force on Victims of Crime* (December 1982) which states succinctly the problem with the exclusionary rule; its impact on criminal court proceedings and its cost and why it should be abolished.

Abuse of Justice by Miranda Rule Interpretation

In 1966, the United States Supreme Court made a landmark ruling in the Miranda v. Arizona case that revolutionized the process of arresting, prosecuting, trying, and convicting criminals. Before the Miranda decision, confessions of an accused could not be received as evidence unless it was shown that the confession was voluntarily made. It only made sense that confessions resulting from physical abuse or mental coercion should not be admitted. The Miranda decision went beyond that, however. The Miranda decision states that anytime a suspect is in the custody of the police for questioning, the person "prior to any questioning...must be warned that he has a right to remain silent, that any statement he does make may be used as evidence against him, and that he has a right to the presence of an attorney, either retained or appointed."[5] A suspect has a right to have a lawyer present and, if he does not wish to talk, he must not be questioned.[6] If a lawyer is present while the police attempt to interrogate him, it is highly unusual for him to let his client talk. It is therefore very difficult for the police to obtain information from a suspect about a crime.

Justice Byron White, writing for the minority in the decision, had great concern about the impact of the Supreme Court's decision. He stated:

> ....The rule announced today will measurably weaken the availability of the criminal law to perform in these tasks. It is a deliberate calculus to prevent interrogations, to reduce the incidence of confessions and pleas of guilty and to increase the number of trials....
>
> There is, in my view, every reason to believe that a good many criminal defendants, who otherwise would have been convicted on what this court has previously thought to be the most satisfactory kind of evidence, will now under this new version of the Fifth Amendment, either not be tried at all or be acquitted if the State's evidence, minus the confession, is put to the test of litigation....
>
> In some unknown number of cases the Court's rule will return a killer, a rapist or other criminal to the streets and

to the environment which produced him, to repeat his crime whenever it pleases him. As a consequence there will not be a gain but a loss in human dignity.

There is, of course, a saving factor: the next victims are uncertain, unnamed, and unrepresented....

Nor can this decision do other than have a corrosive effect on the criminal laws as an effective device to prevent crime. A major component in its effectiveness in this regard is its swift and sure enforcement. The easier it is to get away with rape and murder, the less the deterrent effect on those who are inclined to attempt it. This is still good common sense. It if were not, we should posthaste liquidate the whole law enforcement establishment as a useless, misguided effort to control human conduct.[7]

Cases soon turned up throughout the United States in which the courts, based on the Miranda decision, overturned convictions of criminals. Pandora's box was opened up by the Miranda ruling. Criminals received a new bag of rights, and lawyers received new opportunities to delay trials.

Misuse of the Insanity Plea and Expert Witnesses

In front of a TV audience estimated at 125 million on March 30, 1981, John Hinckley, Jr., shot the President of the United States, a secret service agent, a policeman, and the White House Press Secretary. All four men were seriously hurt. Three of them would suffer the rest of their lives from the shots. Theoretically, with so many witnesses to the crime, a trial for attempted murder should have been held within 60 days and a finding of guilty established quickly by a jury of 12 reasonable people. It was not to be. The trial did not even begin until April of 1982, a year and a month later. While attorneys argued over whether evidence obtained was admissible against Hinckley, the taxpayers paid over $450,000 for his pretrial protection and legal expenses alone.

The trial lasted eight weeks. Most of the time, lawyers, expert witnesses, and psychiatrists argued over Hinkley's sanity at the time of the shooting. Many legal specialists, psychiatrists, and the public spoke out about the inappropriateness of psychiatrists speculating in a court of law as to Hinckley's sanity at a given period of time. To instruct a jury that Hinckley could be judged not guilty of the shooting if he were insane at the time seemed incredible to the general public. On June 22, 1982, unbelievably, the jury returned a verdict of "not guilty by reason of insanity." Hinckley could go free once psychiatrists determined he was well enough.

The total cost to the taxpayers of the trial, defense and prosecution amounted to over $2.5 million. The public's costs for Hinckley's treatment and incarceration will continue, however, until he is released and free to possibly assault someone else.

One Texas District Attorney, Arthur Eads, said, "Only in the United States can a man try to assassinate the leader of the country in front of 125 million people and be found not guilty."

The verdict indicates how fundamentally confused our legal system has become. Many legal analysts believe that the modern insanity defense was expanded to absurdity.

John C. Hinckley's jury verdict generated an avalanche of demands for elimination or modification of the insanity plea. The voices of a few offender oriented people continued their defense of the present insanity plea, but a majority of the voices heard wanted changes. Most citizens, legislators, and lawyers thought the burden should be on the defense to prove insanity; verdicts on similar cases should change a plea to "guilty but mentally ill" and provide commitment of the offender rather than release; and use a state of mind sanity test. California's Victims's Rights Proposition 8 included a test that asked whether the defendant was both incapable of knowing the nature of his criminal act and/or distinguishing right from wrong.

In the four states of Illinois, Indiana, Michigan and Georgia a "guilty but mentally ill" (GBMI) plea is used. These four states are unusual in that the convicted mentally ill offender serves a complete sentence in prison even if insane. The offender theoretically receives psychiatric treatment while in prison serving his sentence but cannot be released early even if he responds to treatment.

States are considering the GBMI with the option that the offender serve a full prison sentence for the offense. While defenders of the present insanity plea point out that only a small percentage of serious crime offenders use the insanity plea successfully, many are dangerous persons.

States and federal legislators should adopt needed legislation and not turn to other matters as the public's clamor for changes quiets down. Victim organizations, prosecutors, and police associations, and the public should lobby legislators to adopt sensible legislation to prevent further misuse of the insanity plea.

Justice Abuse by Social Engineering and Power Seeking Judges

Increasing evidence exists that many judges appointed are overreaching their constitutional authority. In an article "Are Judges Abusing Our Rights?" by the late Representative John Ashbrook, Harvard Professor Emeritus Nathan Glazer stated that we have developed an "imperial judiciary" in which judges "now reach into the lives of the people against the will of the people more than ever in American history."[8] *The Los Angeles Times,* on the subject of judges, said: "More and more judges have developed an itch for more and more power and they are scratching it at every opportunity."[9]

The public has had a problem with judges for a long time. In 1625, Sir Francis Bacon warned, "The judges ought to remember that their office is to interpret and not to make or give law."

Concern exists over the action of justices within the Supreme Court. Justice William H. Rehnquist believed the Supreme Court was going too far when he stated the majority was "fashioning for itself a legislative role resembling that once thought to be the domain of Congress."

The courts have no real administrative hierarchy. Therefore, every judge is independent and little or nothing can be done about judges who are lazy or incompetent. This is especially true in the federal system, where judges are appointed for life and no one, not even the chief Justice of the Supreme Court can do anything about it.

Court Holds Stolen Vehicle Owner Liable For Thief's Accidents

The California Supreme Court, noted for making decisions that puzzle the non-lawyer, have made some that make the victim the offender. In 1984, the Court ruled that a man who was run over by a thief in a stolen truck could sue the owner of the vehicle. They claimed that the victimized owner, the U.S. Industrial Fasteners, was liable because it had not taken enough action to prevent the truck from being stolen. The truck was on a private lot and the keys were in the glove compartment. The thief, Victor Castro, was not held responsible for running over Palma or repaying him for

101

STOP JUSTICE ABUSE

his medical bills of more than $150,000.

The injured man, Richard Palma, sued Fasteners for negligence, but the company asked that the case be dismissed as they were the victim and had no control over what a thief did later. A Los Angeles Court of Appeal agreed with the company and dismissed the action.

Not only did the Supreme Court reverse the Appeal Court's action, but chastized the appellate court for dismissing the suit. Conscientious judges who try to clear the court of frivolous cases like the Palma one must feel frustrated at the state Supreme Court's action.

The stolen truck case is similar to another ruling by one California court in which a bartender or a host in a private home can be held liable for serving drinks to someone who becomes intoxicated and injures a third party later. The state legislature later passed a law to overcome the court's ruling on holding hosts and bartenders responsible for the behavior of guests and customers.

The court seems to be searching for a "deep pocket" as do many litigants. The rulings can be applied to property owners having guns or other equipment that a thief might use to harm a third party after the theft.

In December of 1983, the California Supreme Court made another ruling that shook court watchers. It ruled that the courts must limit the punishment for murder during the commission of a felony where there was no proven intent to kill. The decision means that neither the death penalty nor life in prison without parole can be imposed on a defendant who did not intend to kill or to aid in a killing that occurs during a felony.

The court's action required that a large number of pending death penalty cases and cases involving prisoners sentenced to life without parole be retried at great expense to the public. Robert H. Philibosian, then Los Angeles County District Attorney said the the court's decision "will have a chilling effect on our ability to keep armed robbers from turning into wanton executioners...What will keep a robber from pulling the trigger when he can escape the death penalty just by saying, 'I didn't mean to do it?'"[10]

Lack of Trial Experience by Appellate Court Judges

Many appellate and United States Supreme Court judges have never served as trial judges yet evaluate trial judge actions daily.

102

In 1971, within the United States Supreme Court only two of the
Supreme Court Justices experienced trial work. Of the two, Justice Black was a part-time court judge for one year and Justice
Brenanan was a superior court judge for only one year. The other
jurists had no trial experience as judges. When Justice Black and
Brennan were replaced by Powell and Rehnquist, the court was
devoid of anyone having trial experience. This situation is similar
to "a large metropolitan hospital whose directing board of surgeons consisted of surgeons who had never been in charge of an
operation, some of whom had never been inside an operating theater in any capacity."[11] The situation in Great Britain is different.
In 1971, of 13 of the judges who sat as Lord of Appeal in Ordinary in the House of Lords, 11 had extensive experience as trial
court judges.[12]

Rose Bird, appointed by Governor Jerry Brown as Chief Justice
of the California Supreme Court, never served as a judge in any capacity. As appellate court justices evaluate the work of trial lawyers
and judges, except in unusual cases, trial experience should be required of appellate judges.

The inexperience of Chief Justice Rose Bird caused concern
among the appellate and trial courts. Several state appellate judges
publicly criticized Bird, and others complained about her in private. In June of 1981, Associate Justice George E. Paras of the
Third District Court of Appeals in Sacramento resigned in disgust.
One of the reasons was his

> ...unwillingness any longer to serve in a judicial capacity
> under the domination of the current California Supreme
> Court, an authoritarian body which rules our State like a
> little junta exercising little regard for precedents, statutes,
> constitutions, or the will of the people.
> ...Twelve years of devoted service to the public as a judicial officer in such frustrating circumstances is sufficient. The always-inadequate monetary remuneration of
> the office is no longer sufficiently compensated for by its
> intangible rewards to make further participation worth
> my while.[13]

It was unfortunate Paras resigned because he had designed
many improvements in processing the appellate court's heavy
schedule. In the six years before resigning, Paras developed an

appellate settlement conference procedure for civil cases that helped reduce the court's heavy calendar of cases. His action resulted in more than half the court's civil appeals cases being settled in conferences without the need for briefs, oral arguments, or court opinions.[14]

Two other appellate justices resigned as a result of their disagreement with the Bird Supreme Court appointment. Former President of the California Judges' Association, Robert F. Kane, said when he resigned that he was unhappy with the state of the judiciary. At a later time, he asked for Bird's resignation. Judge Kane believed that the "respect of the community for the Court is at an all-time low right now."[15] He blamed Rose Bird for being partly responsible.

The Governor of California, George Deukmejian, found that the California Court's deteriorating reputation had spread to New York. In 1984, at a meeting with 50 East Coast corporate and finance leaders who have business operations in California, Deukmejian heard numerous complaints about the civil court system. The Governor said: "It surprised us there were questions about the judiciary in California....we generally talk about it in terms of the criminal law, but apparently a number of these companies are experiencing a lot of litigation."

The complaints were about "both the number of suits and the length of time (before trials). In one situation, there was a concern about nuisance-type suits," he said.[16]

In December of 1984, at a news conference, Governor Deukmejian assailed the state Supreme Court's failure to uphold death penalty verdicts and ignoring a deadline in the death penalty law he wrote in 1977. He said, "I'm very disturbed about the way in which the court including, of course, the chief justice and some of these members...have dealt with the death penalty question."[17]

The Governor had reason to be disturbed. In February of 1985, the state Supreme Court for the 30th time in 33 capital cases it had considered since 1978, reversed a death penalty and ordered a retrial of a murderer. Stephen Wayne Anderson, a Utah prison escapee killed an elderly woman, Elizabeth Lyman, 81, in her home in San Bernardino County. He then stole $120, cooked some noodles, and sat down to watch television—where police found him. Anderson confessed to police that he had killed two other people.

The reason for the court's reversal was that the prosecution had failed to prove that Anderson intended to commit a murder. This rationale was based on two previous state Supreme court rulings in 1983 and 1984. Justice Stanley Mosk, who wrote the Court's opinion stated, "it does not prove as a matter of law that he entertained a specific intent to kill at the moment he fired the gun." (People vs. Anderson, crim.22143.) The California Attorney General John Van de Kamp, indicated that some 95 Death Row cases may be reversed because of the Court's 1983 and 1984 intent rulings.

In another speech the Governor expressed the public's frustration with the state Court, he said,

> The United States Supreme Court has ruled that capital punishment is constitutional. Juries, by unanimous verdicts, have convicted and imposed the death penalty on over 170 murderers since 1977. During these past seven years, many innocent people have been murdered, but not one murderer has paid the ultimate penalty. Our California Supreme Court should give greater deference to the vote of the people and the laws passed by the Legislature. The people have been patient long enough.

The Evolution of a Super Government by Appellate Judges

A deluge of decisions by judges occurred in the 1970s and 1980s in which the court imposed its will and created unnecessary government control on the public's lives. While environmental impact reports are required for urban developments, judges have made decisions (bussing of school children, etc.) costing the taxpayers millions of dollars annually and disrupting the lives of millions of people with little concern to its economic impact. A well-known legal historian, Raoul Berger, asks the question, "How long can public respect for the court survive if people become aware that the tribunal which condemns the acts of others as unconstitutional is itself acting unconstitutionally?"[18]

The court of last resort is the United States Supreme Court. No court exists above it. Its powers are almost unlimited as seen by Judge Macklyn Fleming: "For all practical purposes, that Court can issue a ruling on any legal or political question that strikes its fancy, and in so doing it becomes answerable to no one and subject to no review."[19] It is therefore important that men and women with proven ability by experience in court, including trial court experience, be selected carefully before being appointed to the the bench of our state and federal appellate courts or U.S. Supreme Court.

The power of the Supreme Court has developed beyond what many of our judiciary believe is justified. Fleming states:

> In the course of this country's constitutional development, the Supreme Court has acquired absolute power to decide any case or controversy arising within the United States, absolute power to invalidate any act of the President or of Congress, and absolute power to control virtually all acts of a state government, whether legislative, executive, or judicial. This absolute power is exercisable by five of the nine members of the court and is neither limited by precedent nor circumscribed by any requirement that the judgments of the court be accompanied by reasoned opinions.[20]

On the subject of power, Chief Justice Charles Evans Hughes said: "We are under a Constitution, but the Constitution is what the judges say it is...."[21] Justice Oliver Wendell Holmes supports Hughes in his views: "As the decisions now stand, I see hardly any limit but the sky to the invalidating of those rights if they happen to strike a majority of this Court as for any reason undesirable."[22]

Sentencing of Criminals by Judiciary

Many judges tend to be lenient with first offenders. Most state courts believe a pattern of crime must be established before an offender should be sent to prison for a long term. Juvenile and adult offenders are usually given probation for first offenses of non-capitol offense crimes. Only after additional convictions will an offender get a prison sentence in many jurisdictions. Murderers with long criminal records indicate in interviews that if their first offenses had been treated seriously—and stiff jail sentences given—they would not have committed additional crimes. Thousands of offenders are released on probation after serving short sentences only to commit more crimes against the public.

Stopping Abuse of Victim Rights by Judiciary

'Court-watchers,' including members of Congress like the late Representative John Ashbrook, believe that Supreme Court Jus-

CHAPTER SIX

tices have supported a code of criminal procedure that overwhelmingly favors criminal defendants. Ashbrook found that appellate judges all too frequently imposed their personal biases into the decision-making process, especially in death penalty cases. Representative Ashbrook commented:

> State legislatures have sought repeatedly to deter murder by imposing the death penalty. Again and again, they have been thwarted by the Supreme Court that arbitrarily changes the rules. In 1972, five Justices decreed that the death-penalty laws of 41 states were unconstitutional because they left to the 'uncontrolled' discretion of judges or jurors whether defendants should be imprisoned or die. Thirty-six states promptly enacted new laws making death mandatory for specified categories of murder and other crimes. Then the Justices did a U-turn in 1978, holding Ohio's death-penalty law invalid because it failed to give the sentencing judge enough discretion.[23]

In an article by Senator Patrick J. Leahy, Democrat from Vermont and former prosecutor, he offered these comments on sentencing policies in the nation:

> Most criminals are gamblers, They're betting they won't serve any time. Too often, they're right.
> Sentences should be realistic—never shaved and never shaken. When a criminal is sentenced, he should know he'll serve the time.
> Sentences should be applied equally to all criminals who commit the same offense under the same circumstances.
> Sentences should be written with clear guidelines to judges, so that there can be no doubt as to how they are to be applied.
> And we need to give prosecutors the power to appeal inadequate sentences.

At the end of his article, he gave sound advice:

> ....I urge all of you to press your state legislatures for sentencing laws that are fair, firm and easy to understand—

107

both for the judges who will apply them and for the criminals who must come to fear them.[24]

Stopping the Judiciary's Abuse of Democratic Process.

The nation watched on TV as Sirhan Sirhan shot and killed Robert Kennedy. He was convicted of murder and sentenced to life imprisonment. Hundreds of other people present were witness to the assassination. Due to court rules and procedures, four years after Sirhan's conviction, he was eligible for parole. As a result, his lawyer began filing petitions with the Parole Board to have the murderer released.

Due to effective lobbying by various groups, a small segment of the judiciary and society have deemed the death penalty a cruel and unusual punishment. Little thought is given to the victims who were deprived of their lives, often in a brutal fashion, or the emotional or economic impact on the victim's family.

In the dissenting opinion for the case of Coleman v. Balkcom, Supreme Court Justice William H. Rehnquist commented on the need to activate the death penalty in the United States. He stated:

> Although the Supreme Court has determined that capital punishment statutes do not violate the Constitution, and 30-odd states have enacted such statutes, apparently in the belief that they constitute sound social policy, the existence of the death penalty in this country is virtually an illusion.
>
> Since 1976, juries have sentenced hundreds of persons to death, presumably in the belief that the death penalty in those circumstances is warranted. Yet, virtually nothing happens except endless, drawn-out legal proceedings. Of the hundreds of prisoners condemned to die who languish on the various 'death rows,' few appear to face any imminent prospect of their sentences being executed. Indeed, in the five years since the court upheld the constitutionality of the death penalty, only one defendant who persisted in his attack upon his sentence has been executed.[25]

The public pays for these endless appeals and the cost of keeping murderers housed in cells costing the public from $15,000 to

$20,000 per year each. Including construction costs, the annual cost per prisoner is close to $50,000 per year.

Even though voters have indicated that they want the death penalty utilized, most state supreme courts manage to thwart the use of the death penalty. Until mid 1985, no convict has been executed in California since 1967. Despite protests from various groups, a few murderers were executed in Arizona, Florida, and Texas, starting in 1984.

The judiciary has sworn to uphold the laws of the nation, yet they frequently circumvent legally adopted laws because they hold different values than the voters. Do the judiciary have a right to impose their social views on the public?

Changing Judicial Appointment Procedures

In most states judicial vacancies are filled by an appointee of the governor of the state. Federal and United States Supreme Court Justices are appointed for life. In some states, a commission reviews supreme court appointments. The public has no voice in the appointments except to vote on their confirmation at the general election following their appointments. To give the public a greater voice in state judicial appointments, states should require that state supreme court appointments be approved and confirmed by their state senate. The public could then have a chance to protest appointments through their state legislature. Several proposed United States Supreme Court justices' appointments were not confirmed by the Senate because of the public's concern.

At the local level it is recommended that all judicial appointments be approved by county boards of supervisors or commissioners in addition to approvals required by any state judicial commission or bar association recommendations. In many states when an incumbent judge is not challenged at election time, the incumbent's name is not listed on the ballot and the public votes for him unknowingly. The names of all incumbent judges running for re-election should be listed on ballots, opposed or not.

Improving Judiciary Education and Recognition

Continuing education programs are essential for judges to maintain their knowledge and skills concerning new legal issues and problems. All state and federal judges should be required to maintain a minimum level of continuing education in the legal

field. Fortunately many states now require continuing education programs.

Judges who develop court efficiency and have the courage to move
trials along faster need and deserve public and peer recognition. It is
vital that the public and organized citizen groups give positive support
to conscientious and effective judges personally and by sending letters
to the media and legislators. Capable judges deserve better pay and
promotions. When a judge extends his socio-economic goals into the
courtroom, gives light sentences to hardened criminals, or acts improperly, the public and interested organizations should voice their
opinions to bar associations, state commissions on judicial performance, and legislators, informing them of their concern.

Evaluation and Removal
of Incompetent and Irresponsible Judges

The headline read, "Prostitutes Testify at Trial of Judge." Testimony was given that a San Diego Municipal Judge, paid one prostitute $611 for two hours of sex, and paid more than $2,000 to three
other women over a three or four-year period. He was convicted
and sentenced to jail, but refused to resign from the bench until
public pressure demanded it.

A judge of the Eleventh Judicial Circuit Court of Florida was
charged with 13 counts of judicial misconduct. The counts ranged
from "fits of temper, berating and yelling at witnesses, to ordering
a $10,700 attorney's fee be paid to his election campaign manager,
when the attorney was no longer involved in the case." He pleaded
"no contest" to the charges, was reprimanded and fined $3,000 by
the Florida Supreme Court.[26]

Aware of the court's judgment, the Board of Governors of the
American Judges Association nevertheless elected him president
of their 1,600-member organization. Only after the press and public expressed concern and protested did the judge resign as president. His support by the Board of Governors illustrates how lawyers close ranks and protect their own. Unfortunately, the public
seldom hears about other cases of judges' drinking on duty, delaying cases, and other court misconduct as the issues are kept quiet.

Operation Greylord Investigation

In Chicago after a four year undercover investigation called
Operation Greylord, more than 20 judges, lawyers, and police

officers were indicted for corruption in the Cook County court system. In July of 1985, Judge Richard F. LeFevour was found guilty of 59 counts of racketeering, income tax evasion and mail fraud by a federal court jury. The jury heard 163 witnesses testify against the judge. He was the third and highest ranking judge convicted under the federal government's prosecutions. The two other judges received sentences of 10 and 15 years in prison. Fifteen other persons have pleaded or been found guilty. Three others were acquitted.

To avoid jail or heavy fines, people gave the judge money, copying machines, and large 'loans' that were never repaid. Lawyers paid the judge for exclusive rights to work in high-volume courtrooms. During his last five years on the bench, Internal Revenue Service agents testified that Judge LeFevour had more than $143,000 in income for which he could show no source. Dan K. Webb, the United States special prosecutor on the case, said that LeFevour ..."embarked on a course of judicial corruption that is unequaled in the annals of corruption."

In most states the present method of removing judges is not very effective. Once a judge is elected, it's difficult to remove him. The public is seldom aware of the faults of judges except in scandalous situations. When reelection time comes around, the public assumes an incumbent judge is competent if nothing derogatory appears in the newspapers. To remove a judge through impeachment is difficult. Many lawyers who might speak up do not for fear of reprisal when appearing before that judge at a later time. In almost 200 years only nine federal judges have been impeached. Of the nine, four were convicted, four were acquitted, and one resigned before a judgment was reached.

Judicial Evaluation and Removal Procedures

In California during 1984, the Commission on Judicial Performance privately chastised three judges for 'transgressions,' ranging from alcohol abuse to misuse of a judge's contempt power, and wrote informal letters of warning to another 20 judges. Of the judges sent warnings one had jailed a defendant to frighten him, nine had made offensive or discourteous remarks to litigants, and three had endorsed political candidates. None of the judges were named by the commission.

Although most states have commissions on judicial performance, a system of evaluation at the local level should be established that holds judges accountable for their actions. Some states are becoming more active in removing incompetent judges, but most could improve their procedures. Judges can be evaluated in several ways. One is for lawyers to complete carefully drafted evaluation surveys of court management and case decisions by judges. Appellate and supreme court justices can also be evaluated by the bar association and public organizations. Although justices may resent evaluations, most should be responsive and improve their efficiency, knowing their actions will be reviewed.

Citizens for Law and Order (CLO) evaluate problem judges in California by documenting their court records, meeting with them, and telling them directly what they don't like about their court decisions. The CLO believe they have changed judiciary attitudes and the sentencing trends of many judges.

In evaluations, a judge should not be graded solely on the length of time a single case takes. Court rules and the complexity of certain disputes often require unavoidably long trials.

Changing Inconsistent Sentencing Practices

Citizen organizations should identify judges who do not abide by court procedures in sentencing juveniles and adult criminals, lack concern for victims, or use the bench as activists. To prevent inappropriate sentencing practices, public groups should start state ballot initiatives or urge state legislatures to provide sentencing guidelines for offenders and better treatment of victims. Youth and adult correctional agencies should abide by the sentences given offenders by the court, except under court directions or a new court hearing. No prisoner should be released from prison early unless the offender's sentencing court, victims, or their families review the case and take part in the hearing process.

Providing Restitution for Victims

The courts can and should require that restitution be paid to victims for psychological as well as physical damages. To eliminate the need for a victim or citizen to sue separately at great expense in civil court later, judges should assign restitution to the victim during criminal proceedings. The public has a right to expect that offenders will be kept working, in or out of prison, to repay their victims and the public for damages, their processing,

112

and housing expenses.

To impress on the offenders the seriousness of their crimes, judges should consider bringing burglars and thieves face-to-face with their victims when restitution is imposed in court. For three years in Waukesha, Wisconsin Judge William G. Callow held face-to-face meetings in his court of non-violent criminals and victims at the time restitution was imposed. The judge wrote in *The Judges' Journal* that a dramatic drop occurred in repeat crimes of burglaries and thefts in the community.

Over $180,000 was returned to victims during the three-year project. In addition to repaying the value of the goods taken, interest at the rate of 10% was charged to offenders, as the thefts were treated as an "involuntary loan." The judge interviewed offenders in prison and found they rationalized their thefts by saying they had done the victims a favor. The thieves did not think their stealing was morally wrong because they gave the victims an opportunity to rip off their insurance companies. Commenting on the success of the face-to-face meetings, the judge said: "Our records indicate that in almost every case where the victim-offender confrontation was used, the offenders were never charged with new crimes."

Appointment of Task Force to Change Obsolete Court Rules

A presidential blue ribbon judicial task force involving federal, state and local authorities and citizens should be appointed by the President to review the maze of rules and procedures hampering our court process and to recommend changes within the federal and state court systems. The task force should study the efficient British justice system, and consider applying some of their procedures to the United States system. For instance, private practice British lawyers are appointed to serve temporarily as prosecutors by the court, and are not elected to the position as in the United States. This approach seems to improve the efficiency of the courts. As previously mentioned criminal trials are shorter in duration and juries are impaneled in less time than in the United States.

The British courts are less lenient in granting delays and continuances to lawyers and conduct trials speedily. The right of appeal is limited and extended for only a few months, not years. The disruptive actions that can take place in American trials are not tolerated under the British system.

Judiciary Leadership in Preventing Delays in Proceedings

Under present laws judges can play a more active role to prevent lawyers from using ploys and delaying tactics to win cases. Judges should announce to attorneys before trials that frivolous motions and delays will not be permitted and the consequences if the rules are not followed.

Groups should advocate statutory revisions, by the legislative or the initiative process, that will control continuances. Opposing attorneys should be notified prior to the date the continuance is to be requested. If the court finds that no good cause exists, it should impose sanctions that include: reduction of compensation for court appointed lawyers; fines for retained lawyers; fines for prosecutors and public defenders; denial of right to practice in court for up to 90 days; a court report to judicial and bar disciplinary committees; and the use of existing powers such as contempt of court.

Even if a motion is legitimate, lawyers should be charged a fee for the cost of each motion made. Court lawyers should be held responsible for their actions and fined or charged by judges for delaying tactics. Lawyers, not the public or a client, should pay for unwarranted delaying action. Economic penalties may be the only answer to stop irresponsible actions by lawyers.

Action to Restrain Judicial Activism

Concern with judiciary activism in the country prompted the then United States Attorney General William French Smith to tell the Federal Legal Council in Reston, Virginia in October of 1981 that the Justice Department planned to limit "policy-making" by the judiciary. Smith indicated that the courts "have gone far beyond their abilities" to correct perceived wrongs. Smith said:

> Federal courts have attempted to restructure entire school systems in desegregation cases and to maintain continuing review over basic administrative decisions. They have asserted similar control over entire prison systems and public housing projects. They have restructured the employment criteria to be used by American business and

government—even to the extent of mandating numerical results based upon race or gender.

The Reagan administration did reduce judicial activism at the federal level by changing policies within the Justice Department and other federal departments, appointing judges with a different philosophy, appointing new directors of the Legal Corporation, and reducing budgets in operations where they had little control over the personnel.

Judicial Changes By the President

By February of 1985 at the end of his first term, President Reagan had appointed 31 judges to the regional United States appellate courts (23% of the judges sitting) and 130 to the District Court bench (26% of the judges sitting). For 1985, it was estimated that Reagan would appoint at least 115 more to the federal bench. If the turnover rate continued as in the past, Reagan could fill over half of the 744 federal appeals and district court judgeships by the end of his second term. By Reagan appointing over 380 judges as anticipated, he would beat Jimmy Carter's record number of 262 judges.

The appointment of Sandra Day O'Connor to the Supreme Court appears to have changed the direction of the high court. Legal scholars believe that Reagan's court appointees are adhering to the "judicial restraint" he wants. One of his appointees, Judge Robert H. Bork of the United States Court of Appeals for the District of Columbia, defined "judicial restraint" of judges as:

> ...the attempt to discern what was intended by legislators and the framers of the Constitution and then try to do what they intended—without adding your own policy preferences.[27]

Judge Bork was a former Yale law school professor and United States Solicitor General before his appointment. Other law school professors nominated or appointed by Reagan include: Richard Posner, University of Chicago; Frank Easterbrook, University of Chicago; and Ralph K. Winter, Yale University.

While Justice O'Connor is Reagan's only Supreme Court appointee, an additional vacancy or two might evolve. Five of the nine justices are over 75 years of age. With a few appointments to the high court in addition to over half of the federal judges, Reagan could influence court decisions and change the direction of courts on criminal rights, and other issues for decades to come.

Judge Watchers

Because of unpleasant personal experiences with courts and the judiciary, people formed "court watching" organizations in the country and monitored courts and judges. They include Mothers Against Drunk Drivers (MADD), Society's League Against Molestation (SLAM), Citizens For Law and Order (CLO), Judge Your Judges (JUJ), and others.

What Can a Citizen Do to Improve the Court Process?

You can become a court watcher. Observe local judges in action. Real drama better than any TV soap opera is played every day in court and doesn't cost a penny to watch. Talk to local victim/ witness program leaders. Find out who the problem judges are.

Join one of the court watcher organizations. Send them some money to assist their operation. Form your own local group to monitor actions within the court. Establish an evaluation process, but one that takes into consideration the difficulties and legal restraints trial judges face. Let the judiciary know you are watching, but be fair and give them a chance to hear your complaints and improve before voicing opinions publicly. If direct contact with judges fail, then complain to the presiding judge, bar association, and your board of supervisors.

In commenting about a jurist, however, be specific and careful that your facts are accurate.

Support For Quality Jurists

Outstanding trial jurists do their best to keep cases and trials moving through court swiftly and ensure fair treatment to plaintiffs, defendants, victims, and the public. Competent jurists are a frustrated as the public at the lengthy and numerous rules and procedures that bind and slow trials. These jurists should be supported in their attempts to reduce frivolous litigation and control irresponsible lawyers in court without being overturned later by sophist-like appellant judges.

CHAPTER SEVEN

IMPROVING JURY
SELECTION AND MANAGEMENT

Abuse of Courts by
Jury Selection and Management Process

Jury selection is one of the most abused procedures in our court system. In America trials of major significance frequently take weeks and months just to select a jury. The Chicago's "Pontiac Ten" trial took five months alone to select the jury. More than 1,000 potential jurors were questioned in which each side had 120 preemptory challenges. The criminal trial took over eight months. The jury was locked up the entire time.[1]

In Lancaster, California the court finally selected a jury in 1984 after trying for nine months: the apparent American record. The jury selection process cost the community over $250,000 even before the trial started.

In Los Angeles County more than one half of all time in court is given to jury trials, but only 6% of all criminal cases actually go to trial. Obviously offenders could be processed through the justice system faster if jury trials took less time. While the jury selection of the sensitive John Hinckley Jr. case took only five days to seat, it took four months to select the jury for the "Hillside Strangler" case in Los Angeles.

A total of about 3,000,000 citizens are ordered to report for potential jury duty every year in the United States. Most of the jury trials in the world, about 80%, are held in the this country. Of the cases filed in court, only about 10% ever come to trial before a jury. Most are settled out of court or are tried by a judge.

117

LAWYERS AND CLIENTS—"Don't forget to exercise your right of reply. I will exercise mine. That will give our clients two extra speeches to pay for."

Juries do hear about 300,000 cases a year. Unfortunately a large percentage of jurors called (40%) never sit on a jury. Many jurors become quite irritated and hostile about their treatment.

Trial judges interviewed by the authors indicated that permitting the judge alone to question jurors, and changing the present procedures for seating juries, could cut the time of trials thirty to fifty percent. The costs to litigants and the public of trials in turn would be cut considerably.

By speeding up the selection of juries, judge and juror time will be saved, permitting more trials to be held, and reducing the present court backlog. In a study made by three professors from the City University of New York, they estimated that a saving of $9 million a year could be made in New York City courts alone if felony case jury selection was reduced from its present one-third of trial time.

Abuse of Voir Dire by Judiciary and Lawyers

In most state courts judges permit lawyers to use the jury selection process to question prospective jurors (voir dire) as to their ability to serve and as an opportunity to insure that jurors will be sympathetic to their client's point of view. In other words lawyers use jury selection time to "pre-try" their cases. Judges indicate objection to this procedure, but find attorneys for both the prosecution and the defendant in trials want the opportunity to question jurors at length. Both sides hope to select a jury favorable to their cause. With competent lawyers in court, the gain made by one side is canceled out by the other side. Studies indicate that it makes little difference how much questioning takes place as most juries will arrive at similar opinions based on similar facts presented to them. However, judges are reluctant to speed up the selection process and stop lawyers from lengthy questioning for fear of being overturned by appellate courts later.

In federal criminal and civil trials judges keep a tight rein over jury selection, in almost all cases handling the questioning themselves. Because of this federal juries are usually selected within a day, as opposed to states where lawyers have control over the interrogation. Studies in New York State have shown that while a federal judge takes an average of two and one-half hours to select a jury, lawyer-conducted selection in state courts takes five times as long, with jury selection in 20 percent of the state cases taking as much time as the actual trial. The 28 states using the inefficient voir dire system can change the jury system if they have the courage to fight the trial lawyers.

"Brainwashing Expeditions"

At the end of 1984 Chief Justice Warren E. Burger spoke out against proposals that would require federal judges to allow attorneys to question prospective trial jurors. This process, used in many states, has resulted in what Burger called "brainwashing expeditions" by lawyers.

In his 1984 annual year-end Report on the Judiciary, Burger wrote that "Under no circumstances should Congress change the jury selection procedure in federal courts. When lawyers are allowed 'free rein' as is true in some state systems, (jury questioning) is often exploited to become a 'brainwashing' expedition as lawyers use the process to influence jurors, not simply to select them."[2]

Burger found that the increasing role of attorneys in the jury selection process has proved "increasingly disruptive." He said that it could result in "incalculable delays" in the federal system. He pointed to the case of convicted Trailside Killer David Joseph Carpenter, whose trial in Los Angeles in 1984 required seven months to select the jury. "By contrast," he said, "in England I have observed a jury selected in a criminal case in six minutes."[3] Burger's attack continued the debate over the role lawyers should play in jury selection.

States should be encouraged to follow the federal plan, and Congress should not weaken to pressure from lawyers and interject the state jury selection process into federal courts.

Treatment of Jurors

Many jurors become hostile to the court system after serving One woman psychologist, Sally Grodsky, learned the hard way what it's like to be a juror. In a letter to a newspaper editor, she said she looked forward to her experience as a juror. After serving she became disillusioned and thought the jury system was a complete waste of her time and the taxpayers' money. She left home at 8:00 a.m. and got home between 5:30 and 6:00 p.m. She spent most of her time in a large assembly room with 80 other prospective jurors

120

The day started with a jury orientation lasting about half an hour, followed by another half an hour of suggestions as to where to eat or shop while waiting for assignment. She had a ten-day tour of duty. She was excused quickly the first day when lawyers discovered she was a psychologist and that her husband and one of her sons were attorneys and another son a medical doctor. She said in her letter that:

> ...The other eight and a half days, we were left to our own devices and were instructed to remain in the assembly room except when dismissed for lunch or at the end of the day. We spent our time sleeping, doing stitchery, playing cards, watching television (and usually the TV was turned to soap operas), reading books or magazines if you could read above the distractions of a large, buzzing room. One man occupied himself for two days completing a jigsaw puzzle.
>
> On the fourth or fifth day of my duty, I was assigned to traffic court. Since I was curious as to how many people were waiting in the room for a call, I inquired of the jury supervisor. There were 88 that day, and no person was called. We were all milling around aimlessly.
>
> It should be noted that many companies pay their employees for the time they are called for jury duty, so that there is an economic loss not only to the taxpayer, but to the employer as well, while the employee sits helplessly performing his civic duty. Something has to be done to improve the present system.[4]

Although many jurors report a negative experience in serving, their major complaints stem from wasteful waiting, the attitude of the court system personnel, the waitingroom environment, and the sloppiness of the system. Even with the problems, jurisdictions report most jurors find it worthwhile and are willing to repeat the experience.

The public has a right to a more efficient jury system. The public should demand higher quality jurors, better juror treatment, better pay, and an enriching experience for them. All will benefit from a better jury system.

Is there a Need for Specialized Juries?

Many cases going to trial are concerned with highly complex matters involving scientific and complex corporate anti-trust disputes. These cases take a long time to try because the jurors, knowing nothing of the subject, must be educated to a point where they can understand the issues.

If jurors for specialized issues were selected from professional groups or from people with skills or knowledge in the area of dispute, trials would move faster. Complicated disputes could be settled faster and with wiser verdicts with specialized jurors. The jurors should be paid well for their time; the cost being borne by the parties involved. Higher fees for a quality jury would be minimal compared to the cost of a battery of lawyers for an extended period of time.

Starting in 1970, the National Union Electric Corporation of Philadelphia, which makes televisions, radios and air conditioners, filed a $1.5 million suit against 27 of its Japanese competitors. The company claimed the Japanese used unfair business practices. The case was not ready for trial until nine years later. By that time, the various parties had generated more than 100,000 pages of depositions and 20,000,000 pages of documents, of which many were in Japanese.

Realizing the case was very complex, 14 of the Japanese firms asked the U.S. District Judge to hear the case without a jury. The firms believed that the case was so complex that it would be "beyond the practical abilities and limitations" of a normal jury. The District Judge did not agree. The Third Circuit Court of Appeals overruled and said that certain extraordinary cases indeed may be too complicated for a typical jury.

In a case in Seattle in 1976, the Boise Cascade Company created 900,000 documents involving 50,000 lawyer hours. Equally complicated cases, with thousands of pages of documents, are thrust often upon the courts and jurors ill-equipped to comprehend the technical arguments.

It becomes important that judges in complex cases be familiar with the subject and trained in conducting them in an efficient way, just as Judge Green did in the AT&T case. Unfortunately lawyers benefit from slow-moving cases and will continue to submit document after document, until instructed to stop. Judges must be wise to lawyers and prevent endless documents from being submitted to the court. Taxpayers would obviously benefit from a more efficient court operation.

Chief Justice Burger did appoint a panel of federal judges to consider the use of "special" or "blue ribbon" juries, especially created from a selection process to require jurors with specific qualifications. Another alternative being considered is the expert non-jury tribunals, staffed by judges rather than jurors, with special technical backgrounds and training to make decisions on special cases.

Recommended Changes to Jury Selection Process

The extended time allowed lawyers to question jurors is not necessary to safeguard an offender's rights or to safeguard the public's rights. A number of improvements can be made to speed up the jury selection process. The following basic changes in the jury system when made would greatly reduce trial time and save considerable amounts of money without depleting the rights of defendants. All states should pass legislation permitting only the trial judge to question prospective jurors. Jury instruction and questioning should be permitted with all jurors present. Attorneys should be permitted to submit questions to the judge for juries, but the judge should have full authority to decide what questions will be used.

Juries should have a "right to privacy" and be protected from frivolous questions about their sex partners, religion, political views, social life, etc., that have little to do with being objective in making a decision on evidence presented to them.

Voir Dire in Capital Cases

In many states, court rules require that all prospective jurors in capital cases be questioned individually and out of hearing of the other jurors. This procedure is not only unnecessary, but is expensive and does not improve the quality of justice for either offenders, victims, or the public.

Non-Unanimous Jury

It has long been a tradition that in criminal cases a person cannot be convicted unless the jury vote is unanimous. In federal trials it is still a requirement. The federal Constitution, however, does not require that state juries reach unanimous verdicts. In the case of Johnson vs. Louisiana and Apodaca vs. Oregon, the United States Supreme court ruled in 1972 that the Constitution did not require unanimous decisions for state trials. Since 1972 several states enacted non-unanimous juries in criminal cases, except in capital cases where the death sentence was a possibility. Some legal analysts claim that the unanimous jury requirement results in hung juries due to the bias of one or two jurors. In a recent trial in San Diego the mayor was tried for election fraud, but it resulted in a 'hung' jury. The jury had voted to convict him on an 11 to one vote. The one holdout was a city employee.

In a *Los Angeles Times* article about the non-unanimous jury system in Oregon, Judge Robert E. Jones, a Justice on the state Supreme Court, said:

> After sitting for 20 years as a criminal-felony trial judge in Oregon, where jurors in all but first degree murder cases are allowed to return a verdict if 10 out of 12 agree, I believe that such a system delivers fair, if not perfect, justice to both the state and the defendant. In my experience, no one who was convicted by a non-unanimous jury later was shown to have been innocent.[5]

Judge Jones asked Chief Judge James M. Burns of the United States District Court in Oregon, who had seen both types of jury systems in practice, to compare the two. Judge Burns said: "I don't think it makes a damned bit of difference. A good or bad case will be spotted by either type of jury. The only difference seems to be that unanimous juries deliberate several minutes or sometimes several hours longer."

Judge Jones summed up his experience by saying:

> I believe that non-unanimous jury verdicts have no harmful consequences for our criminal justice system. However, in a system that allows a 10-2 vote, the jury selection process is shorter, yet the deliberations are just as robust, the defendant receives just as fair a trial and justice will not be frustrated by a holdout juror who is irrational or simply mistaken about the facts in evidence. So even though I cannot prove it, I believe that the non-unanimous system provides a model that other states should follow.[6]

124

The authors recommend that each state prepare a constitutional provision providing that in criminal trials, except those involving the possibility of the death penalty or life imprisonment without possibility of parole, a verdict can be reached when ten or more jurors agree. The initiative route should be used by the public if their legislature will not cooperate. A provision should be included, in the interest of speedy case resolutions and to avoid doubtful retrials, that would prevent further prosecution of an accused offender when the jury could not reach a verdict and where more than six voted not guilty. An exception should be made if the prosecution finds new material evidence to strengthen their case.

MEN OF JUSTICE—The defense counsel dispensed full justice to the rare talent displayed by the public prosecutor in his indictment. The Attorney General is eager to render merited praise to the admirable eloquence of the counsel for the defense. In conclusion, everyone is extremely satisfied except the accused.

CHAPTER EIGHT

CHANGING
COURT BUREAUCRACY
AND OBSOLETE PROCEDURES

The civil and criminal courts are saturated with rules and procedures established by jurists for a variety of reasons. Attempts have been made by judges to speed up the slow process of cases in court, but matters seem to get worse not better. Joseph McNamara, San Jose, California Police Chief and author, writing about court bureaucracy in the *California Lawyer*, said:

> Virtually every major legal change promulgated by appellate judges, the upper echelon legal bureaucrats, has resulted in more costs, more delays and more need for lawyers without any noticeable increase in public satisfaction with the courts. For example, take pre-trial discovery, the much heralded legal reform of 10 years ago, intended to unclog court calendars. Witnesses now are doubly inconvenienced, court calendars are more clogged than ever and costs of adjudication have soared and of course, there is a good deal more work for lawyers.[1]

On the troubled state of the legal system in California, Dale Hanst, President of the California Bar Association in 1984 said in an interview:

> I think that the system creates for itself a lot of problems and I think that our society remains overly litigious. And, I think our lawyers are overly litigious and not as oriented

127

toward amicable resolution of matters as they ought to be.

But, I think the State Bar and other organizations are beginning to take steps to make the public and lawyers more aware of other means to resolve disputes short of litigation. I just don't believe that our system can continue to handle the volume of litigation that's it's been trying to handle in the last two or three years for much longer without failing of its own weight.

Filing a Complaint—Going to Civil Court

Normally civil cases do not go to trial until the opposing counsel is ready. The judge has an umpire role, ruling on matters presented before him. He is not responsible for gathering and presenting evidence and initiating trials. Attorneys ready to go to trial file what is normally called a 'Notice of Trial Certificate of Readiness.' The opposing counsel receives a statutorily specified period of time to plead his preparation for trial or inform the court that he is not ready. If the court is not informed otherwise, the case is placed on the trial calendar. No civil case can be held for trial unless the attorneys have filed a Notice of Trial.

Delays and Continuances

Counsels for both parties provide the initiative to move a case into court. Clients are not protected against lawyers who are dilatory and neglectful. Lawyers, although theoretically ready for trial after filing, frequently are not. When the court time finally arrives, attorneys often ask judges for more time. Delays are expensive to both parties and the court. Witnesses have to be paid whether they testify or not. If the judge disciplines a dilatory lawyer, the client may be hurt financially by action against the attorney.

Lawyers often file the Notice of Trial only to get on the agenda. The court has no way of knowing which cases are actually ready for trial. Presiding judges, aware of lawyers' tactics and settlement patterns, schedule more trials for each day than the court can process. This is done to insure a full calender and to utilize the time of the judges. Court overbooking occurs sometimes as a result. Unfortunately, such arrangements result in highly paid lawyers, witnesses, and assistants spending most of a day waiting to be heard, only to be re-scheduled for a later date—an expensive process.

Pretrial Conferences

To prevent postponements and continuances, some courts schedule 'status conferences' or 'pre-pretrial conferences.' A judge, a magistrate, or even a para-judge meets to review case situations with lawyers for both sides. If lawyers are not ready, trials are re-scheduled to a mutually agreed time.

Pretrial conferences can prevent what is known in American law as ' settlements at the courtroom door'. Lawyers often use a 'trial bluff' to intimidate opponents into settling issues on favorable terms rather than going to trial. When the trial date actually approaches, litigants not ready for a showdown often settle. Many 'courthouse door settlements' can be prevented by holding pretrial settlement hearings before judges.

The atmosphere in a pretrial settlement conference is very different from the courtroom environment. Courtroom procedures, being stiff and formal, discourage discussion or compromises to reach a settlement. Conferences are usually held in a judge's chambers in an informal arrangement with counsel from both sides present. When the counsel for one party indicates a condition of settlement that seems unfair, opposing counsel or the judge can comment and discuss it. The judge can informally give an idea to counsels as to how the court might rule, but with no guarantee. These proceedings help bring lawyers with outrageous claims back to reality. Settlements can be reached in a few minutes, an hour, or more than a day for complex matters. The same cases in court might take weeks to reach a decision.

Pre-settlement conferences are helpful to the public in that more cases are settled and kept out of court. Trial calendars are kept clear for complex cases that involve expert witnesses and require a trial to settle issues. Mutually agreed upon settlements are usually better for both parties than one imposed by a judge or a jury in a courtroom.

Many lawyers believe clients are the problem in settling disputes and prevent them from reaching an agreement. Clients frequently want to have their 'day in court' to fight their adversary. When informed of the true cost of a court fight, however, many find a settlement agreeable.

Pretrial Conferences Management Skills

It requires a special art to handle pretrial settlement conferences well. A judge needs knowledge and skill to bring people to a compromise that is fair to both sides. It takes special sensitivity to move hostile and stubborn people to a settlement. A judge must act as a mediator and as a conciliator. At times a judge may feign anger with a stubborn person to move them to compromise, yet not go too far. Judges often remind litigants of the estimated cost of a trial if they do not settle.

To enhance the conference skill of judges, regularly scheduled training sessions for pretrial conference skill development should be conducted in states by continuing education programs. The public and litigants will benefit greatly from judges with settlement skills.

Even if cases go to trial, pretrial conferences ensure trials will be conducted more efficiently. Litigant counsels will be better prepared and will spend less time conducting trials, saving taxpayers and litigants inestimable amounts of money.

Changing Pretrial Discovery Process

'Discovery,' as used in trials, is a legal 'show and tell' process. It means that each side must show the other party the documents and evidence that they intend to use in court. Before the system was introduced, lawyers used their evidence like a trump card: to surprise their opposition in court and defeat them. Instead of speeding up trials, the discovery process has caused numerous documents to be traded back and forth; and more and more data to be demanded from the opposite side. The process escalated trial costs, not reduced them.

In a famous trial between United Nuclear Corp. and the General Atomic Co., a unit of Gulf Oil Corp., New Mexico District Judge Edwin L. Felter found Gulf lawyers and the company guilty of "obstruction of justice and ...a willful, deliberate and flagrant scheme of delay, resistance, obfuscation, and evasion in discovery matters." He ordered Gulf to transfer to United Nuclear $8.25 million in cash and the disputed market rights to almost $1 billion worth of uranium. Judge Felter took this action because he believed Gulf had abused the discovery process during a two year trial in 1978.

United States Supreme Court Justice William H. Rehnquist is one of many jurists concerned about the misuse of the discovery process. In a speech at the University of Florida Law School in 1984, he proposed that discovery be abolished in cases in which lesser amounts of money are at stake. He said, as an alternative, discovery should be sharply limited to instances in which it is essential for a 'just result' in a case.

Courts should require that pretrial 'discovery' be limited in use, reduced in quantity of contents, and length of depositions. Actually, the use of the discovery process should be abolished, as Justice Rehnquist suggests, in cases not involving much money. Until its use is controlled, judges should require an early time frame for discovery to enable disputants to realize how weak or strong their case may be. Judges have authority now, as evidenced by Judge Felter, to prevent the misuse of the discovery process. Many cases could be settled earlier as a result of their assertive action. If the jurists do not change the process, citizens should use the 'initiative' process to change discovery's misuse.

Reducing Court Workload

To stop delays in civil cases, courts should require that hearings be on a specific date within 60 days of filing. Lawyers should sign affidavits that they are ready to go to trial and be held accountable and fined if not. If lawyers are dilatory in proceedings, they should be held in contempt of court. Clients should also be required to be present when a case is being discussed in court.

Reduction of Civil Court Cases and Speedups

The best way to ease the flow of cases in court is to prevent some from ever reaching court. Civil matters such as divorce, probate, traffic, personal injury, and some condemnation suits could be settled by alternative means and never go to trial except in special situations. To insure that those not requiring a trial are screened out, pretrial conferences, mediation, arbitration committees, and minitrials should be made available and built into the court system. Mediation and arbitration are being used more and more in the country, but often on a voluntary basis.

Victimless Crimes

Thirty to fifty percent of the criminal justice system's resources are directed toward so-called 'victimless crime' laws—laws that make it a crime to participate in voluntary acts that violate no other person's rights. For over ten years groups such as the National Advisory Commission on Criminal Justice Standards and Goals, the American Medical Association, and the American Bar Association have expressed support for the decriminalization of some of these crimes. Civic organizations such as the Alliance for a Safer New York and the San Francisco Committee on Crime have joined in urging a closer look at some of these now-illegal activities.

With the serious backlog in courts, any reduction in the case load should be welcomed. The filing of marijuana possession cases as misdemeanors rather than felonies in Los Angeles County resulted in a 25% reduction in felony cases. By utilizing a policy of down-grading victimless crimes to the lowest level of priority, more of the system's resources would be available for serious crimes. Justice and economy would be better served and the efforts of the criminal justice system can be used to protect people from aggressions against their persons or property.

Diversion of Offenders

'Diversion' means steering first-time offenders from normal criminal processing in court into less expensive alternatives. Diversions can reduce the costs of courts and correctional institutions and is used with increasing frequency in the nation. The process requires that prosecutors refrain from pressing charges if defendants agree to take part in a rehabilitative program. If the assigned program is completed successfully, charges are dropped and the arrest record is erased or sealed. If the defendant fails to complete the program, the initial criminal proceedings are resumed.

In three Massachusetts' counties near Boston, a diversion program called the Court Resource Project has experienced excellent results. On a daily basis, the arraignment list for persons between 17 and 22 years old who have committed misdemeanors or minor felonies is reviewed. If the detainees meet criteria set by project personnel, they receive a 14-day continuance of the arraignment to allow time to work out a rehabilitative plan. If the plan is accepted by the Court Review Project, the court is asked to allow a 90-day continuance to implement it. If not, the defendant is returned to court for prosecution under the original charges.

After three years, 1,000 detainees were screened and 1,000 assigned rehabilitative plans. When arrested, 68% were not employed. After 90 days in the program, 97% were employed and only 8% were rearrested. The cost per successful case was $1,000. This compares favorably with the estimated $12,000 spent for court processing costs per offender.

Changing Court Organization

Small Claims Court

Little need exists for qualified judges to sit in small claims courts. Those proceedings can be handled by lawyers or non-lawyers with adequate experience. State legislatures should pass legislation enabling lawyers or experienced non-legal individuals to administer small claims court. Cases allowed in small claims court should have the financial limit raised to $25,000. This action would permit more of the public to settle their differences without hiring a lawyer.

Traffic Court

The processing of moving vehicle violations should be removed from traffic courts and shifted to state motor vehicle administrative divisions. An experienced and highly paid judge is not needed to hear traffic ticket cases. They can be heard by a lower paid magistrate or administrator.

Changing The Dual Court System

To provide swift and efficient justice again, it will be necessary to change the basic structure of courts. Either one system of courts should be organized or what is to take place in state courts and federal courts should be carefully defined and the overlapping between them reduced. The change of responsibility within the two-court systems in the decades of the 1960s and 1970s generated costly problems. Justice Macklyn Fleming comments on how the present dual court system has harmed the justice system:

> These developments have brought about the current phenomenon of two systems of courts operating simultaneously on the same subject matter, and the ensuing tug of war, waste, confusion, and plain muddle are painfully evident to anyone involved in the process. Yet the mischief goes beyond inefficiency brought about by duplication of effort. This by reason of the fact that lower courts continue to retain the provincial outlook associated with courts of limited jurisdiction. Normally lower federal courts assume no share of responsibility for protection of the community against disaster; for maintenance of public order; for en-

forcement of laws against murder, robbery, burglary, aggravated assault, theft, and rape; for continuance of municipal services; or for maintenance of local jurisdictions. From these responsibilities, lower federal courts disassociate themselves almost completely in their concentration upon protection of federal constitutional rights.

Lower federal courts in areas where their jurisdiction overlaps that of state courts suffer the weakness of being one-interest courts—courts which concern themselves exclusively with protection of personal rights and privileges and not at all with performance of personal duties and obligations. Too often, this one-sided viewpoint upsets the balance of right and duty within our dual court system and produces irresponsibility, much as though a government were to operate with duplicate legislatures, one concerned solely with spending money, the other solely with imposing taxes.[2]

Fleming has found that Canada's and Australia's unitary court system operates well without overlap or duplication. The judiciary, legal profession, and the public must understand how expensive the present dual system is in terms of inefficiency, injustice, and cost of operation. Citizens should comprehend what a unified or unitary system, with responsibilities clearly defined, could be like and how it could operate.

Alternatives to Our Dual System

Fleming believes that a basic change in the American court system is overdue and that it can be made without great pain to the present court participants. A single system of courts could be obtained by "abolishing the lower federal courts and relying exclusively on state courts to handle cases arising under both state and federal law. Alternatively, the same result could be achieved by abolishing the state courts and relying exclusively on federal courts to handle cases arising under both state and federal law."[3] Congress has used the latter system in establishing court systems in some American territories. A combination of the two systems might be established which is similar to the system used in Canada. Within Canada's unitary court system, Judge Fleming says:

The provincial (state) courts possess original jurisdiction over civil and criminal cases arising under most federal and all provincial law; the Federal Exchequer Court has exclusive original jurisdiction in cases involving patents, copyrights, taxation, admiralty, disputes between provinces [states], and claims against the crown; and the Supreme Court of Canada serves as the final court of appeal from the provincial and Exchequer courts. Judges of both provincial and federal courts are appointed by the federal government.[4]

To gain support for a major change in the American court system, the present court personnel should continue to operate it. While it would be difficult, the original federal system could be refurbished and the lower federal courts restored to their position as courts of limited jurisdiction. Fleming describes how this could occur:

> ....Congress retains exclusive control over the jurisdiction of the lower federal courts and, by amendment to the United States Judicial Code, it could reinstate the lower federal courts as courts of limited jurisdiction (bankruptcy, copyright, patents, admiralty, anti-trust, federal taxation, claims against the federal government, and so on) and remove their jurisdiction over matters that duplicate the work of the state courts. Federal law and federal rights arising out of the work of the state courts could be enforced in the state courts, as they are in Canada and Australia. State court judges are sworn to uphold the Constitution and the laws of the United States, and they could be made federally accountable on their oaths. The jurisdiction of the United States Supreme Court over all courts would continue as before, and cases from the highest state courts involving federal law would be reviewable by the Supreme Court. But final judgments of state or federal courts would not be subject to further review in the lower federal courts.[5]

Congress has the tools to control our disordered court system. The problem warrants Congress' reviewing the situation by appointing a task force to suggest alternative court reorganization plans. The federal courts, in any case, should stop reviewing state court actions.

Separate Civil and Criminal Courts in State System

To create more efficiency within the state court system, it is recommended that the present system of magistrates, municipal, and superior court systems be revised into a separate civil and criminal court system. Judges could sit on either civil or criminal cases, depending on the workload. This system would insure that civil cases are heard promptly. Duplication of effort within the criminal system would be eliminated with the division.

In a criminal case in which restitution is justified, the judge should be given the power to make binding judgments for recovery. If state legislation is not adequate, state legislators should propose legislation permitting judges to provide restitution to a victim in criminal or civil court.

Anatomy of a Murderer's Trial

Elected state prosecutors (district attorneys) decide which cases presented to them by the police, grand juries, or their own staff will be prosecuted. Once a case has gone to trial, a criminal defense lawyer is expected to do whatever is possible to protect his client. He is allowed and even encouraged by appellate judges to use trial delaying tactics if it will benefit his client. The following case illustrates the procedures that can be used in a murder trial and how careful a judge must be to avoid violating court rules and inadvertently establish grounds for an expensive retrial.

McLain's Trial for Murder

The McLain case shows how judicial rules make trials involving the death penalty long and costly even with an experienced and conscientious judge presiding. Jody Whitman and her friend were headed home after a swim at the Ventura, California High School pool. The two 11-year-olds took a short-cut through Cemetery Park in the city on evening of August 12, 1971. A man wearing dark glasses followed them into the park. He came up behind and ordered them to keep walking. Aiming a gun at them, he told the girls to stop, get down, and disrobe, keep their eyes shut, and not tell anyone.

The two girls, frightened at having the gun held to their heads, did what they were told. Both were painfully sexually assaulted by Robert Cruz McLain. He warned the girls not to talk or he would find them and kill them. He meant it.

Jody had nightmares for two years after the 1971 rape. Her body would be soaked with sweat. The family had no conversation about the incident, and Jody never cried about it. McLain was caught and tried in Ventura, County. At the trial both girls identified McLain as their rapist. McLain received an "indeterminate sentence" of three years to life in prison as a result of the 1971 conviction. His parole date was set for 1986. However in 1972, California's state parole officials considered granting freedom for Robert Cruz McLain. The County Prosecutor sent a letter to the officials with the following warning:

UNDER NO CIRCUMSTANCES SHOULD THIS HIGHLY DANGEROUS PSYCHOPATHIC AND TOTALLY IMMORAL CRIMINAL EVER AGAIN BE RELEASED TO SOCIETY TO PREY ON INNOCENT AND DEFENSELESS YOUNG GIRLS.

Deputy District Attorney Pete Kossoris told the Parole Board that McLain had a criminal record of assaulting girls which stretched back to 1953. Even when he was 13, he had sexually assaulted a 3-1/2-year-old girl. Kossoris said, "His past history indicates to a near certainty that [future crimes] would be the result if he were ever released again." He was not released at the time.

Unfortunately the flaws in the justice system became apparent later. The correction agency and parole officials released McLain in August of 1979 without notifying the Whitman family or local authorities.

When Jody Whitman, now 19, returned to her apartment in November of 1979, she didn't notice immediately that the rear entrance to her apartment had been tampered with and that the screen was off and the window glass had been cut. McLain had tried to get in Jody's apartment.

The next day after the attempted break-in, McLain and two others, Willis and Ketcherside, picked up a woman hitchhiker, Joannie Donell Kelley, 20 years old, of Saticoy, California. Kelley was a cook on a fishing boat and was on her way to work. McLain and Willis raped, beat, and shot her to death. They dumped the body in a park near Santa Paula.

Strong evidence exists that McLain, frustrated by not being able to get revenge by torturing and killing Jody Whitman, murdered the first woman he came across. Tragically, Joannie Kelley was hitchhiking and vulnerable to attack. She paid with her life for being available at the wrong time.

A few days after the murder and attempted break-in, Jody received a frightened call at work from her mother. Asked to return to her apartment, a sheriff's homicide detective gave her some startling news. After inquiring about the attempted break-in to her apartment, the deputy sheriff said, "...we want you to know that McLain has been picked up on two counts of murder, and we have reason to believe that he came down here to kill you." Jody was lucky.

Meanwhile, McLain and Willis had returned to Solano County in northern California and within a week had robbed and murdered Diana Cheryl Bazargani, 31, of Concord, California. In the process they strangled, stabbed, and slashed Bazargani's throat. Her body was dumped alongside a road near Benicia.

McLain and Willis were caught, tried, and convicted of the murder in Solano County. At their trial for the murder, the northern California forensic pathologist who examined the remains of the 31-year-old Miss Bazargani said, "It was the most severe [strangulation] I've ever seen." The jury in Solano County found McLain guilty of murder, along with Willis. McLain was sentenced to life imprisonment without parole. Willis, 17 years old at the time, was given life imprisonment but, because he was a teenager, was eligible for parole in seven years.

Lloyd Ketcherside, who had accompanied McLain and Willis on their trip to Ventura, was granted immunity by agreeing to turn state's evidence. With a strong witness to the Ventura murder, a second lengthy trial was to start in Ventura County.

The district attorney brought McLain and Willis to Ventura County. He charged them with first-degree murder with intent to obtain a death sentence for them. It was reported that McLain was willing to plea bargain with the District Attorney and plead guilty to the Kelley murder, if his sentence would be life without possibility of parole. Willis was too young to receive the death penalty, anyway. Due to the nature of the crime the District Attorney chose instead to try them for the death penalty. This meant an additional, expensive trial with lengthy, costly appeals, all paid for by the public.

At the start of the trial, McLain's attorneys used a variety of defense tactics that delayed the trial. They made one pretrial motion after another, totalling over 30, which took five to six weeks to process. Motions were made to change venue, to have a separate trial on the issue of guilt and punishment, the constitutionality of the death penalty, to exclude certain types of professions from the jury, and numerous others.

One issue was whether the defendant was incompetent to cooperate with his counsel. This position was supported by the testimony of two psychiatrists for the defense. A position was taken by Judge Lawrence Storch that sufficient prima facie evidence had been made to warrant a trial. Under California law the defendant had a right to a jury trial on that issue alone. As a result, a jury was impaneled. A four-week battle of psychiatrists then took place on the question of his competency to stand trial. During this time, McLain maintained the look and demeanor of an incompetent person. He gave the impression that he had no interest in what was occurring in the courtroom and role-played the 'incompetent.'

The jury concluded that McLain was competent to stand trial. The jury was correct in its findings. Immediately after the jury returned its finding of competency, McLain suddenly became very attentive and alert. He thereafter conscientiously cooperated with his lawyers in reviewing police reports, engaging in vigorous discussions with them and taking copious notes.

The jury selection process for the new case was then started. When a jury is impaneled for a capital case under California law, they must be selected in a procedurally different manner from that used for a jury in a noncapital case. In this situation, each juror must be examined outside the presence of the other jurors. This procedure added a considerable amount of time to the selection of the jury. In a capital case, where there is a possibility of a sentence of life in prison, each side is permitted 26 preemptory challenges; that is, a right to excuse 26 people without the necessity of stating any reason for the decision. Each side can make unlimited challenges for cause, actual or implied bias, in addition to the 26 preemptory challenges permitted for each side. It took almost a month just to select and seat the jury. The trial phase then started which took more than two months.

Because the California Supreme Court is likely to free an accused defendant if some technical error in trial proceedings occurs, Storch, a highly respected judge, monitored proceedings carefully. Before the trial he called in the local press for an informal conference and told them of the horrendous expense that would be involved in the trial, and asked them not to print any information concerning the defendant's prior conviction of murder or of the prior convictions that had occurred in other parts of the State. The press cooperated. Storch was pleased that it was not necessary to use a gag order.

Jody Whitman, now 21 years old, took the witness stand and recalled to the jury her rape and assault by McLain as an 11-year-old. The horror of the experience had to be recalled again. This time her rape became public information, and her brothers found out about the previous secret.

When Whitman testified for the first time against McLain, face-to-face, she said, "I was just scared. I didn't want to look at him." When asked to point him out in the courtroom, she was hesitant. "But once I did, I mean it was weird," she said. "I just sat there and just glared at him. I just wanted. . .[to] burn a hole through him,...He just glared right back at me, and it didn't bother me a bit."[6]

At the trial, some embarrassing moments occurred. While Whitman was waiting outside the courtroom, the mother of Joannie Kelley, who was killed by McLain, approached her and spoke to her several times about the death of her daughter. She told Jody about five times that "...if you would have been home, maybe my daughter wouldn't be dead."[7]

After a seven-month trial that was estimated by authorities to cost over $500,000, the jury found McLain guilty of first-degree murder. Because it was a capital offense, an additional or separate "penalty" trial was started, but with the same jury. After weeks of more testimony, the background of McLain's previous offenses against young girls were introduced to the jury. The jury never learned of his past during the first trial. The jury recommended the death sentence for his heinous crimes. He was sentenced by Judge Storch to die in the gas chamber in California.

This was not the end of the case, however. In California automatic appeals are required when the death sentence is given. The appeals took over a year to process and cost the taxpayers another large sum. Officials estimated that the trial and appeals of McLain cost the public(not including the Solano trial) one million dollars. Neither Jody Whitman nor the murdered girl's family received anything from the state for their victimization.

Theodore Willis, 18, was convicted by the jury of rape and murder of Joannie Kelley. He was sentenced to life in prison without parole. He could not be given the death sentence, however, because of his age, 17, at the time of the crime. A later construction of the statute by the California Supreme Court prevented his serving a sentence of life without parole. He was later resentenced to 25 years to life with the possibility of parole. The public would support the two in prison at the rate of about $40,000 per year. It is not likely that McLain will ever be executed.

After all the careful work of Storch, by mid 1985 the state Supreme Court had not yet heard the case on appeal. The view in legal circles is that the case may have to be retried because of a later California Supreme Court case that held that instructions given to the McLain jury pertaining to the Governor's power to commute the death sentence was unconstitutional.

Impact of the Trial on Jody Whitman and Her Family

The Whitmans were angry that a vicious person like McLain could be released without any warning to them. They found the 'State' and the 'law' amorphous. They could not find any one government person or office responsible to focus their anger against. Jody's father believes dangerous criminals are being released all over the country and that the legal system must change. Like many other families who have become victims, the Whitmans changed their way of life. They bought two large black Labradors to serve as watchdogs. Doors are carefully locked and information is carefully given out to strangers.

Speeding Up Personal Injury and Liability Cases

In accident and personal injury cases, settlement conferences should be required in an attempt to force the plaintiff and defendant to come to agreement, Settlement conferences should be organized in such a manner that a party not satisfied with an arbitrator's award takes a chance on appealing the award, and could end up paying legal fees and court costs for both parties if the appeal is lost. Court procedures should discourage a party from going to court in hopes of getting a big profit from a jury by preparing a clever case. The court should make it risky for anyone to use public facilities to gain more than is considered reasonable by a qualified arbitrator.

Approximately three to six months before a trial date settlement conferences for accident and personal injury cases should be held by a settlement judge. The court should be able to order arbitration when a judge believes a case is not worthy of trial. Incentives should be built into the process to prevent cases from going to trial.

Lawyers claim that insurance companies gain from delaying the settlement of accident and personal injury cases. It is also true that when insurance companies go to trial, they run up big expenses for their attorneys and staffs to try cases. Usually arbitrators in accident and personal injury cases are lawyers. Many believe that arbitrators should not be lawyers. It is suggested arbitration committees consist of possibly three people: one representing the industry involved in the dispute; one a lawyer to review the legal aspects; and the third, a non-lawyer picked for an objective viewpoint.

Insurance companies find that auto accident cases where bodily injury occurred settle much faster without lawyers representing the client. In a 1979 national study of 29 major insurance companies, writing 62% of the auto injury coverage, it found that "Claimants with economic losses greater than $2,000 received a larger net return if they were not represented by an attorney." For bodily injury claims, "those with attorneys took an average of 500 days from first report of injury to final payment, compared with an average of 100 days for non-represented claims."[8] The 29 companies paid out an estimated $2,512,200,000 in 1979 to auto accident claimants. The insurance industry study showed also that while claimants got a bigger settlement with lawyers the net amount they received was less than those not having lawyers. Based on the findings of the study, it appeared that lawyers created work for themselves at the expense of their clients, the insurance companies, and the public.

Because of some recent cases in the country referred to as 'bad faith' cases, insurance companies are paying what they consider blackmail money, over and above the policyholder's policy limit to avoid being sued by a policyholder for making a 'bad faith' mistake.

In criminal cases there is a limit to the length of jail sentences or fines a defendant must pay. In civil cases no protection exists for a party going to trial. An award can range from zero to several million dollars. Courts should impose reasonable limits, or safeguards in civil trials as in criminal court.

When an enormously high award is given to a person which in reality represents punitive damages, the public is victimized. Consumers absorb these enormous awards by increased insurance fees or costs of products.

142

Some lawyers claim that because insurance companies can obtain an estimated 20% to 25% per year return on their investments, the longer they hold out paying an accident victim the more money they make. For example, if sued for $100,000 but not paying for four to five years, the company can make an additional $100,000 to pay off the victim.

The famous trial lawyer, Melvin Belli, responding to questions on how to speed up settlement from insurance companies and prevent trial delays, said:

> ...fix interest from the happening (accident or injury) of the event and at around 17%. Alaska has 15. Then the insurance companies wouldn't hold out and use your money that they eventually have to give you and gain interest on it. An insurance company can make 25% easily and inside of four years they've made what money they're going to give you, so it costs nothing. Alaska speeded up its calendars by pro tem judges and by fixing the insurance.
>
> And then you have to get a hard-nosed judge who won't take any excuses and you have to get all of the plaintiffs' lawyers to sign affidavits that they'll go to trial when the case comes up. We've got to do something about the trial delays or the whole system is going to come tumbling down, an otherwise good system. I think a lot of stuff should go to arbitration and we ought to have more of these pre-trial settlements.[9]

By insurance companies being required to pay current market interest rates from the date of an accident to settlement, companies probably would settle faster with claimants. California does have a 'pre-judgement' interest law that requires insuring companies to pay 10% from the date settlement demand is made. Trial judges should take the responsibility to prevent delays and require companies to settle within a prescribed time limit.

Multiple-Disaster Cases

In a speech to the American Law Institute on May 14, 1985, Chief Justice Burger spoke about how to hasten the hearing of multiple-disaster cases and to provide more equitable treatment to victims of them. He suggested that accident cases from plane crashes, building collapses, fuel explosions, or gas leaks be handled by special tribunals with authority to resolve claims outside the courtroom. These tribunals would operate similarly as do workers compensation claim boards.

Antitrust, Securities Fraud and Complex Cases

Burger thought that juries formed by specialist judges should hear complex cases on antitrust, securities fraud, and financial issues. He believed as do the authors that well informed judges can better understand and reach logical decisions on complicated legal and technical issues than a lay jury.

Solving Civil Disputes—Alternative Justice Programs

Most divorce and probate proceedings should be taken out of civil court and handled through the arbitration and administrative process. No need exists for divorce or probate to be in court, except in disputes over the meaning of a will or where large sums of money are involved. Simple estates should be settled administratively, without the need for lawyers or judges, in a matter of a month or two as done in most European countries.

Divorce Mediation

To avoid court battles in divorces, a psychologist, Randy Wood, and a lawyer, Christopher Danch, formed a team to do divorce mediation and work out voluntary agreements to avoid expensive litigation. The team, working in Ventura, California, are hired by both spouses which eliminates the adversary relationship that occurs when each hires a separate attorney in a normal divorce action.

Danch says that mediation costs one-third less in most cases than do legal fees in a contested divorce and the mediation process takes about one-third the time. The team said the total cost for mediation cases ranges from $300 to $1,500. They obtain a $750 retainer of which the first $100 is applied to a joint session with the team and additional sessions are charged against the balance on an hourly basis. If the $750 retainer is not fully used, the remaining amount is returned to the couple.

Organizational Changes

'Rent-a-Judge'

With civil cases backlogged four to five years in most California jurisdictions, two lawyers in 1977 discovered a California law that authorizes litigants to hire a referee to hear civil cases. With approval of the Presiding Judge of the Los Angeles County Superior Court, Jerome Craig and Hillel Chodos hired a retired judge to hear their case. They obtained a decision in seven months, not four years, and saved their clients an estimated $100,000 in legal fees.

The advantages of the system are that litigants can pick judges with expertise in the field of dispute, trials can begin when litigants are ready, money is saved for litigants, and other cases are not held back. In fact the legal backlog is eased by removing cases from the normal court system. The 'rent-a-judges,' usually retired judges, are doing well, making $125 to $150 per hour or more hearing cases.

By 1984 rent-a-judges were used in several states including New York, Rhode Island, Washington, Oregon, California, Idaho, Nebraska, and Utah. The well known celebrity Johnny Carson used a rent-a-judge to solve his contract dispute with NBC.

Some critics objected, claiming that the hearings were secret and that private courts were discriminatory as they provided swift justice only to those who could afford it. These freedom-of-press objections do not make much sense as the public has little interest in private disputes not affecting them. The hearings can be made public if the press is interested. The use of private judges frees court time to more litigants and helps clear the court backlog. The American Arbitration Association has been resolving malpractice and construction suits privately for years. A law professor at University of California at Berkeley, Preble Stolz, said: "If the cases that this system takes out of the pipeline are the ones that take several months to try normally, then that amounts to quite a bit of time saved to try many other cases in the normal court system."

Private Tribunal or Mini-Trials

Many companies involved in disputes with other companies and dissatisfied with the court system sought a faster, inexpensive, and private alternative way of finding solutions. The 'tribunal' or 'mini-trial' evolved. The tribunal was formed, not by judges, but by an executive from each company and a neutral adviser.

How does it work? In 1983, two large companies, the American Can Co. and Wisconsin Electric Power Co. were embroiled in a dispute when Wisconsin Electric stopped burning garbage-derived fuel provided by American Can. Suits were filed claiming a loss of $61 million and a lengthy expensive trial was anticipated.

With the assistance of a company called EnDispute Inc., the two companies argued their case before a tribunal, made up of a high executive from each company and a neutral adviser. The system worked. A solution was reached, the suits were dropped, and the companies continued their normal relationship. Both companies saved large sums in legal fees by using a private mini-trial as it is called.

EnDispute is operated by a lawyer, a law professor, and three management consultants. In 1982, it opened offices in Washington. D.C. and Los Angles, and offers advice on how to avoid litigation and to reach an early settlement. In 1984, its fees were about $150 per hour.

Other firms offer similar services. Washington Arbitration Services Inc. was started in Seattle in 1981. It provides arbitrators who handle disputes between companies selling and companies buying computers.

In 1984, two other companies, Judicate Inc, and Civicourt Inc., started private court systems for corporate use to settle claims ranging from insurance claims to personal issues such as divorce settlements. Judicate judges received $600 per half day and $1,000 for more complex cases.

Most of the mini-trials focus on business concerns and not legalism, as would happen when lawyers are used in a traditional court of law. For example, when TRW Inc. and Telecredit Inc. became involved in a dispute over a patent infringement case, they decided to use the mini-trial process in which abbreviated presentation of evidence was made to executives who were not lawyers.

In a mini-trial involving pipeline contractors and Standard Oil Co. (Indiana) in 1982, all lawyers were dismissed from the conference room. An Indiana Standard attorney, Matthew Gallo said it was necessary otherwise "the power play is in the hands of the attorneys." He indicated that with the lawyers not present, within a day executives had settled all of the claims which concerned construction cost overruns.[10]

Mini-trials cannot be used for every dispute, but appropriate

146

time and large sums of money can be saved and relationships continued amicably. This occurred in an issue between Texaco Inc. and Borden Inc. By the time a mini-trial was used over 300,000 pages of documents had been produced in litigation. In a private room in New York, claims of $200 million were settled in 1982; and the companies continued to work with each other afterwards.

Dispute, Arbitration and Neighborhood Justice Centers

'Dispute Resolution Centers,' or neighborhood justice centers, are using arbitrators and mediators, and speeding up the processing of civil cases by keeping cases out of court. In 1984, over 170 Dispute Resolution Centers existed in the country. Under the mediation process a third person listens and talks to the two sides and tries to get them also to listen and talk to each other so that they can work out a compromise and settle their dispute.

Some dispute centers are funded publicly and some privately. In Tampa, Florida the Citizen's Dispute Settlement Program receives all its financing from county government, and provides its services free. The University of Massachusetts has a program oriented toward students, faculty, staff and campus area residents and business people. The Brooklyn, New York Mediation Center depends on law students to process its disputes. In Framingham, Massachusetts elderly people operate its neighborhood justice center. The earliest alternative justice centers were in urban centers like Philadelphia, New York, Atlanta, Los Angeles, and Kansas City, Missouri.

As a result of complaints from consumers and disputes with industrial firms, companies have set up channels in which consumers can list grievances without filing a legal claim in court. This system works in the following manner: first, a complaint by a person is filed with a court clerk or prosecutor's office. The court clerk, instead of setting this up on a court calendar, refers the issue complaint to a mediation center. A meeting is held in the mediation center with the complaining party and the industrial representative to discuss the issue. This is frequently done with a volunteer mediator. In the District of Columbia a large trained mediation staff assists in resolving problems. When a solution is reached, an agreement is prepared and signed by the parties involved. The mediator checks with the parties afterwards to insure they are complying with the agreement. When the parties in dispute cannot come to agreement, claims are submitted to an arbitrator who makes a decision. Nationally the American Arbitration Association handles over 40,000 cases annually.

Arbitration is used by many major companies. In arbitration an impartial third person hears both sides and then decides for one or the other. In a three year period General Motors had a reported 3,350 cases, of which about three-fourths were resolved by a mediator and the rest by an arbitrator. The savings in legal and court costs to complainants and the companies involved is considerable. The Ford Motor Company reported that in 3,200 arbitration cases 60% went against the car owners, but only 23 went on to court. Mediation is also used in personal disputes concerning family violence and child custody.

Out-of-Court Settlements

Court officials are beginning to realize the importance of keeping some disputes out of court. Chief Justice Herman Lum of the Hawaii Supreme Court, addressing the American Arbitration Association's conference in 1984, indicated that new ways were needed to settle disputes outside the court system. He said that the civil cases in Oahu increased by 161% and the number of cases pending increased by 271% from 1972 to 1982, and:

> The time has come when we must greatly expand our use of arbitration, mediation, conciliation and other alternatives to court litigation. Those of you who over the years have been working in the fields of arbitration and mediation have gradually laid a solid base upon which we can build. But my message to you today is that right now there is a pressing need to rapidly develop and spread throughout our society the use of alternative methods of dispute resolution.[11]

Judge Lum explained that the alternative of adding judges is expensive. Just to add one judge increases the cost to the public of $350,000 a year, he said, including the "cost of court personnel (clerks, secretaries, baliffs and court reporters), plus supplies and the cost of operating court facilities and the cost of administration."[12]

Success of Dispute Centers

Mediation centers are widely used in China. An estimated 90% of China's minor criminal and civil cases are resolved through people's mediation committees. The country of one billion people has only half as many lawyers as the State of Wisconsin.

A study by the National Law Journal found that a typical lawsuit takes 10 times longer to resolve as in an alternative justice center. In a study of the civil court system by the Rand Corp., they found that mandatory mediation for minor cases could relieve court congestion, save time and money for litigants, and give them a feeling of satisfaction.

Streamlining Court Case Administration

Handling Routine Court Work

An abundance of routine work is attached to any court system. It was customary for judges to handle much of the routine pre-hearing work. For years federal courts have utilized magistrates to assist district court judges. This has proven satisfactory and increased productivity. In criminal cases magistrates can handle initial appearances and preliminary hearings for detainees, bail hearings, issuance of search and arrest warrants, and preliminary reviews of applications for post-trial relief for the purpose of making recommendations to the judge concerning the desirability of a hearing. Under the federal system, magistrates can also try petty offenses.

In the state systems, magistrates can process several types of civil cases. Magistrates can conduct status, discovery, and pretrial conferences. Magistrates can also decide on pretrial motions of a non-positive nature relating to venue, pleadings, joiner, or discovery. With the consent of both parties, magistrates can even preside over civil trials.[13] Courts should consider using magistrates to help, especially in systems having a backlog of cases.

Court Management

Simple reforms can make dramatic improvements in court management. The mechanics of preparing schedules to increase efficiency through systems analysis was pioneered in Denver, Colorado by the Institute of Court Management. Computer-based information systems were developed to keep track of cases, provide access to needed records, and to assist in producing efficient schedules.

Recently in Los Angeles Municipal Courts the calendaring judge ruled that no more than three continuances would be granted. This cut the waiting time for civil cases from an average of six months to less than three months. In San Francisco reforms that included a change to 8-member civil juries speeded up civil trials to a point where four civil courts were transferred to the criminal side. This reduced the criminal case backlog by 25%.

Through professional court administration, Pittsburgh, Pennsylvania developed a number of time-saving management processes. This included pre-selection of Monday morning's juries on the preceeding Friday, a tough stand on granting continuances, pre-trial conciliation conferences, as well as last-chance settlement conferences. The conferences settled 25% of the cases. New York City, assisted by the Economic Development Council, designed a new administrative structure that cut the criminal court backlog by 5% in 10 months.

Civil Trial Advancement Plan

Starting in 1981 under the leadership of Ventura County, California Superior Court Judge Lawrence Storch, felony cases were settled more rapidly than usual permitting trial courtrooms and judges to try more civil cases. The five year civil case backlog was attacked at the same time under a program by the then Presiding Judge Jerome H. Berenson. Later in 1982 as Presiding Judge, Storch supervised the ambitious plan to reduce the civil suit backlog. During one week every three or four months, all seven judges heard only civil cases that would take no more than one week. Storch impressed on lawyers that when they filed a civil case they had better be ready to go to trial. He urged litigants to settle in conferences and to avoid a trial. Storch let lawyers know that continuances and delays would not be tolerated. He urged fellow judges to suggest pre-trial settlements and to process more criminal and civil cases.

The program was successful. By the time Storch had finished a two year stint as Presiding Judge, the backlog of 1,800 civil cases and five year wait was reduced to a normal 800 case backlog and a

90 day wait. Storch was successful because he obtained the cooperation of the district attorney's office, private attorneys, and the courts' superior and municipal judges.

Conference Telephone Calls

Various courts and judges throughout the country are experimenting with a variety of means for speeding up the processing of cases. The use of conference telephone calls by judges has worked well. In Atlantic City, New Jersey, Superior Court Judge Phillip Gruccio disposed of 60% more civil cases in a year after hearing argument motions by telephone. It was estimated that the cost of divorce cases was reduced from an average of $250 to $87 per case in the New Jersey courts by the use of telephone conference calls.[14]

Reduction of Unnecessary Paperwork

In submitting questions for written depositions lawyers have a tendency to ask the other side to do an unnecessary amount of work. In Kentucky the Chief Justice of the Kentucky Supreme Court, John S. Palmore, said that in a court system experiment, 70% of the civil cases were disposed of in no more than nine months, less than half the time it normally took.[15] The Kentucky court specified a maximum number of pages a lawyer could use in filing a written argument for appeal cases. Oral arguments were also eliminated.

Kentucky judges made more case decisions without writing elaborate opinions explaining their opinions, a time-consuming and expensive process. In court lawyers were required to stick to the issues of a case. Judges also reduced the number of questions and the amount of time permitted in questioning potential jurors. Concerned with the time and cost of litigation, Palmore stated, "We must throw the shackles off our traditional way of doing things. That's the only way we can make litigation faster and cheaper."[16]

Use of Computers In Court

Because courts must keep masses of records, they could benefit from greater use of computers, by recording and keeping information current on offenders, rapidly retrieving data needed for trials and case processing, reducing storage needed by keeping data on disks, and sharing offender information quickly with other jurisdictions.

Judge Robert G. Crouchley in the Providence, R.I. court has used a computer in his courtroom and found it useful in handling the growing caseloads and finding ways to curb crime. Crouchley found that the computer provided more detailed data quickly that he wanted in court, and saved time. He said,

> We handle four to five cases a day and for each one of those cases, a clerk has to bring up the necessary paper-work from four floors down.
>
> That interrupts her work and when she brings up a stack (a foot high)..., you can imagine what kind of time we're running into.[17]

Judge Crouchley believed that the computer had potential for helping authorities to identify potential problem kids early, enabling intervention and help before they get into serious trouble.

Los Angeles Superior Court Judge Lester E. Olson uses a computer for a variety of uses:

- Drafting opinions on the computer rather than in long-hand and inserting 'boilerplate' data from computer data.
- Completing letter-perfect daily 'minute orders' of trials in a minute (A "minute order" is a daily record of what happens to a case when it is before a judge).
- Maintaining a list of witnesses for use in non-jury trials, including data about them and their testimony.
- Creating a list of numbers for the clerk to use in 'inventory control' of exhibits.[18]

Olson strongly believes the computer can make work easier. He said:

> We have burned-out clerks, burned-out law clerks and burned-out judges, partly because we are doing dumb-dumb things. Computers are not going to replace judges or clerks, but they are going to make our jobs easier.[19]

In Ventura County, California Presiding Judge Lawrence Storch, arranged to use television for communication between the Simi Valley, an hour away, and the courthouse to handle some civil cases and routine court matters. The TV arrangement saved lawyers and their clients the need to travel to Ventura for court business.

The Superior Court Executive Officer Hank Rodgers said, "It is a little like taking the judge to the people instead of the other way around."

Recommended National Action

Public organizations should 'encourage' their state and federal legislators to pass legislation providing time limits for insurance companies to settle personal injury and accident claims or pay current interest rates to them until final settlement.

Judicial Task Force

A special judicial task force needs to be appointed by the President to review the opportunities for changing our maze of rules and procedures to speed up the court process. The task force should carefully examine the qualities of the British justice system and the impact on civil rights.

Justice Rehnquist's Proposals to Reduce Court Delays

At a speech at the University of Florida Law School, Supreme Court Justice William H. Rehnquist offered several suggestions for reducing delays in our nation's courts. He said the legal profession should consider "radical change" in the court system to reduce costs and delays in civil cases.

The justice found that law schools were "seriously wanting" in research and instruction in areas of the law involving persons who are neither very rich nor poor—but the vast majority of the civil litigants.

To reduce court delays, he would:

- Change the type of faculty members that law schools hire. He thought the schools employed too many persons who had served with big law firms or worked as judges' law clerks.
- Abolish 'discovery,' the time-consuming pre-trial exchange of evidence between parties in lawsuits, in cases in which lesser amounts of money were at stake.
- Abolish the absolute right to appeal in civil cases from federal

153

district courts to appellate courts and, instead, allow such review only at the discretion of appellate courts. This action would reduce the burden on the federal courts of appeal.
- Raise to $5,000 the jurisdictional limits on cases heard in small claims courts.[20]

Rehnquist believed that too much focus was put on cases involving the poor who may receive free legal aid or the rich, who can afford expensive law firms, while the rest are told to find "alternative methods of dispute resolution." He said "To tell 50%, 60%, or 70% of such potential litigants that they ought to find a form of 'alternative dispute resolution' is a gross abuse of the monopoly of judicial power..."[21]

CHAPTER NINE

MAKING CORRECTIONAL INSTITUTIONS COST EFFECTIVE

The prison population in the United States more than doubled in ten years to almost a half-million inmates by 1984. To house the increased number of inmates, improve the rehabilitation process of prisoners, and make the correctional system more effective, fundamental changes should be made. Money cannot solve all the inherent problems, even though the nation is in the midst of a multimillion dollar prison construction program.

Stopping Correctional Institution Abuses

Chief Justice Warren E. Burger asks, "Will we build more 'human warehouses,' or will we change our thinking and create institutions that are training schools and factories with fences around them...We pay at least $17 million each day to run the nation's prisons."[1] He made more suggestions that are included later in this chapter.

In discussing the problems of the criminal justice system with court officials, they stated repeatedly that corrections needed changing the most, and had the greatest opportunities for improvement. They said offenders were not being rehabilitated, and those victimized were not getting sufficient justice or restitution.

The parole and correction system abuses the court system and the public by not making prisoners work to earn their keep, not

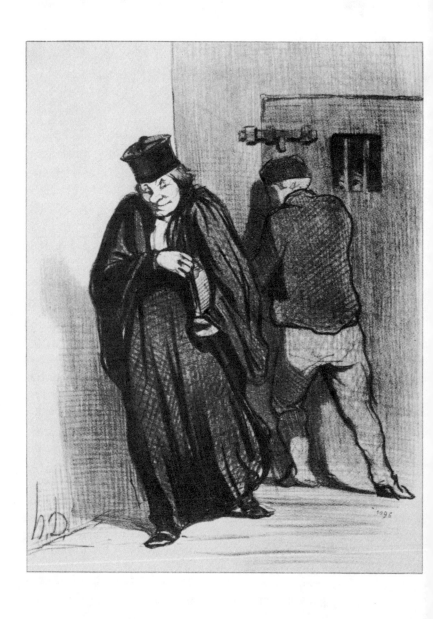

MEN OF JUSTICE—It seems that my client is a scoundrel.
Good. What honor for me if I get him acquitted!

teaching them skills to use in normal community life, and by releasing dangerous offenders prematurely.

Who Determines Sentences for Murderers?

Did you believe that, when a judge sentences a convicted killer to life in prison, the offender would stay in prison for his lifetime? If you did, you were wrong. Unfortunately, trial judges have less to say about how long a criminal stays in prison than the public realizes. Parole and correctional boards usually make the final determination of a prisoner's term.

Changing Parole Boards—Another Judiciary

As presently constituted, parole boards serve as a second judiciary in most states and decide release dates of criminals based on their own criteria, not the courts. As the public became aware that parole boards were releasing dangerous criminals before they had completed their sentences, letters were sent and petitions signed to prevent early releases of brutal murderers. As a result full fledged trials, involving high paid consultants, usually psychologists and psychiatrists, with a jury have evolved to determine if a convict should remain another year or more in prison. The legal maneuvering and trials over early release are held at public expense. At some parole trials victim/witnesses must testify again about the offender's attack on them.

A juvenile, Tony Matzen of Oxnard, California was convicted of murdering Paul Yenney, Jr. and raping and beating his girl friend nearly to death. The Oxnard Police Chief, Robert Owens, said the crime was one of the worst he had ever seen. Based on state correctional laws and procedures, Matzen was to be released on his 21st birthday. The public erupted with a flood of angry protest letters. Under public pressure the parole board voted to hold Matzen for two years past the normal release date in California for a juvenile, no matter how vicious the person. Before Matzen could serve another two years however, a hearing, really a trial, was required to be held before a juvenile court judge.

The trial and jury deliberations lasted almost three months at great public expense. The jury decided that Matzen was still a threat to society and prevented his release for another two years. At the end of the two year term Matzen was released under a cloud of protests from the public, police, and the district attorney's office. Why should a trial of this sort be held at all? It was nothing but a duplication of the court's functions by corrections. Parole boards should be reestablished with new guidelines and procedures. A sentence should be reduced only in accordance to the offender's providing restitution to the victim and doing work in the prison as scheduled under terms of the trial court's stipulations. The right of a parole board to hold expensive hearings and establish a separate criteria from the court for the release of offenders should be taken away from them. If legislators will not take action, the public should use the initiative process to obtain needed parole board reform.

Until action can be taken to abolish parole boards in their present form, interim action is necessary. Legislation should be passed requiring that victims of crime and their families be notified by parole boards of any pending hearings for the release of their offender. Victims or their representatives should be allowed to attend parole hearings and express their views on the damage done to them. Parole hearings should be open to the public.

How Long do Murderers and Violent Offenders Serve in Prison?

In a study made by the United States Bureau of Justice Statistics of 29 states, it found that in 1982 half of the murderers released from state prisons served less than six years and that the median time served had dropped to a new low. Director of the Statistics Bureau Steven R. Schlesinger said that increasing numbers of inmates were serving sentences for violent crimes, but that the amount of time they served was declining. Of those admitted to prison in 1982, 37.5% had committed violent crimes and faced a 51-month median sentence. The majority, however, served less than one-third of it after being granted allowances for good behavior and paroles.

The study found that about 3% of the total inmates entering prison faced life sentences, but that the 'lifers' served only five years and nine months, on average. Rapists released in 1982 served a median sentence of 36 months and those in for manslaughter served a median time of two years and four months. The study results were announced in July of 1985.

In 1901, the California Legislature decided that criminals sentenced to life in prison would be automatically eligible for parole after serving seven years. Other states took similar actions. In 1978 however, under public pressure the minimum time to be served by convicted murderers was increased to 16 years and 8 months. Actually the State Board of Prison Terms, appointed by the Governor, determines the length of sentence after the minimum term has been served.

In 1975, under guidelines prepared by California Adult Authority Head Raymond Procunier, the parole of Sirhan Sirhan, the convicted murderer of Robert Kennedy, was scheduled for 1984. When the media reported his possible release, the public responded in anger and disgust with the correctional system. In an article by Bill Farr, a *Los Angeles Times* reporter, he found that:

- Of 2,173 men serving life sentences for murder in California, only 167 had been in prison more than 10 years.
- Of 99 women serving life sentences, only three, (part of Charles Manson's 'family') remained in prison 10 years.[2]

During 1981, 50 male murderers were released, serving a median time of 10 years and 11 months. The median time served by 90 killers released in 1971 was only slightly longer, 12 years and one month. The parole board has been more lenient with women murderers. Over a 30-year period, women have been released after serving an average term of about seven years and seven months.

With increased public pressure not to release prisoners early, parole is being delayed longer to around 13 years for male murderers. In 1982, 379 of the 873 murderers eligible for parole were given release dates.

Only through the public's efforts was a life sentence required for some criminals that the Board of Prison Terms could not change.

In 1984, a survey by the Justice Department's Bureau of Justice Statistics reported that violent criminals spend more time in prison, but less time, percentage-wise, than those who commit property crimes. Using information from a survey of actual prison time served in 12 states for certain crimes between 1977 and 1983, the survey found that the average prison stay for violent felons extended from two and one half to four years. The survey indicated that an automobile thief serves up to twice as large a percentage of his sentence as a convicted murderer.

The Justice Department found that the trend "appears to be universal: there is an inverse relationship between the seriousness of the offence and the percentage of the sentence that is served. That is, those who are imprisoned for the most serious crimes (and therefore receive the longest sentences) serve the smallest percentage of their sentences."

Attorney General William French Smith said, after reading the report, "The public has assumed that the worst offenders—murderers, rapists, drug traffickers—serve substantial terms. The bureau's study ...shows how easy it is for hardened criminals to get back on the streets to commit new crimes...This erodes public trust."[3]

Who is in Prison?

Even with most states providing parole and probation liberally to offenders, the population of state and federal prisons moved upward to 438,830 inmates by the end of 1983. The Justice Department's Bureau of Justice Statistics reported that the number of prisoners in state and federal institutions increased 24,468 or 5.9% during 1983. The growth rate was 12.2% in 1981 and 12% in 1982. California had the dubious honor of leading the nation with the largest inmate population of 39,360; Texas was second with 35,259 inmates, and New York was third with 30,489. Nationally the number of inmates increased from a ratio of 98 per 100,000 people in 1969 to 140 by 1980. Internationally, the United States leads the free world in the number of people in prisons.

Prisons throughout the country are overcrowded due to increased crime, and renewed interest in putting dangerous criminals in prison. Many county jails are holding felony suspects awaiting trial because state prisons have no space to house them.

Most offenders in prison are under age 30. Chief Justice Burger pointed out in his address to the American Bar Association in 1981 that a majority of the prisoners cannot meet minimum standards of reading, writing, and arithmetic. Inmates unable to read or write will naturally have difficulty finding jobs when released. Educational and vocational programs are needed to prepare and equip released prisoners for jobs in society.

Prison Sentences Within the States

In a study conducted by the National Law Survey completed in 1981, it was found that the average length of time criminals spent behind bars differed drastically from state to state. The survey revealed that often the nature of the crime mattered less in determining a sentence than the state where it took place. The survey conducted in 37 states found that the average person convicted of robbery in one state would serve more time in prison than convicted killers spent behind bars on the average in six other states. The study was based on the number of months defendants actually spent in prison for various crimes, rather than the terms imposed on them at sentencing by judges.

Persons convicted of felonies in the United States averaged 25 months in state prisons before parole. This compares to 27 months convicts averaged in federal prisons for federal crimes. The total average time spent in prison ranged from a high of 53 months in Massachusetts, which gives very stiff sentences for murder, to a low in South Dakota of 15 months.[4]

The Juvenile's Contribution to the Crime Rate

An average of 10,000,000 juveniles and young adults are involved with the Criminal Justice System in some form. One study found that 190,000 people between the ages of 18-22 entered the penal system in 1979.

Unfortunately, a large percentage of juveniles have contempt for the juvenile justice system, and have little fear that it will harm them. Many officials involved with juveniles believe they should be treated as adults when they commit adult-like crimes. In a study conducted at Virginia Polytechnic Institute Center for the Study of Public Choice, it was estimated that, while "an adult burglar has only one chance in 412 of going to jail for any single job,"[5] the odds for a juvenile burglar under 17 ever going to jail are even slimmer. The Institute found that one in 659 juvenile burglars will go to jail, and if so, only for a nine-month term if caught and sentenced.

Juvenile Crimes against Persons and Property

Of all crimes against persons and property nationally in which arrests took place, about half were committed by teenagers and young adults. The estimated peak age for violent crime was 15 years in 1975. Of the murders in the United States, over 45% were committed by those 25 or younger, and about 10% by those under 18. About 75% of those arrested for street crimes, not including murder, were under 25, and 45% were under 18.

The public is victimized by a court and probation system that prematurely releases dangerous juveniles to prey on them and that naively assumes that juvenile offenders can be rehabilitated with conventional probation and counseling.

Abuse of Public by Correctional Policies

Release of Child Abuse Offenders

Little Amy Sue Seitz was only 2-1/2 years old when she was kidnapped, raped, horribly tortured with pliers, and strangled to death in 1978. She was murdered by Theodore Frank, who had been under treatment at Atascadero State Hospital in California as a Mentally Disordered Sex Offender (MDSO). He was released shortly before her abduction. Frank had a 20-year history of molesting children. Amy Sue's family and the community of Camarillo, California were so outraged at her murder that they formed SLAM, Concerned Citizens for Stronger Legislation against Child Molesters (later Society's League Against Molesters).

While SLAM founders were concerned with the amount of child molestation, their main complaint was with the criminal justice system's inability to imprison offenders, keep them there, and prevent them from continuing to prey on innocent children. SLAM, founded in February 1980, grew into a national organization with over 100 chapters and 30,000 members by 1985. It had obtained tougher laws in more than seven states. In April of 1984, President Reagan presented Patti Linebaugh, grandmother of Amy Sue, a certificate at the White House for starting SLAM in 1980.

The reasons for SLAM's formation are easily understood after examining the treatment of molesters nationwide as well as in California:

- Of 396 convicted child molesters in California in 1979, 236 (60%) were released on probation, 102 (26%) were sent to state hospitals, and 58 (14%) received prison terms.
- A convicted rapist was four times more likely to go to prison than a convicted child molester(62%, as opposed to 14%).
- Child molesters incarcerated by the state as mentally disordered sex offenders are released after an average of 18 months. Those sent to prisons serve an average of 41 months.

• Only one of 100 child molesters is apprehended, and of those apprehended, only one out of 10 is convicted.[6]

Patti Linebaugh and SLAM members were horrified to learn in June of 1985 that the California Supreme Court had overturned Frank's death sentence. Another expensive trial at public expense was held to redetermine Frank's sentence. Chief Justice Rose Bird in a separate opinion, stated that she would have reversed both the penalty and the conviction.

The criminal justice systems in other states have a similar statistical pattern. In fact, an abused child is quite often revictimized by the child protective and criminal justice systems. Courts often make it difficult for children to testify about their abuse. Because of the way the court system works, children are sometimes required to take the stand as many as seven or eight times to testify and be cross-examined.

Children and the Courts

Judges often believe children are unreliable witnesses in family sexual abuse cases. In a case in Compton, California Superior Court, a clinical psychologist said that one abused girl spoke clearly and calmly about her abuse. She was consistent in her descriptions of the time and places of abuse. Two other children told of similar incidents, and medical examinations confirmed what the three children had said. However, the judge dismissed all charges because he believed the children had lied.

Molestation and Restitution

Families of abused children are starting to sue offenders for restitution. The family of a 14-year-old girl who was sexually assaulted when she was nine and ten was recently awarded $25,000 by the court from the man who assaulted her. The defendant had been convicted on three counts of child molestation and spent a year in Atascadero State Hospital. He was later released and placed on three years' probation. The family of the girl later filed a successful civil lawsuit. The suit claimed that he sexually assaulted her over a period of a year, damaging her physically, mentally, and psychologically.

Child molesters when caught should be required to pay restitution to their victims. Restitution determination can and should be made during criminal trials. A separate civil trial at additional time and expense to the family should not be necessary.

Stopping Public Perks to Criminal Inmates

Should the public send Social Security payments to convicts in prison? Unbelievably, many convicted criminals continue to receive such monthly benefits. In addition, the inmates receive room and board and free medical care while in prison at a cost of about $20,000 a year to taxpayers.

In an analysis Representative James Collins of Texas found that, during 1980 over 30,000 convicted prisoners received $60 million in Social Security benefits because of a loophole in the law. They received disability checks because they were taking part in rehabilitation programs while in prison. Responding to the situation Collins introduced a bill in the House of Representatives, HR3274, that proposed to change the present federal system of sending checks to convicted prisoners who are "involved in rehabilitation projects while in prison." The congressman stated in a *Los Angeles Herald-Examiner* article:

> These are tax-free payments to convicted mass murderers, child molesters, and other hardened criminals whose daily needs are already being taken care of at the public expense. How can we justify to the Americans, especially the elderly citizens who are honest and deserving of their Social Security benefits that we continue to condone criminal acts by paying the Social Security and Disability payments?[7]

Collins described the benefits received by a convicted child molester of a six-year-old girl. The prisoner was awarded $3,624 in back disability payments because he claimed he had "dizzy spells" from a police beating. When apprehended, he had no visible injuries and an x-ray examination showed no evidence of any other injury.

Collins cites another inmate who was convicted of stabbing a person 66 times with a hunting knife while under the influence of LSD. He received a monthly Social Security disability check for $214 because a psychiatric report declared him "unemployable in American society." The prisoner had saved about $6,000 in four years from his payments.

Another young man who killed his mother and sister five years ago received around $21,500 in Social Security Survivor Benefits upon his parole in January of 1982 from the California Youth Authority. The irony is that Charles Patterson, by killing his mother, became a survivor, and therefore eligible for Social Security benefits. He was being rewarded with thousands of dollars for killing his two family members.

When questioned about the situation, Social Security Administration Regional Office spokesmen said that crimes committed by parent killers are not officially called felonies under juvenile law. The Administration puts their benefits into a trust account until they are released from the Youth Authority.

A Youth Authority spokesman, Art German, said, "People are probably horrified to find out a person gets benefits as a result of killing a person. The Youth Authority has no way of stopping it. Look at it this way. If they didn't get Social Security, they probably would go on welfare."[8]

Another Youth Authority inmate, Dwayne Peel, reportedly was credited with receiving $8,000 in benefits since April 1977 when, at 14, he killed his father. The legal system works in mysterious ways.

Compensation to Criminals for Movie Rights and Book Royalties

After fouling up his attempted bank robbery in Brooklyn, John Wojtowicz held a bank officer hostage for 13 hours. Caught and sent to prison for a short term for the holdup, Wojtowicz was paid $80,000 for the movie rights of *Dog Day Afternoon*. Fate was with him. A successful robbery would have netted him only $29,000. Under a 1977 law in New York, first in the nation, $20,000 of Wojtowicz's movie fund went to Bob Barrett, his bank hostage who suffered physically from the ordeal.

The "Son of Sam" murderer, Sam Berkowitz, received $80,000 for his story rights. Fortunately the money went into a trust fund and is to be used to repay his victims for their injuries and to the relatives of those he killed.

Probably the highest paid convicted criminal is G. Gordon Liddy. He wrote a book, *Will*, which sold well and sold movie rights to NBC television for a reported $100,000 or more. Liddy's lectures throughout the country are received enthusiastically and pay him well. Other former inmates are doing well with their books and story rights, including several others involved in the Watergate conspiracy group.

Making Restitution Available to Victims

In nonviolent crimes or crimes against property, convicted persons should provide restitution for their victims. This includes burglary, embezzlement, shoplifting, computer crimes, and other 'white-collar' crimes. Individuals involved, men or women, should be kept working in their communities, wherever possible, in programs to repay persons who were victimized, or companies, for their losses and damages. Restitution programs in Ventura County, California and in other centers of the United States require repayment to victims, but also help rehabilitate the offenders. Offenders learn that it is costly to steal when they are forced to get a job and repay their victims. Restitution specialists believe that offenders relieve some of their guilt, and become better citizens by repaying victims for their actions. Restitution programs can be a satisfactory alternative for prison in many cases. Offenders who have violated the rights of others should expect to have their liberties curtailed as punishment. But the lockups can be on weekends and nights, enabling the offender to work, continue to contribute to his family and victim, and keep himself in the mainstream of society. Offenders need not have an easy time under restitution programs. The profits are taken out of crime when the burglars and thieves must pay back their 'takings.' As a priority, a greater percentage of correctional funds should go into juvenile programs; not to 'coddle' them, but to make them repay victims and learn job skills. They should receive prompt hearings and decisions on their cases. While incarcerated for offenses they should get remedial education: learn to apply for a job, how to work and behave while on a job, and learn to cope in society without criminal activity.

Changing Prison Patterns

Jails throughout the nation are overcrowded. In California by 1985, county jails held over 25 percent more prisoners than they were designed to house. If present lockup trends continue, counties face a building fund need of over $400 million before 1990. In addition 23 percent of the prisoners are in jails more than 40-years-old; and over 10 percent are in facilities the state fire marshal has declared unsafe for staff and inmates. The problem of separating prisoners into sub-groups for the safety of convicts and staff alike is almost insolvable under present conditions. To compound the situation, inmate lawsuits against city and county jails continue and pose a serious financial threat to local governments.

Probation Alternatives For Adult Offenders

A recent legislative report in California dealing with crowded prisons suggested three alternative sentencing and punishment methods. They are community-based restitution centers, so-called 'shock probation,' and home incarceration. The report, issued by the Legislature's Joint Committee for Revision of the Penal Code in 1985, is titled *Prison Overcrowding: Emergency Measures and Alternative Forms of Punishment*. Stating that the state's prison system is at 150 percent of design capacity, the report concludes that "The need for alternative forms of punishment that maintain the punishment and restrictiveness of incarceration should be the primary concern of correction officials in California." The report suggests that community-based restitution centers could house and closely supervise certain inmates while they earn money to pay restitution to victims of their crimes. They have operated successfully in Georgia and Iowa since 1975. These centers could function with local advisory boards, with locations subject to local government approval. Inmates could contribute to family support and to their own upkeep.

The second alternative of 'shock probation' would permit the Department of Corrections to file a recommendation with the court within 150 days after imprisonment of specified non-violent offenders to suspend further time in prison and put them on probation. Such prisoners would not be aware they are candidates for probation during the time they spend in prison. This has been in effect in Ohio since 1965 and in Texas since 1977.

Prisoners Confined to Homes

The third option of home incarceration confines prisoners at home, instead of in prisons. They are allowed to leave their homes only for work and emergencies. Home incarceration has been used successfully in Illinois since 1980. Three counties in California instigated this alternative in 1982 and 1983, reporting a positive result from keeping certain non-dangerous offenders out of crowded institutions and under strictly enforced home incarceration.

In Palm Beach County, Florida experiments have shown that non-violent offenders can be kept at home by an electronic device attached to a prisoner. Called the 'In House Arrest Program' a device, attached to an ankle permits an offender to move within 200 feet of the monitoring instrument in the home, a telephone, except when cleared to go to work or to report to a probation worker. Prisoners under an In House Arrest serve a longer sentence than those given a jail sentence. County officials have found that the program allows offenders to keep working, makes restitution possible to victims, is cheaper than housing a prisoner in a jail, and keeps offenders in the mainstream and away from hardened criminals.

Establishing Restitution Programs in Penal Settings

An adult restitution program called Inner Voices, located in Virginia, was founded by Rhozier T. Brown, a former inmate at Lorton Reformatory in Virginia. Inner Voices was originally a prison-based music and drama group. In describing the program, Brown says, "The way we ordinarily deal with offenders, particularly those convicted of non-violent offenses doesn't make sense. We talk about making convicts pay their 'debt to society,' but we forget that the actual debt is to the victims of their crimes. Our program gives them a chance to really balance the books and most of them are glad for the opportunity."[9]

The top student in the class at the time, a woman, had developed word-processing skills that could lead to a career for her. She had recently been convicted of a criminal offense. Brown believed her progress was evidence that "restitution as an alternative to prison can work, that it can save money and reduce recidivism."[10]

Brown and Chris Singletary, coordinators of the program, found that: "The overwhelming majority of those who come into the program do well; if they don't, they go directly to prison. Of 275 men and women, all serious offenders, who have come to the program during its three years, only 30 have failed to complete their one-year contract with Inner Voices."[11] Participants in the program are required to sign a commitment to vocational and psychological counseling and "an agreement to repay in cash or services the victims of their crimes." Of the 30 who failed the program, some were arrested for new offenses; but none involved physical assault.

Brown indicated that the program works better than sending a person to prison and costs less money. Brown said: "It costs a minimum of $12,000 to $20,000 a year to keep an inmate in prison, and that's a conservative figure based on outdated statistics. We take 80 clients a year on government funding of $150,000 a year."[12] That amounts to around $1,875 per person. The two coordinators have been in prison and know from personal experience what it is like. Brown finds that most crime-oriented people, from a correctional viewpoint:

> ...have a negative self-concept. The way we usually treat them gives them an even lower self concept by making them feel that once they make a mistake, they are no more good to society. We work on their self-concept through rap sessions, through job training and counseling, and by providing a solid, constant support system to help them deal with their problems. Job training by itself isn't enough. Often people with job skills don't have the skills to get jobs. We show them how to keep from losing the job during the job interview."[13]

Based on their experience, Brown and Singletary believe that prison can do more harm than good for nonviolent offenders. They found that convicts who completed victim restitution had a lower recidivism rate than those sent to prison. Restitution programs also are less costly and more beneficial than the prison alternative.

Prison Sentencing Based on a Restitution Model

It is possible to establish restitution programs within prison walls; but the attitudes of labor unions, industry, correction officials, and the judiciary must change. A British penal specialist, Kathleen Smith, has advocated a unique restitution program in England that could work in the United States. Smith refers to her restitution system as a 'self-determinant sentence.' The length of a sentence an offender serves is based on an inmate's own responsibility and actions. The length of a sentence is determined "first by the type of crime he commits and second by the effort he makes during his sentence to compensate for his crime." The sentence policy applies equally to men and women. Smith believes offenders should be given a minimum but not a specified length of time to serve in an institution. Instead, the court should sentence the offender in terms of "money to be earned." Offenses involving victims would be assessed in two ways: "First, by the restitution due to the victim for the physical, material and, in cases of terrorization, for psychological damage sustained." She suggests that "psychological damage, which is often the most serious of harms suffered by victims, is at present too often disregarded by the courts and should have more consideration given to it in sentencing. Second, fines should be levied at the court's discretion in relation to the offender's persistence and intent."[14]

Fines received from an offender's work would be directed into a fund which would reimburse victims. "Offenses involving no victim—drunkenness, prostitution, drug-taking—would be subject to fines that would be paid into the National Compensation Fund."[15]

If the system was used in the United States, the courts should decide and direct what part of a fine or compensation should be paid from an offender's earnings in prison or what part, if any, could be paid from an offender's private funds. In Smith's opinion, crimes against property should be assessed,

> ...according to the value of the property damaged or stolen, and stolen property voluntarily restored might, as the court directed, be deducted from the compensation ordered. This would not, however, provide an automatic discharge for offenders who restored all their ill-gotten gains. Few crimes can be so simply dismissed. If property owners were terrorized during an offense committed, they would be compensated for and fines levied according to the record of the offender and the strength of the deterrent deemed necessary.[16]

When stolen property has been voluntarily restored, the court should take this into consideration and reduce required compensation. This would also encourage the recovery of stolen property, which is an incentive lacking in our present system.

Smith believes that,

> While it is laudable that victims of violence now receive compensation for the damage done to them, it is heinous

that assailants are not required to pay for the injuries. If they were obligated to compensate for the harm they inflicted through the self- determinate sentence, it is reasonable to predict that crimes of violence would be less frequently resorted to.[17]

While it would be difficult to establish a self-determinant sentence for the compensation due for murder or manslaughter, (because it is difficult to assess the value of a life taken) she would like the self-determinate sentence to be based on the motive, provocation, and method of the killing by the offender. She finds that,

> ...a killing in which the motive was to release a person from suffering is less culpable and would attract less compensation than a murder committed in order to obtain the victim's property. Similarly, there are exonerating degrees of provocation. Some murders are committed under provocation of such intensity and duration that the victim of the killing becomes almost as responsible for the killing as the assailant himself. Murder provoked by personal relationship is more excusable than one committed on a passerby whom the criminal regarded as an obstruction or as fortuitous prey. As to method, homicide with an instrument picked up in the heat of the moment is less to be condemned than, for instance, murder by systematic poisoning over a period of time.[18]

A thoroughly mean individual who has killed and feels no remorse, is incorrigible, and will not cooperate with authorities in prison perhaps should be executed, as he is a menace to society. Even in cases where a murderer has been sentenced to life imprisonment or a long term, the self-determinant sentence could require all killers to use their time to compensate the dependents of their victims. Where a victim had no dependents or a victim with dependents unwilling to accept compensation, it could be paid into a National Compensation Fund. In a case where a victim was killed by more than one person, but only one could be convicted, by that person being required to repay the victim's family might induce him "to name his confederates, assist the police in making arrests, deter gang crimes, and break up the solidarity of the underworld."[19]

171

When the court determines the amount of compensation where several accomplices are involved, it could order a proportion to be paid by each according to the available evidence "as to the degree of participation and anticipated gain of each offender. Likewise, fines would not necessarily be imposed equally on all offenders."[20] In cases where offenders volunteer information that helps to convict others, the compensation order or fines against them should be reduced as an incentive to assist authorities.

While an offender is in prison working, Smith believes that person should contribute part of job wages to pay for state provided food and clothing. A prisoner should be permitted to save money while in prison for use upon release. A little nest egg saved could help tide a person over while making adjustments outside prison.

To provide incentives for prisoners to develop skills, work, and to prepare for leaving prison, Smith believes prisoners should be given opportunities to live like normal people as much as possible. Based on satisfactory work and attitudes, after approximately 50 weeks of work, prisoners not considered a threat to society should be given one or two weeks vacation with pay. She states, "Prisoners completing their sentences before becoming eligible for an annual vacations would be paid on release the appropriate vacation pay which is due."[21] Those considered a threat to the public would still be given a vacation or rest period within the prison due to their satisfactory work. Other benefits should be provided such as more visits from family and friends; other personal comforts, for example, better quality food or more entertainment, occasional beer or wine. Rewards should be given for working, cooperating, and developing work skills.

To provide an incentive for prisoners to continue working, parole could be granted to those not regarded as a menace to public safety, when three-quarters of their restitution has been paid. This would permit prisoners to repay the final quarter of their debt from work in civilian life. Failure of parolees to maintain regular payments would mean a return to prison.

The self-determinant sentence concept should attempt to make work attractive to prisoners. Smith finds, "The overriding factor that would persuade most prisoners to make an effort would be that their pay would depend on their work and their release date would depend on their pay. Few would consider it worthwhile to sabotage a system that settles the length of their sentences in their own hands."[22]

On preventing offenders from resorting to crime again Smith states:

> This system would give the greatest possible encourage-
> ment to offenders not to offend again, as well as to poten-
> tial offenders not to offend at all, for it would reduce the
> value of crime as an investment. At present, major rob-
> beries represent a very good investment: the larger the
> robbery, the more it is worth the risk of the criminal hav-
> ing to wait a few years in prison before enjoying the pro-
> ceeds... The self-determined sentence would offer no
> such bargain. There would be very little attraction in salt-
> ing away a stolen fortune for enjoyment after the sentence
> if the sentence consisted of working until the fortune was
> restored.[23]

Kathleen Smith makes an excellent case for changing our correctional system to one that provides restitution for victims, re-
spects the rights of victims, and help offenders improve themselves. The concept should be incorporated, on a pilot basis, at the
earliest possible time within the federal and state penal settings.
Smith's concept could help to take the profit out of crime. Unfortunately, in our courts a sentence for one burglary is no greater
than for ten burglaries. While out on bail waiting for trial, burglars
often pull off more jobs since their sentence will be no greater if
they are convicted. If a burglar had to pay back $20,000 for ten
jobs rather than $2,000 for one, he might be more careful about
committing additional crimes while on bail awaiting trial.

Smith's concept takes into consideration that victim needs come
first and that they should be reimbursed for losses and damages. In
cases where no personal victimization occurs, the offender must
nevertheless make restitution and payment to a National Compensation Fund for a crime against the public.

The public should help the judiciary, legal profession, legislators, businessmen, and labor unions to change their attitudes toward offenders working and restitution by using the initiative
process if legislators will not act. The 'self-determinant' or 'restitution sentence' concept gives offenders a better chance to become
responsible citizens by teaching needed work skills and helping
them survive in our society. With this system the cost of prisons
should be reduced.

Establishing Juvenile Restitution
as an Alternative to Prison

The states have tried numerous new approaches to stop juvenile crime and rehabilitate young criminals. Situations only get worse. Training and reform schools have not helped. Juveniles are off the streets but they are not rehabilitated. Foster homes had some success but juvenile offenders were not rehabilitated. In several states, large juvenile institutions were shut down and other residential type programs, such as group and foster homes, were tried. There are no clearcut winners, but restitution programs have proven successful in many instances.

Many seasoned probation officers, judges, and lawyers willing to try new ideas believe that juvenile restitution programs represent an important concept that works for victims as well as for juveniles. In one of the best programs to come out of the Law Enforcement Assistance Administration's (LEAA) activities, several probation departments were selected and funded to receive federal funds for juvenile restitution studies and programs. A total of about 80 juvenile restitution programs were funded in 1981 under the Office of Juvenile Justice and Delinquency Prevention. Five of the 80 projects were classified as 'intensive evaluation sites.' One of the most outstanding projects was in Ventura County, California.

Ventura County's Juvenile Restitution Project

The Juvenile Restitution Project (JRP) operates successfully because it's in a cooperating environment with the Probation Department, the District Attorney's office, the courts, and the public. The personnel administering it are enthusiastic and well qualified. The Project is a part of the Ventura County (California) Corrections Services Agency. A young probation officer, Calvin Remington, administered it for the first three years. He and his staff were dedicated to providing restitution to victims by offenders and insuring that offenders learned something in the process of repaying their victims.

The program's major goal was to hold juveniles accountable for their actions and to provide restitution to the victims. The program was conducted in two phases: 1) a work-release program, and 2) a field supervision component. Under the work-release program, juvenile offenders stay in a work-release center adjacent to Juvenile Hall in Ventura. Juveniles are required to attend school, work on jobs, and repay their victims. Under the field supervision component, the staff stays in contact with offenders who live at home or in a foster home to insure they are working and providing restitution as established under their contract.

Juveniles are selected for the project on a random basis by the juvenile court judge as cases proceed through the juvenile court system. Probation officers or social service agency personnel normally make recommendations for restitution and disposition of juvenile offenses to the court. When there is a possibility a juvenile will have to pay restitution, victims are notified by probation officers prior to the offender's disposition or court trial, called a 'contest.' The victim is asked to prepare a 'loss statement' indicating the amount the juvenile court should consider when deciding the total of restitution. Occasionally a difference occurs over the amount of loss. In these cases the judge determines what the juvenile must refund. Before each hearing, the judge reads reports from Social Services, Probation, and the District Attorney's Office concerning the offender in order to arrive at a carefully thought out sentence. Victims are kept well informed of proceedings and the amount of restitution ordered.

Normally, Ventura County has about 1,200 juvenile cases on probation. The project staff handles about 50% of these cases. During a two year period, the project handled over 550 cases. Juveniles spend the first 45 days of their time in the Restitution Program Center. After that offenders are released to their home or foster home, depending on their situation. As many of the juveniles have not had work experience, they're carefully coached on how to apply for a job, fill out application forms, act on the job, and conduct themselves to hold a job. Before starting to work, the staff prepare, discuss, and sign a contract with the offender. The contract includes the offense and the obligations of the offender. Restitutions for offenders have ranged from $100 to a high of $3,500, but average around $240. Based on the contract, the offender can reduce his time period on probation by paying off his obligations earlier.

In some cases offenders are too young or cannot get a job. In these cases, the youth are required to do a minimum of 100 hours of community work for various organizations such as the Park Department, Salvation Army and Goodwill. The staff has found ample firms and agencies that will accept offenders for work.

At first, some people were skeptical that kids from broken families and low income families could get jobs and pay back their obligations. They were wrong. Cal Remington found that over 85% of the offenders completed their obligations within six months. In 1980-81, the staff collected over $80,000 from the juveniles. These funds went to the victims of the offenders' crimes. The rate of restitution has increased almost every month. By April 1981, money was coming in at the rate of $6,000 per month.

Before the restitutional center project started in 1977, the court had ordered juveniles to pay slightly under $12,000 in restitution for the previous year. At the end of the year, slightly more than $4,600 was collected. This included all juvenile offenders throughout the county. Under the center project program, more money was collected in one month in 1981 than during the entire year of 1977 from all juvenile offenders in the County. The project handled only about a third of the total juvenile offenders in the County at that time.

Most of the offenders understand their punishment because they are repaying funds directly to their victims who suffered losses. Occasionally a victim personally meets with an offender. In one such case a youth had damaged several cars belonging to a dealer. He went to work for the same person to repay $3,500 in damages. Several juveniles have received jobs from places they worked after paying off their obligations. The project staff find that young offenders usually feel good about themselves when they hold jobs and repay their debts.

In an analysis of the amount of restitution paid to victims during 1984, the Ventura County Corrections Services Agency collected $32,833 from the Juvenile Restitution Program, $204,881 from adults (on Probation), $38,351 from juveniles (on probation) and $6,603 from the work furlough program for a total of $282,669. Including income from offenders on work furlough and weekend sentence programs, the County collected a grand total of $2,397,461 which was turned over to crime victims, families, or returned to the County. An additional 167,043 hours of public service work was performed by juveniles and adults that benefitted public agencies and taxpayers. Who says you 'can't get blood out of a turnip?'

Reduced Recidivism

One method of testing the success of a juvenile program is by the recidivism rate of offenders, or the number who end up in juvenile court again. It is not uncommon for juveniles who have been on probation, fined, or sent to Juvenile Hall to have as high a recidivism rate as 55% to 80%. In a preliminary analysis of the JRP by the Institute of Policy Analysis, they found that it "has a much lower in-program re-offense rate than youths receiving more traditional treatments (home on probation, incarceraton)."[24] The total re-offense rate or recidivism rate for JRP was about 27.5%, while the rate for the control youth group (non-project) was double, or 54%. The investigators analyzing the program indicated that, considering the full 12-month follow-up period of the program, the JRP youths had an even lower likelihood of re-offending while fulfilling the terms of their disposition than those of a similar number going through the normal juvenile punishment process.

The victims involved in the program seem quite pleased. They believe the justice system is working and offenders are paying their debts to society. Most victims are refunded for damages and losses to them. The offenders are aware of the seriousness of their crimes when they must repay full value of thefts. The more they steal, the longer they work (if caught) to repay their victims. Several victims indicated that their own children learned a lesson from the process. Jean Caldwell stated:

> I was so thrilled when I got the letters (from the probation officers). I had thought the only way to get any kind of reimbursement was to hassle the parents in court....I was glad for my own kids to see you'll get caught sooner or later. It wasn't a good image for my boys to see them (the offenders) getting away with it. Now my kids are glad they've never done anything like that.[25]

If the recidivism rate can be cut from 50% to 25% and offenders are learning new skills, getting and holding jobs, the program is well worth the money spent. It takes a good team to make this program work. In an interview with then Juvenile Court Judge Steven Stone, who contributed to the success of the program, he said: "The program works well because there is close cooperation between the staffs of the JRP, Probation, Social Services, District Attorney, and the court." It's also important that the juvenile court judge believe in restitution.

Project Environment

At the project center, offenders can walk away if they wish. There are no locked doors but only a few juveniles under court order have ever run away from work or the Center. As community work projects are under supervision, offenders learn work skills which help them get a job at a later time. Offenders become involved in the community and avoid being locked up 24 hours a day. Cal Remington has found that:

> When you lock up juveniles, or adults for that matter, you set up a special community in which they try to beat the system and the people who lock them up. It establishes a negative environment. By the kids getting out into the community and working with an adult figure, they have a different role model and spend time with someone other than kids with similar troubled backgrounds which doesn't help them too much. When an artificial community is created, the offenders only try to beat the people who lock them up. The Center provides a structure to their lives.

Project youths seldom commit crimes, don't run away, and come back on time. The positive role model of adults in the program is beneficial to them. The staff's goal is to integrate the young offenders, as they grow older, into the mainstream of the economic system. They're expected to get to their jobs on their own through public transportation, a bicycle, or with the help of friends. The staff makes it clear that offenders are not to break the law. Until they honor their obligation and provide restitution to the victim, they will not get off probation. They work themselves off probation by getting a job and paying back victims.

The staff finds that juveniles mature more through restitution programs than through all the counseling and special treatment they might get in some other rehabilitation approach. An offender returns something to the community for the trouble he has caused people. Restitution is a more positive way of dealing with the problem, and it is more cost-effective.

Remington found that:

> A lot of people going through the criminal system are not hardened criminals, but irresponsible, impulsive peo-

ple, who have lifestyles that don't conform to the mainstream. If there is a structure provided for them in which they must work to provide restitution, they'll follow through.

Offenders in prison are in a very dependent situation. They normally do not learn skills that will help them outside. When convicts come out of prison, they are bewildered by the outside world. As a new probation officer, Remington told of meeting a parolee at a bus station for the first time. He said,

> You can always spot them. They have the same haircut, the same clothes. They have a dazed look on their faces, carry their belongings in a paper bag, and really don't know what to make of the outside world. You take them to a cheap hotel, find them a room, and tell them to start looking for a job.

If juveniles can find jobs, adult offenders can. Many adults choose not to find work, but when they have to, they will. The jobs are out there. Remington cited a serious problem Ventura County had with divorced husbands' not paying alimony and child support payments. When pressure was put on them by their former wives, the men would skip town. There was no way the women could get paid. As a result, family support units were set up in district attorneys' offices, subsidized by the federal government. The district attorney and the probation officers worked closely in operating the program. As a result, if a spouse failed to provide, he was prosecuted by the D.A. and put on probation. It was amazing how much money started to flow in when pressure was put on the men. They got jobs.

Juvenile Work Habits

You can't talk to a teenager very effectively about career planning and career growth when he doesn't know what he's going to do from day to day. Young offenders must learn how to work. The restitution center's experience indicates that even though young kids start out working at minimum wage at fast food restaurants, doing tree trimming and manual type labor, they are still learning how to work, which is very important to them. It's important that kids learn how to fill out an application properly, print it neatly, and have a nice appearance when appearing for a job, and to feel that they can do the work.

Permanent restitution programs should be established nation wide for both juveniles and adults. While many officials within the justice system believe in restitution programs, a large percentage have a negative view. Not all judges are familiar with the process. Many believe "you can't make people work." These myths have been shattered by successful restitution pilot projects. If low income youths who never had a job are able to find work and repay obligations, adults should be able to do the same thing, in or out of prison. The positive results that can be realized in our correctional and probation systems will be helpful to victims and the offenders themselves, but also to the taxpayers.

Ventura County's restitution program was enhanced when the Proposition Eight initiative was passed by California voters in 1982. Under a follow-up bill that went into effect in 1984, restitution was made mandatory in all criminal cases—juvenile or adult. In the case of a victimless crime, the offender must contribute to a state Restitution Fund. Only in special cases are offenders not required to pay restitution. Under this law, the result of the efforts of Paul Gann and many public-spirited citizens, California became the strongest restitution state in the Union.

CHAPTER TEN

WHAT DOES
THE JUSTICE SYSTEM COST?

Criminal Court Procedure Costs

The elaborate court rules and procedures concocted have made justice expensive and hard to obtain except for the indigent criminal offender or the wealthy. As the public pays for 'free' legal service for criminal offenders, delays, appeals, and motions are made freely by public defenders or court appointed lawyers.

Crime Costs to Nation

In an analysis of the national costs of crime in 1970, *U.S. News and World Report* estimated that it was $50.8 billion. This amount included: $19.5 billion for organized crime (gambling, narcotics, loan-sharking and other illegal activities); $13.1 billion for crimes against property and business (kickbacks, shoplifting, burglary and larceny); $8.5 billion for Law enforcement (police, courts and corrections); $5.5 billion for private security/protection (over and above federal, state and local law enforcement); and $4.2 billion for Medical costs, loss of earnings and property damages (due to assaults, homicides and drunk driving). By 1974 they found the costs had jumped to $88.6 billion. During 1982, the Justice Department's Bureau of Justice Statistics estimated that crimes against persons and households of individuals cost Americans $10.9 billion up from $4.4 billion in 1970. The Bureau's report, issued in April of 1984, covered only part of the cost of crime to the public as it did not include computer fraud, arson for profit, embezzle-

LAWYERS AND CLIENTS—"Finally! We finished the division of the divorcees; property."
"It's about time, the case ruined both of them."

ment, white-collar and organized crimes, and 'victimless crimes.' The total cost of crime to the nation in 1982 was estimated by the authors to be $145 billion.

National Cost of Justice System

The Bureau of the Census reported that the Criminal Justice System expenditures in 1976 amounted to $3.3 billion at the federal level and $18 billion at the state and local level for a total public cost of $21.4 billion. Not including law enforcement expenditures, the justice system cost $10.2 billion in 1976. By 1982 justice costs reached an estimated $4.3 billion at the federal level and $51.6 billion at the state and local level for a total of $55.9 billion. Without police costs of $42 billion, the figure drops to an estimated total of $13.9 billion.

Federal Criminal Justice
System Expenditures (Millions of $)

	1976	1982
Judicial	$219	$ 285
Legal Services	149	194
Public defense	104	135
Administration, etc.	948	1,200
Police	1,616	2,000
Corrections	286	500
	$3,322	$4,314

State & Local Justice Expenditures

Judicial	$ 2,297	$3,000
Legal services	908	1,200
Public defense	236	300
Administration, etc.	833	1,100
Police	9,513	40,000
Corrections	4,269	6,000
Total	$18,056	$51,600

Federal Court System

In 1982, the taxpayers paid $2.3 billion to process civil and criminal cases through the federal justice system not including law enforcement costs. For 1983, the budget of the Federal Courts was

$796,044,000, exclusive of the Supreme Court, but including the salaries and expenses for all federal courts. The 1984 budget was projected to be $867,434,000. In 1984, 16,867 persons were employed by the federal judicial branch of which clerks, secretaries and related positions made up 50%, probation personnel made up 17%, bankruptcy judges and staff 18%, and the balance were federal judges, magistrates, public defenders, and other employees. The payroll of all federal court personnel amounted to $36.4 million in 1984.

The cost of each judge in the United States District Courts, including his salary, benefits, and supporting personnel (clerks, secretaries, court administrators, bailiffs, court reporters, and court operation expenses) was $752,000. The number of full-time support staff for each judge was 11.9 persons compared with 5.7 to 8.0 persons per judge in three state courts analyzed.

State Justice Systems

The cost of the criminal justice system for all state and local government including law enforcement, prosecution, public defense, courts, and corrections, totaled an estimated $51.6 billion in 1982. Not including law enforcement expenses, it totaled $11.6 billion. In 1982, the justice system costs in California alone totaled $4,954,238,000, including $2,741,479,000 for law enforcement, $260,477,000 for prosecution, $96,737,000 for public defense, $468,518,000 for the courts, and $1,387,027,000 for corrections. To run the California justice system it took 104,648 persons, including: 71,071 for law enforcement, 7,401 for prosecution, 1,972 for public defense, 1,400 for the courts and 22,794 for corrections (California Department of Justice, Bureau of Criminal Statistics).

The cost per judge in California, including court reporters and bailiffs was $402,917 for the superior courts and $389,157 for the municipal courts in 1983. In 1983, California1 had 302 judges operated the state court. This included seven for a supreme court, 5 for courts of appeal, 646 for superior courts, 503 for municipal courts, and 87 for justice courts. An additional 16 federal judges were in the Federal 9th Circuit and 50 judges in the Federal District Court.

The total state operating budget for California's civil and criminal courts rose to about $650 million in 1983-84. With the State'

10% contribution, the counties had a hefty sum of about $590 million to budget for trial court costs.

In Florida $324,000 was expended for each judicial position in 1982, with 35% provided by the state and the balance by the counties. In the State of Washington, a much lower amount, $261,000 was allocated for each judicial position and 13% was provided by the state.

The National Center for State Courts report that 16 states (including New York, Massachusetts, and Connecticut) provide between 80% and 100% of court funding, and fourteen states pay 25% or less. The balance is provided by counties.

Total Public and Private Litigation and Justice Costs

The authors estimate that the total costs of private and public litigation and the justice system added up to approximately $40.9 billion in 1982. The costs included $13.9 billion for federal, state and local justice; $2 billion for state civil processing; and $25 billion for private civil litigation costs. With the addition of $42 billion for law enforcement, justice costs soar to $82.9 billion.

Legal Profession Costs to Litigants

The practice of law in the nation is big business. Based on a Census Bureau report for 1982, the nation's law firms increased their income from $17 billion in 1977 to $34 Billion in 1982, a hefty rise. As might be expected California's law firms led the nation with a gross annual income of $5 billion, up 134% from 1977, and almost 15% of the total legal income for the country.

Most of the income to firms came from business interests, with individuals a close second at 44.7%. Private litigants paid legal fees to law firms amounting to $25 billion during 1983.

California had the largest number of law offices (15,447), the most lawyers (80,000), the highest number of employees, (76,000), and paid the biggest payroll ($1.9 billion). The states following California in highest annual legal-service revenue were New York: $4.9 billion; Illinois, $2.2 billion; Florida, $1.8 billion; District of Columbia, 1.6 billion; and Pennsylvania, $1.4 billion.

Cost To Public For Indigent Defense

The cost to the public for legal representation of indigent defendants in 3.2 million cases tried in state and local courts in 1982 was $624.6 million, according to a United States Justice Department report in 1984. California had the most cases, 661,000 or 27% of the total cases in the country. The $624.6 million was 44% above the estimated $435 million for 1980.

Civil Legal Services For the Poor

The cost to the public of the federally supported Legal Services Corporation was $321 million in 1980. After cuts by the Reagan administration, it was reduced to $275 million during 1984. The Legal Services Corporation provides free civil legal assistance for items such as divorces and tenant-landlord disputes. Up to 1982, the LSC had a staff of 6,000 lawyers.

Cost To Public of Civil Litigations

To process the 8 million civil lawsuits in state and federal courts during 1982, the Rand Corp.'s Institute for Civil Justice estimated it cost the taxpayers $2 billion annually. This does not include the private costs of civil litigants, which was $25 billion as indicated above.

Who Should Pay Court Costs?

Should the taxpayers—state and county—or court user pay for court costs? Do courts exist to serve individuals or society? California's Chief Justice Rose Bird, contends that "the business of the trial courts is the people's business...It is the state's obligation to pay for the cost of the public's business conducted by the legislative and executive branches of government."

Some members of the legal profession like attorney David Bergland, Libertarian Party presidential candidate for 1984, claim that forcing litigants to bear all court costs would reduce the size of courts and their budgets and thereby reduce the tax burden on the middle-class. In a recent article he said:

> Justice is not free. Some of us use the court system and some of us don't. Those who are getting the benefit should be those who are paying for it, as opposed to having the general taxpayer pay. If you knew you would be paying a $1,000 fee instead of a $100 fee, you would probably be more circumspect about going off and filing a lawsuit. It

would not squeeze anybody out of court. It would mean more disputes would be resolved out of court.

One of the objections to state funding of the courts is the fear of state control. Cities are concerned also about loss of revenue if states take over court funding. Proponents of state funding are growing in the states as court costs continue to rise.

High Cost of Criminal Court Trials

The cases below illustrate the unnecessarily high cost of court procedures and the need to change. For a private citizen, even with assets, defending oneself in criminal court can wipe out resources; and leave a person or a family destitute. The trial of Fred Roehler, Jr., a person with considerable resources, shows what can happen to anyone forced to defend themself in criminal court, innocent or guilty.

Murder at Little Scorpion

The headlines were bold, "Mother, Son Die–Effort to Save Dog Ends in Sea Tragedy." The pictures of Fred Roehler, Jr., 38, of Malibu, California being taken from a Coast Guard helicopter to an ambulance were dramatic and empathy provoking. But some experienced sailors became suspicious of the handsome marine consultant as his story unfolded in the newspapers. Except for an anonymous telephone call, Fred Roehler could have collected $820,000 in insurance money for the "accidental death" of his wife and stepson.

The tragedy began on the second day of the New Year 1981. Fred Roehler anchored his 50 ft. yacht, *Perseverance*, at Little Scorpion Cove at the east end of Santa Cruz Island, in the Santa Barbara Channel on that fateful morning. The island is about 26 miles south of the coast from Santa Barbara. On board were Fred Roehler, his wife Verna Jo, his stepson Douglas, Verna Jo's daughter from a previous marriage, his mother and father, two children from Roehler's previous marriage, and his brother and his wife.

After lunch Roehler, Verna Jo, Douglas, 9, and their beagle puppy, Lady, rowed their 16 ft. dory around a nearby rocky outpoint called Bird Rock to take some pictures of Douglas and the beagle with the *Perseverance* in the background. Douglas was wearing a life jacket and Roehler a 'float coat.'

Roehler was an expert diver and a former Navy frogman. While manuevering the dory into position to take a picture, Roehler claimed that Lady sprang at one of the sea gulls swooping around them and fell into the water. He said Douglas lunged to reach the dog, he reached over the side to get Douglas, Verna Jo shifted her position, and the dory flipped over spilling all of them in the water.

Roehler claimed he was unable to get out from under the dory for 30 seconds to a minute because his camera strap was caught on something. When he got to the surface Roehler said Verna Jo and Douglas were not breathing. While treading water, he kept them afloat and gave them mouth to mouth resuscitation alternately, but it was difficult because the dog kept trying to climb on to his head and shoulders. Rather than put the two on top of the floating dory, he took them about 100 to 150 ft. up wind to Bird Rock where he put the dog ashore. He claimed he was unable to put his wife or Douglas ashore because of the rock's steepness. He continued dog paddling until a motor boat, the *Sound of Music,* came by, heard him calling, and lifted them out of the water. Attempts to revive Verna Jo and Douglas were fruitless. Roehler was cold but conscious, alert, and had no injuries. He was brought to the St. John's Hospital in Oxnard, examined, and released later.

A routine autopsy was made of Verna Jo and Douglas by Dr. Craig Duncan of the Ventura County Medical Examiner-Coroner's Office who reported that they had died from accidental drowning. The case was about to be closed.

Strangely the Santa Barbara Sheriff's Office received some anonymous phone calls asking them if they knew about the unusual death of Roehler's first wife, Jean, and the large amount of insurance carried on Verna Jo and Douglas. Investigators found that Roehler's first wife had been found unconscious and face down in their swimming pool. She died a week later—never regaining consciousness. Roehler carried an accidental death insurance policy on her.

Suspicions aroused, Santa Barbara County had a second autopsy made of the two bodies by Dr. DeWitt T. Hunter, Jr. Doctor Hunter found that each had been hit in the back of the head by blows. The tragedy was no longer just another unfortunate drowning in the Santa Barbara Channel. It looked like murder.

Fred Roehler, Jr. was arrested April 3, 1981, and charged with the murder of his wife and step-son. He was held without bail from the time of his arrest. The longest criminal trial in the history of

Santa Barbara County was about to begin, from October 26, 1981 until May 7, 1982. Just to select the jury took seven weeks. The trial was held in Santa Barbara County as Santa Cruz Island was in their jurisdiction. The total testimony amounted to over two million words.

The Santa Barbara County Prosecutor, Stanley Roden, built a strong circumstantial case around the fact that Roehler took out an accidental death portion of the insurance policy he carried on his wife only three days before she was drowned. He had taken the original insurance policy out shortly after they had married. Roehler also carried a $120,000 policy on his nine year old stepson. One insurance man testified that he had never heard of such a high amount being carried on a child who has no earning power to protect. Roehler was the beneficiary of a total of $820,000, tax free, on the accidental death of his wife and stepson.

The prosecutor attempted to prove that the two victims could not have been hit on the head with enough force by the dory to have killed them. Films were made showing three similar sized people attempting to tip the dory over, in the same location and under similar sea conditions as originally happened, according to Roehler. The trio could not tip the boat over except by great effort. Expert witnesses for the prosecution said death could not have occurred as Roehler claimed. One well known pathologist, Dr. Joseph H. Davis, said that he believed Douglas had been struck in the head with a "considerable amount of force."

Roden alleged that Roehler positioned the dory behind Bird Rock where they were out of sight of the boats anchored in Little Scorpion cove. He then hit both of them with an oar knocking them out, enabling him to drown them, and making it look like an accident. Instead of holding on to the dory to help save them, he swam 150 feet to a place on Bird Rock out of sight. The dory oars have never been found.

The defense lawyers countered the prosecution's case with a group of pathologists who claimed that the blows to the heads of the victims occurred after death and that their deaths were accidental. A total of eight pathologists testified, often contradicting each other. The eminent pathologists came from Canada, Alaska, Florida, Michigan, Maryland, Texas, and California to testify.

The District Attorney called over 36 witnesses in the three months he put on his case. The defense lawyers called 11 witnesses in only 16 days, considerably less than the prosecution.

The trial attracted a big following of newspaper and television reporters, detective story writers, retired lawyers, and the general public. One had to be very aggressive on some trial days to get a seat or even standing room.

The courtroom had a strange aura about it with exhibits including the pink 16-ft. dory, a model of the murder site, marine and weather charts, a skeleton, and a head and brain model on display in front of the judge and jury. From the day the trial started Roehler's parents and Verna Jo's mother sat together in the front row listening to the proceedings. Verna Jo's mother, a religious person, believed in her son-in-law's innocence throughout the trial.

The prosecutor indicated that Roehler did some strange things for a man who had not worked since December 1978 and was deeply in debt. Family expenditures exceeded their income in 1980 by $12,000. The taxes on the house had not been paid. Yet Roehler planned to go on a six-month vacation to Mexico and bought a 50-ft., $155,000 boat with payments of $1,056 a month. The prosecutor disclosed that Roehler had stashed $30,000 in cash in his deep freezer. Why? How was he going to pay for all these expensive items with only a tiny income? Murder was an option with a $820,000 pay-off.

On May 7, 1982, the packed courtroom waited tensely for the court clerk, Judy Austin, to read the jury's verdict. Roehler's supporters gasped and groaned when the guilty finding was read. The decision stunned Roehler's lawyers. They thought that the jury believed in their case.

Under California law a second penalty trial was necessary to determine if Roehler should be given life imprisonment without possibility of parole or the death penalty. Two months later on July 26, 1982, the same jury decided to spare Roehler and sent him to prison for life. The longest and most expensive trial in Santa Barbara finally came to an end. The Judge, John T. Rickard, 69, also decided to call it quits and retired at the end of the trial.

To pay for the cost of his defense, Roehler utilized all of his money and assets. He expended $600,000 from a trust fund that represented every asset he possessed to pay for attorneys and investigators and expert witnesses. The public had to pay an additional $1,000,000 for most of his trial costs, prosecution and defense, when Roehler and his family ran out of funds. At the end of the trial over $1,600,000 had been spend for the trial. More would be needed.

A few months later Roehler's lawyers filled an appeal. At tax payers expense the lengthy and costly appeal process started. In April 1985, an appellate court upheld his conviction on a 2-1 vote. Roehler's lawyer indicated at the time that he would appeal to the supreme court. If a court later decided to free Roehler, he would re-enter the world economically broke because of his defense. Because of the media interest in the case, he might make some money by selling his story. Most accused cannot. The defense costs to most private citizens, with savings and assets, because of the nature of the criminal court system, would bankrupt them, innocent or guilty.

High Cost of Trials For Indigent Offenders

Mass Murderer Juan Corona

In 1971, one of the country's most notorious mass murders occurred in Marysville-Yuba City, California. Juan Vallejo Corona was convicted of killing 25 farm workers and burying them in shallow graves. Most of the victims were found on a ranch and in peach orchards along the Feather River. After a long trial and appeals costing an estimated $1 million, Corona was convicted of murder and sentenced to life imprisonment. Later however, a new court-appointed attorney for Corona, in an appeal, said that the original attorney for Corona was incompetent and that Corona should be retried.

In 1978, six years after the original trial, the California Court of Appeals overturned the conviction, based "on the grounds his trial attorney had provided inadequate representation." The court also found "that the lawyer had a conflict of interest because he had entered into a book contract about the case." After the 1978 decision, the case was appealed to the State Supreme Court. Attorneys then became involved in a lengthy dispute over what evidence could be admitted at the retrial.

Even Chief Justice Rose Bird of the Supreme Court, sternly criticized by court watchers for making decisions slowly, expressed "dismay that it had taken five years for Corona's conviction to reach its first review by the State Court of Appeals." The Supreme Court settled the evidence issue clearing the way for a new trial.

The State Appellate Court held that evidence concerning a pistol, ammunition, two hunting knives, an axe, an ice pick, and other items could be admitted. The items argued about for years concerned eight other items, including some bullets and rent receipts. The court ruled that some of these items could not be admitted as evidence because they had been collected on the basis of legally faulty search warrants.

The costs of collecting evidence, interviewing witnesses, and preparing for Corona's new trial alone reached an estimated $4 million, according to a Sutter County deputy county auditor. One court administrator estimated the total trial costs and appeals may reach $6 million. The auditor became concerned about how the county would pay the costs.

State Controller Ken Cory, upset at the bills being charged to the state, revealed that attorneys and investigators had charged high expenses to the case. One investigator spent $423 for a four-night stay in a high-class San Francisco hotel. The state protested another bill in which three lawyers traveled to London for nine days in December of 1981 at a cost to state taxpayers of more than $10,000. Previous to that, members of the prosecution team went to Mexico for three days and billed the state for $2,400.

Even though the State Appellate Court panel found overwhelming evidence that Corona was the murderer, the public had to pay for a retrial based on a legal technicality. In March of 1982, the second trial actually started. It took the prosecutor three months alone to introduce 620 items of evidence and 135 witnesses before concluding his case. The defense lawyers took less time to present their case, but a month nevertheless. Finally on September 23, 1982, the jury found Corona guilty of 25 counts of first degree murder, same as the first jury, for brutally chopping to death 25 farm workers. The second trial cost the public $5,000,000.

A few days after the trial, the Chief Counsel for the State Board of Prison Terms announced that Corona was now eligible for parole. He had served enough time after his first conviction and the second trial to be eligible for parole. A hearing was held shortly after, but the public protested and his release was denied—for the present.

A day after the jury's findings, an article appeared in the *Oakland Tribune-Eastbay Today* claiming that Corona had agreed to plead guilty at one time. Court records indicated that Corona did confess his murders to a Roman Catholic priest, but the information was not permitted to be introduced as evidence. If the confession had been admitted in court or Corona's lawyer, knowing he was guilty, had acknowledged it, the $5 million trial could have been avoided.

Once Corona was arrested and convicted, no more farm workers were killed. If the appellate court did not doubt Corona's guilt, why did the public have to pay for a $5,000,000 second trial? What was proven by the second trial? Did Corona achieve more justice through the second trial? Or was the public victimized by a short-sighted legal system? Who gained? Only the lawyers, investigators, and court personnel involved in the case benefited from the lengthy appeals and trials. Of all the money spent, not one dollar went to the families of the slain farm workers.

High Cost of Criminal Case Delays

Thompson and Wisely Case

To illustrate the results of court delays and continuances on victims and the public, another California case is cited. In February of 1981, Phillip Arthur Thompson and Willie Ray Wisely robbed an antique store owner in San Gabriel, California. Property valued at close to $174,000 was taken by the two men. After intensive detective work by the Los Angeles County Sheriff's Department, Wisely was apprehended and arrested in March of 1981. Most of the property taken was recovered by the police. After questioning by the Sheriff's Department, Wisely confessed to the robbery and implicated Thompson.

On May 15,1981, Wisely was arraigned and a preliminary hearing held. Evidence presented at the preliminary was sufficient to set a pretrial hearing for June 8th. Defense tactics then came into play.

At the June 8th hearing the case was continued to June 15th. The motions started. Based on a motion on June 15th, the case was continued to June 18th. Another continuance from the 18th to June 25th. The case was continued several more times, first to July 6th, then to July 13, then to July 28th, and to August 18th. Wisely had a good reason for not making the August 18th hearing. Another jurisdiction, Orange County, charged him with murder and commenced proceedings against him. Wisely was then taken to Orange County pending his appeal from his conviction of first degree murder and the death penalty.

Thompson was another matter. The police found Thompson

lodged in the San Mateo County jail and brought him to Los Angeles County in July of 1981 to face robbery charges. As the Sheriff's Department collected information about Phillip Arthur Thompson, they realized he was a clever and dangerous person. Thompson's record revealed that he intimidated any witnesses to his crimes with threats of bodily violence. The police suspected Thompson had murdered as many as twelve potential witnesses although he had never been convicted of their deaths. His record did show many attempts at witness intimidation.

A preliminary hearing was held for Thompson on August 10, 1981. Trial date was scheduled for October 24th. Unusual circumstances entered the case. Thompson managed to make bail and was released on September 23rd. Knowing of Thompson's record of assault, solicitation of murder and attempts to kill witnesses, the sheriff immediately placed the antique dealer, Arthur W. Suel, and his family under protective custody around the clock. The court delays increased the cost of Suel's protection to nearly a quarter of a million dollars. It would have been much cheaper to simply deny bail to Thompson and keep him in jail.

Even before Thompson's trial could begin, his lawyer had the case continued to October 14th. The judge allowed him to change the trial date to October 27th, to November 12, to November 24th, and to January 20th, 1982. Thompson then fired his lawyer and requested another one. On January 26th, the court granted another continuance. Mr. Suel and his family, fearing for their lives, stayed locked in their home. Due to Suel's absence from his business, it started losing money.

The Sheriff's office concerned about the court delays, cost to their department for providing protection to Suel's family, and preventing three deputies from performing other work, appealed to the court to stop the continuances and try Thompson. The court agreed. On February 9th the trial was to start. But the delays continued. At each hearing lawyers, witnesses, and court personnel were present at great expense ready to proceed.

On February 17th however, Thomson's new lawyer filed a motion delaying the trial to the 18th when he filed an emergency writ. The trial was continued again from February 23rd to the 24th when Thompson finally agreed to submit to a trial based on the preliminary hearing transcript.

During the time the trial dates were being postponed, the Sheriff's Department discovered some Federal agency had approached the court and was attempting to have Thompson released. Upon investigation Sheriff detectives were angered to find that the San Francisco office of the Federal Bureau of Investigation had indeed tried to have the court go easy on Thompson. Allegedly the FBI was using Thompson for some type of undercover services. The sheriff complained to the FBI about the interference and told them that Thompson was a dangerous man. Apparently, the Los Angeles FBI had not been informed of the northern office's interest in the case.

Finally, at the March 26, 1982 hearing, Thompson was found guilty of robbery and sentenced to prison. However he did not go to prison. Based on a plea bargain agreement, the district attorney agreed to drop several counts on the condition that Thompson remain free on bail while his conviction was appealed. Thompson's high bail was made by someone and he was released. He was free again. Sheriff office personnel wondered who actually put up the bail money.

The Sheriff's Office terminated Suel's protection after Thompson was sentenced. The police had no record of Thompson killing anyone after testifying against him, only before. The Suels hoped they were correct. The cost to the County taxpayers for the Suel family protection alone was estimated at over $200,000. After being imprisoned in his house for over five months, Arthur Suel's business was ruined. The cost to the county for legal services, custody and processing of Thompson through the court was estimated at around another $40,000.

When asked what he thought of the justice system after his experience, Mr. Suel said: "I don't really have too good a feeling about the system and the way it works for the victim. I just have the greatest feeling for the police, but the attorneys, no; It just didn't improve my image of them at all."

Is Thompson's case an unusual one? Not at all! The Los Angeles County jail houses an average of 12,500 to 13,000 inmates a month. Seventy percent of these inmates are awaiting preadjudication or a decision on their case. Some 600 accused murderers have been waiting a year or more to go to trial. The "Hillside Strangler" suspect, Kenneth Bianchi, was jailed from 1977, and his co-defendent Angelo Buono, from 1979 until their trial in 1983. When the Strangler case finally went to trial, it took three months alone to select the jury.

Other pre-trial murder suspects still housed in the Los Angeles

County jail over four years include: James "Doc" Holliday, Michael Delia, and hundreds more.

People vs Daniel Thompson— A Lengthy Pre-Trial Grand Theft Case

A grand theft case in Santa Clara County, California against Daniel Thompson took over five years to reach trial. As the case crawled along, a total of six defense attorneys and five prosecutors were involved. One of the prosecutors died and the chief investigator had a heart attack during this period. Eight dates were set before the case actually went to trial. It was all in vain. Daniel Thompson took a powder and left the state.

Cost of Robbery Trials

In Los Angeles County the average robbery trial lasts a week and court expenses cost $10,000, not counting the time of the prosecutor, public defender, witnesses or the police. As in most criminal cases described, the public pays while the lawyers gain.

New Bedford's Tavern Rape Case

California's not the only state having expensive trials. The seven-week trial of six men for the rape of a 22-year-old woman on a New Bedford, Massachusett's tavern pool table cost taxpayers of that state over $500,000. The total included $265,000 for attorneys, court officers, the judge, and other officials. Another $239,000 was spent for jury and trial-related costs, including $89,000 to house, feed, and pay 32 jurors. Two sequestered juries and four court-appointed attorneys were used. Other costs included $300 to build a model of Big Dan's bar, where the crime took place, $200,000 for the district attorney's staff salaries, and $90,000 for the four court-appointed attorneys.

Reducing Public Defender Costs

One of the most significant costs of the public defender system in the country is the need to hire additional attorneys to represent each individual defendant where two or more people are involved in the same crime. Under many state laws a conflict of interest exists if a public defender provides legal defense to multiple defendants. These so-called 'conflict' cases often result in excessive budget overruns that cause financial problems to governmental entities.

Jurisdictions have attempted to address this problem by a variety of methods. Several alternative programs are outlined, all of which require that the prevalent civil service form of public defender's office be eliminated or drastically curtailed.

In Pomona, California the Municipal Court contracts out to selected law firms for the defense of indigents when the public defender is unavailable or has a conflict of interest. This system replaced the former method of appointments by a judge on a rotational basis from lists of available lawyers. Although opposed by the local bar association and many criminal lawyers, the new program has resulted in substantial cost savings.

Los Angeles County developed a program to determine the financial capacity of defendants represented by attorneys at the county's expense. After investigation, defendants capable of paying the cost of their own legal defense are made to repay the county. The procedure followed by the courts is simple and direct. At the termination of a case, the judge sends the defendant to a Department of Collections finance officer. Assets and liabilities are listed and an agreement is reached on the total defense costs and the amount the defendant will reimburse the county. Payments are made on a scheduled basis to Collections who treats them as any other bill owed to the county. The cost recovery has been so significant that the courts endorsed the project.

Los Angeles County initiated another program in which paralegals perform the routine administrative tasks previously done by higher paid deputy public defenders. After meeting resistance from the county public defender's office, the program remained in pilot form. Once instigated, an annual savings of over $200,000 a year was anticipated.

Santa Barbara County, California has contracted with a consortium of private attorneys to handle conflict cases at a set amount. This limits the total costs of court-appointed attorneys to the contract total and eliminates costly budget overruns. As an example of possible savings, a case involving Dennis Boyd Miller cost taxpayers about $175,000 for his defense. The consortium type contract could have handled Miller's case and provided all other conflict assignments for less than $78,000 for six months, a considerable savings.

The Long Beach, California Municipal Court created panels of private attorneys who take conflict cases at a reduced hourly fee. This system resulted in large savings to the court. The Criminal Court Bar Association proposed expanding the program estimating initial savings at about $250,000 annually. Regardless of the method used, the present system of providing for the defense of indigents needs to be changed. The number of criminal cases is climbing rapidly because of the increased penalties for drunk driving, new criminal legislation, and criminal filings. With public defenders now representing over 75% of criminal defendants and with the mounting costs of court-appointed private attorneys involved in 'conflict' cases, it is time more cost-effective methods be employed. The use of contract private attorney firms and consortiums seems to be the most logical solutions for the present.

Public Abuse of Justice by Court Inconsistency

Murder Trial Costs—Nevada vs. California

The two trials of Gerald Gallego for multiple murders in two different states, under the same Constitution, but at great differences in costs and time, illustrate how state court management and policies can vary. In late 1980, Gallego was arrested in California for murdering two Sacramento college students. He was suspected of killing eight or more other women. It took two and one-half years to convict Galelgo at a cost to the taxpayers of an estimated $1 million.

Gallego was sought in Nevada for killing two 17-year-old girls. Nevadans could have let California handle the murderer, but officials and the public feared he would be released on a technicality or let out on parole in a few years. In an almost cloak and dagger environment, authorities spirited Gallego to Pershing County, Nevada to be tried. In three months at a cost of only $90,000, he was tried, convicted, and sentenced to death. Because the county had little money budgeted for murder trials, local citizens donated over $30,000 to defray the costs.

The Pershing County District Attorney Richard Wager said the county tried Gallego because "I really don't have a great deal of faith in the California system to carry out any death penalty."[1]

A Nevada utility company worker, Sue Taylor, commented: "If California had been able to finish the job with this guy, I'd say why spend the money (on the trial). But as long as there's a chance he'll escape the death penalty, I say the only fair thing to do for those girls' families is for us to follow through with the trial."[2]

Mary Vincent's Rape/Assault

Within the same state and under the same law but in different courts, decisions with such wide variations are reached that it boggles the mind. Victims in civil court can sue for huge amounts and get them while a victim in criminal court often gets nothing. In the following example the manner in which Mary Vincent was treated by the State of California in comparison to how Evelyn Walker fared in civil court in rape cases illustrates the inconsistency of the system and the cost to the public indirectly.

At age 15, Mary Vincent, a runaway from her home in Las Vegas, was hitchhiking in Northern California. A man picked her up and raped her near Modesto, California. He then cut off her arms with an axe and left her to die in a remote area.

Tough and determined, Mary Vincent did not die. She staggered for two miles nude to a nearby road where she was picked up by a motorist and taken to a hospital. The man who raped and mutilated her was identified as Lawrence Singleton, a 51-year-old merchant seaman. He was convicted and sentenced to prison for 14 years and four months for the crime. Mary managed to recover and learned to use artificial arms. She returned to her Las Vegas, Nevada home where she attended high school. At 18, Mary graduated from high school dressed in the traditional cap and gown. She marched with the other students into the assembly room, pushing the wheelchair of another graduate.

Mary, wanting to develop a career in dress designing, enrolled in a fashion design school. The high school graduation ceremonies were touching. As Mary Vincent accepted her diploma from the principal with her hook on her left arm, she shook hands with the principal with her right hook.

Shortly after the assault, Mary applied for compensation under the State of California's Victims' Indemnity Fund, but was turned down on legal technicalities. Because Mary was not employed at the time, she was declared not eligible. Mary Vincent took the case to court and finally won in June of 1982, four years later. The court ordered the State Board of Control to pay Mary $13,000. The court determined the Board had not interpreted the law properly. Mary Vincent will suffer her mutilation for the rest of her life.

The taxpayers will continue paying approximately $20,000 a year to support Lawrence Singleton while he is in prison. If he should serve a 14-year sentence, the public will pay out over $250,000, not counting his trial costs. He does no meaningful work in prison, and will contribute no restitution to Mary Vincent for making her a handicapped person for life. Based on actions of the State Department of Corrections, he will be free on parole much sooner.

Evelyn Walker and Her Psychiatrist Offender

A very different situation occurred in Evelyn Walker's case. In San Diego a psychiatrist was accused of having sexual intercourse with a patient over a two-year period. Found guilty, the psychiatrist was ordered by the court to pay $4.6 million in damages to the woman, Evelyn Walker. The trial lasted for five weeks. Walker claimed the doctor-patient relationship had damaged her emotionally and ruined her personal life.

Walker originally asked for $6.9 million. Faced with an appeal, she later agreed to settle for $2.5 million. Her lawyer, said, "I'd rather get her the money now. She needs to get well. A lot of people think lawyers are greedy. I have to think of this woman's health."[3] The appeal could have taken another four or five years. Assuming the lawyer received the normal fee in cases like this (one-third of award), he would have received close to $750,000.

Walker's psychiatrist should obviously be punished. His behavior was unethical and improper in every way. But was Walker damaged as badly as Mary Vincent who got nothing at first for losing two arms and suffered a worse fate? Does it seem fair that for being brutally raped and assaulted, Mary Vincent had to fight for four years to get $13,000, while Evelyn Walker became a millionaire? Did Walker suffer any more psychologically or physically than Mary Vincent? The insurance company covering the psychiatrist will pass on its costs to their premium holders and the public will pay in the end for the excessive award.

Individual Action to Reduce Legal Costs

Individuals needing legal assistance in the areas of uncontested divorce, bankruptcies, author's rights, establishing a corporation and wills could review books on the subject. Thousands are doing this annually by purchasing books from several do-it-yourself legal publishers.

The Nolo Press, a Berkley, California publisher, has been producing do-it-yourself legal kits since 1971. Their first, a divorce manual, continues to sell about 30,000 copies a year. In 1984, a personal-bankruptcy book issued two years previously was selling at the rate of 700 copies a month. Self-help legal action will allow a larger percentage of the population to save money and avoid paying unnecessarily for expensive legal services.

Use of a Legal Clinic

If one does require a lawyer, another alternative is available in the form of 'walk-in' legal clinics. Hundreds of legal clinics are now available that charge lower fees than the traditional law firm. Over 1,000 clinics have emerged after Jacoby and Meyers opened their clinic in Van Nuys, California in 1973.

Probably the largest clinic, the Hyatt Legal Services of Kansas City, had 117 locations in 17 states and was serving 15,000 new clients a month in 1984. Most of their business was related to divorces, wills, adoption, real estate transactions, and traffic offenses. The Hyatt clinic's charges vary somewhat by locality, but are considerably cheaper than a regular law firm.

Most legal clinic lawyers make less than traditional law firms. In 1984, the firm employed over 300 lawyers. The founder, Joel Hyatt, a Yale Law School graduate, claims that the "middle 70% of the population" has not been adequately served because they are "not poor enough to qualify for free government-funded legal aid and not rich enough to afford the traditional law firms which have always served the affluent."

Avoiding Litigation by Legal Prevention Work

"Prevent Litigation—See Your Lawyer Early," should be every businessman's theme. The public could avoid a myriad of legal problems if they would consult with a lawyer or specialists before entering into an agreement, or contract with someone. An hour or so discussing one's plans ahead of time with a lawyer could save days of grief and expenses later. Have periodic legal checkups.

Results of Justice System Reforms

The preceeding suggested legislative, educational, court administrative and organizational changes and personal actions could reduce the costs of trials and total court costs from 20% to 30% for the nation, a considerable saving.

MEN OF JUSTICE—"Lost again in the lower courts and he laments as if he couldn't still appeal."

CHAPTER ELEVEN

HOW DID WE GET IN THIS MESS?

To better understand how to change our justice system, we need to look at its history if only briefly. How did American courts evolve into their present form? By reviewing the history and evolution of the legal system, the reader will understand why judges and court analysts refer to it as medieval and why the adversary system is used. The reader will also understand why restitution was abandoned for years and American courts differ from those of Western Europe.

Need for Laws and Court System

People found over the centuries that they could not trust their rulers to make decisions based on their own subjective interpretation of what was good or bad. It was necessary to have written laws to insure an even standard of justice. In our democracy citizens delegate power to state and federal legislative representatives, enabling them to make laws concerning our health and welfare. Legislators are expected to make laws that apply equally to all parties. At election time, we can vote those legislators out of office if they do not perform in the interests of the majority. The laws must not only be fair, but be enforced and be upheld by the judiciary.

Law Development and Historic Settlement of Disputes

The processing of criminal disputes and treatment of victims has changed considerably since ancient times. Our contemporary judiciary seems more interested in adhering to the rules of the legal process than meeting the needs of litigants and victims. In primitive and biblical civilizations victims settled disputes with offenders by retaliation. If a person stole or trespassed on one's property, the victim personally reacted in kind. As clans and tribes developed, an act or offense against one tribe resulted in a vengeful movement by the offended clan or tribe. Retaliation by an entire group became known as a 'blood feud.'

Primitive cultures soon learned that feuds between groups were very unsettling and caused problems to everyone, not just those in an altercation. Large groups became embroiled in fighting which was disruptive to the normal process of working, preparing food, sleeping, and surviving. As tribes and clans accumulated economic goods and wealth, the simple rules of retaliation gave way to repayment of an injury in the form of goods or money. A slow change evolved from unregulated revenge to a system of negotiation between the offender's family and the victim's family. Victims were paid for physical or mental injury in goods or money in place of physical abuse.

The behavior of people, tribes and communities was regulated by custom and unwritten codes long before laws were put in writing. With the advent of writing, laws were translated into written documents.

Code Of Hammurabi

The earliest known laws were made by King Ur-Nammu of Ur, a city in ancient Sumer, a part of Babylonia, in the Twenty-Fifth Century B.C. The first surviving code was that written by Hammurabi, King of Babylonia, around 1750 B.C. During Hammurabi's 43 year rule, he compiled a new code from the older existing Sumerian and Akkadian legal codes, some 300 years old. He revised and expanded the older codes into one covering some 300 provisions including land and business regulations, family laws, false accusations, witchcraft, property rights, loans, and even medical malpractice. The code was unique in that its major principle was that "the strong shall not injure the weak." It gave rights to the individual. Simple rules were developed which permitted the victim or wronged party to get revenge. The policy of "an eye for an eye and a tooth for a tooth" prevailed. The code was known also for its severity. For instance, if a father was struck by his son, the son, if convicted, would have his hand cut off.

The practice of providing restitution to victims prevailed at one time over most of the populated world. As tribes assembled into villages and communities became larger and more structured, leadership became centralized and laws were enacted to define acceptable behavior. Most of these early laws provided for the payment of goods or money for offenses as compensation to injured victims. Victims were provided indemnification under the early laws of Babylonians, Hebrews, Greeks, Romans, ancient Germans, and the English.[1] Under the law of Moses, if a person stole another party's sheep, he had to make a four-fold restitution. Stolen oxen required a five-fold restitution.[2]

Between 1200 and 400 B.C., the Hebrews assembled their various social and religious laws. The laws were known as the Mosaic Code, as they were reportedly formulated by Moses. The Ten Commandments included within it influenced Western civilization for centuries. Other countries such as India and China codified their laws around 500 B.C.

Development of Law in Greece

Most of the original written laws had an aura of "coming from the gods." The priests or leaders claimed the laws were given by God. The 'people' had difficulty changing these laws because of their high source or origin. The ancient Greeks, however, had a different philosophy. They were among the first to believe that laws were made by men and could be changed by men when the need arose. The Greeks believed that citizens and a country should be ruled by law rather than by men. Their laws regulated property, inheritance, contracts, trade, and other matters.

Roman Law

Because Roman citizens believed that they could not get fair treatment from hearings before Roman judges, written laws were developed. The laws were codified on 12 tables about 450 B.C. by a council of ten men. The tables described the customary behavior expected of citizens. These tables or laws continued to be a force in the Roman Empire and Italy for centuries. As a result of written laws, legal schools evolved to interpret them, and law became a profession in Rome.

Under the Law of the Twelve Tables in ancient Rome, a thief had to pay double the value of property stolen. If a house search was required, the offender had to pay three times the value. If the offender resisted the house search, he paid four times the value. If property was taken in a robbery, the offender had to pay four times the value of the items taken.[3]

Early codes accepted cruel punishment as a deterrent to crime. The ancient Germanic codes provided compensation based not only on the nature of the crime, but also in accordance with the age, rank, sex, and prestige of the injured party. According to Schafer, a free-born man was worth more than a slave, an adult more than a child, a man more than a woman, and a person of rank more than a free man.[4]

The Roman Emperor Justinian I codified all Roman laws into the Justinian *Digest* and *Code* in Constantinople in the Sixth Century. This code influenced European law, and continued in use until the Eastern Empire of the Byzantium collapsed in 1453 A.D.

Medieval Europe

As the Roman Catholic Church became strong in medieval Europe, canon or church law evolved for a period of time. Canon law was based on Roman legal principles. Roman law prevailed, and replaced many feudal laws in Western Europe.

England's Legal System in the Middle Ages

Due to its isolation from the Continent, England developed a different kind of legal system. Justice was administered throughout Britain by way of royal courts that operated on the basis of established customs. As a result, this type of law became known as 'common law.' The word 'court' that we use today comes from the king holding court throughout the country to settle disputes among his subjects.

In medieval England many disputes were settled through trials by compurgation, ordeal, and battle. Under trial by compurgation the principals in the dispute would swear along with their friends that their position on a dispute was correct. The other side would swear equally that their side had the correct viewpoint. Somehow the judge, usually a lord, would determine which side was telling the truth.

In trial by ordeal the accused was tested by a variety of painful or dangerous actions. One method was trial by fire. The accused was made to grab hold of a red-hot rod. After three or four days, the bandages were removed. If the person's hand was blistered, he was guilty. He was in the clear if his hand had not been harmed. Not good odds!

In trial by battle the parties often hired a champion to fight for their cause. The champions frequently fought each other with staffs. A decision was reached at the end of the day, based on whose champion had won. If the defendant's champion had not been defeated by the plaintiff's champion or given up, the defendant won. Our modern-day lawyers developed from this primitive, medieval champion concept. Present lawyers, of course, are higher paid and take less physical chances.

Under the English offender-victim system, an offender could "buy back the peace he had broken." He paid what was called 'wer' for homicide, or 'bot' for an injury to a victim or his kin in accordance with a schedule of injuries and their fines.[5] In King Aldred's time, for knocking out a man's front tooth, the fine was eight schillings; for an eyetooth, four schillings; and for a molar, 15 schillings. The term 'outlaw' came into existence at that time, around 870 A.D. If a victim demanded compensation and the offender refused to pay, the offender was declared an outlaw by the community for not paying for his offense. The outlaw could then be killed by any member of the tribe or community with impunity.[6]

Over a period of time in England the king, lords, and clergy took more responsibility within their territories and became involved in the compensation process. For conducting a hearing between an offender and a victim, lords demanded a commission called 'wite' for their time and for their protection of the offender against retaliation by the victim or his clan.[7]

By the Twelfth Century, English lords increased their power over communities in settling disputes. As a result, a victim's share of compensation for a crime committed against him was decreased. The king and his lords slowly increased their wite and finally took over the entire payment. The offender was assessed a fine and the money paid to the court or state. As occurs now in the United States, the state became the offended party in criminal law and had the right to punish offenders and receive compensation or fines. Victims no longer had a right to restitution.

Before the Magna Carta was signed in 1215, conflicts grew among the regional lords, barons, and the king over who had power to settle disputes. As barons and lords became more unfair in court procedures, British citizens complained loudly, and court procedures slowly changed. The Magna Carta's signing in 1215 defined and limited the rights of kings to settle disputes, and established the civil rights of citizens.

Victims Lose Out to State on European Continent

From 1600 to 1800, most Continental European countries modified the use of Roman law. Under Napoleon Bonaparte, scholars codified the French law after 1800. This effort, known as 'Code Napoleon,' employed a mixture of Roman law and French legal customs. Victims gradually lost their restitution rights in most Western European countries. Germany clung longer to the personal restitution process than the other Western European countries.

Under the 'adhesive' procedure, developed within the German legal system in the Sixteenth and Seventeenth Centuries, a judge, while hearing a criminal case, could consider the claim of the victim for restitution during the same hearing. Technically criminal and restitution hearings were heard separately in court, yet heard at the same time. The adhesive procedure is still used in several other countries as well as in Germany. The victim seldom receives full compensation for the loss of property, damage, and/or personal injuries suffered; but he receives something.

Various leaders have made attempts for centuries to provide more restitution to victims. In 1516, Sir Thomas Moore wrote in his book, *Utopia,* that "restitution should be made by offenders to their victims and that offenders should be required to labor on public works projects to raise money for such payments."[8] A similar position was taken by Jeremy Pentham in the Eighteenth Century. He believed that offenders should provide restitution to a victim and that restitution should be in the form of money or in-kind service for property offenses. When an offender could not be found, he wanted a public victim-compensation fund established to help the victims of offenders who were not caught or convicted. A state compensation system was necessary for people victimized by insolvent offenders.

European Restitution Reform Movement During Modern Times

At the International Prison Congress in 1878 held in Stockholm, the Sixth International Penitentiary Congress in Brussels, and in many other international penal conferences, reformers and

208

penal specialists recommended that criminals provide restitution to victims.

Very little was actually done about the plight of victims until the 1950s, however. One English penal reformer, Marjorie Frye, offered fresh insight on victims' need for restitution in her book, *Arms of the Law,* and in her 1957 article entitled "Justice for Victims." Frye believed that not only should victims be compensated for injuries, but that offenders could learn much from paying directly to victims for their offenses. She believed that offenders would receive some rehabilitative value from taking part in providing restitution to victims. Marjorie Frye's writing stimulated interest in compensating victims. She asked that a national fund be established and administered by the state to compensate victims. To Frye restitution meant that offenders provide indemnification directly to the victim for their criminal actions.[8]

The British Parliament initiated a study resulting in a White Paper in 1959 entitled "Penal Practice in a Changing Society." An excerpt on victim rights from the White Paper stated:

> The basis of early law was personal reparation by the offender to the victim, a concept of which modern criminal law has almost completely lost sight. The assumption that the claims of the victim are sufficiently satisfied if the offender is punished by society becomes less persuasive as society in its dealings with offenders increasingly emphasizes the reformative aspects of punishment. Indeed in the public mind the interests of the offender may not infrequently seem to be placed before those of the victim.
>
> This is certainly not the correct emphasis. It may well be that our penal system would not only provide a more effective deterrent to crime, but would also find a greater moral value, if the concept of personal reparation to the victim were added to the concepts of deterrence by punishment and of reformation by training. It is also possible to hold that the redemptive value of punishment to the individual offender would be greater if it were made to include a realization of the injury he had done to his victim as well as to the order of society, and the need to make personal reparation for that injury.[9]

A number of victim compensation programs were initiated as a result of Frye's writings and Parliament's actions. Programs were developed in Great Britain, New Zealand, Australia, Canada, and the United States.

The New Zealand government passed the New Zealand Criminal Injuries Compensation Act in 1964, which established an administrative tribunal. The tribunal had the power to conduct hearings on compensation claims and to make awards to victims. The awards were limited to cases of criminal violence involving personal injuries. During the same year, the British government set up a non-statutory program in which an administrative board could assess and award compensation to victims. California followed quickly in 1965 with a program providing compensation to victims.

Since the 1970s, several other states established compensation type programs. These include Alaska, Hawaii, Illinois, Louisiana, Maryland, Massachusetts, Nevada, New Jersey, New York, Rhode Island, and Washington. Most of these programs do not require offenders to pay victims for stolen property or for injuries. Instead a compensation fund pays the victim for personal damages and losses. In the late 1970s and 1980s, American authorities showed increasing interest in requiring restitution for victims by the offending person, whether directly or through a compensation fund. The latter covers those instances where the offender cannot be found, cannot be convicted, or is unable to pay.

In general the punishment of criminals and treatment of victims went through the following evolutionary stages: "1) private vengeance on offender; 2) collective vengeance; 3) the process of negotiation and payment of wrongs to victim; 4) the adoption of codes containing preset compensation amounts to be awarded the victim in the process; 5) the gradual intervention of lords or rulers as mediators and payment to them of a percentage of the compensation award; and 6) the complete takeover of the criminal justice process and the disappearance of restitution from criminal law."[10]

Growth of American Law
and Criminal Court Procedures

The majority of early American colonists were from England making British Common Law the accepted law. The concept changed somewhat however, due to the different problems faced in the colonies. British Common Law was concerned with protecting scarce land while the opposite was true in America. In the eyes of the newcomers, the vast amount of land needed exploration and development. Common law was adjusted in America to encourage expansion of the West, despite Indian land holdings. Indian property rights and way of life suffered drastically under the new laws.

Compliance to government laws were viewed differently in America. William Penn decided to follow his God and preached the use of an outlawed Quaker doctrine rather than obey government law, which he perceived to be unfair. During Penn's trial, in defiance of all evidence and harsh treatment and threats by the judge, the jury refused to return a guilty verdict. They perceived the law to be improper.

Lawyers were not respected by early colonists. Lawyers were actually banned from some of the new settlements and not permitted to serve on councils or the legislature in others.   It is interesting to read the following oath that the clerk of the court administered to constables in Colonial America:

> You shall well and truly keep every person sworn of this jury together in some convenient room, without meat, drink, fire, candle or lodging, and you shall not suffer any person whatsoever to speak to them, or any of them; neither shall you yourself speak to them, until such time as they be agreed of their verdict, unless it be to ask them, if they be agreed of their verdict. So Help You God.

Obviously, enforcement of such an oath resulted in a quick verdict by the jury.

Present day Libertarians believe that judges try to veto the rights of juries. They find that judges mislead juries by telling them to accept the law, and judge only the facts. In opposition to attempts to allow less than unanimous jury verdicts, Libertarians advocate that juries be allowed to refuse to convict someone if one or more jurors believe the legislation itself is unwise or unjust.

The Thirteen Colonies developed a court system by the early 1700s and a law profession soon began to practice in the court system. Of the 55 men who drafted the Federal Constitution in Philadelphia in 1787, two-thirds were lawyers. The makeup of legislatures hasn't changed significantly since.

The framers of the Constitution were concerned that too strong a president would result in a monarchy, and that the big states would dominate the small states. They therefore made the Constitution a document full of checks and balances. The powers of the three branches of government (legislative, executive, and judicial) were established and their powers carefully defined. In 1789, the Constitution was ratified by nine states and became the law of the land. In 1791, ten amendments were added to the Federal Constitution, commonly referred to as the 'Bill of Rights.' They insured freedom of speech, freedom of worship, right to trial by jury, the sanctity of private property ownership, and many other civil rights that are considered important to our democracy. After almost 200 years the Federal Constitution has been amended only 16 more times. It is truly a remarkable document.

The legislative and executive branches of the new government were stronger than the judiciary branch. This power balance changed in 1801 when John Marshall became Chief Justice of the United States. Marshall strengthened the judiciary system when he established the right of the Supreme Court to review laws to determine their constitutionality. The court's power of judicial review, although passive in nature, is a powerful tool. The court acts as a brake on the legislative branch of government and sometimes the executive branch.

With new laws came government agencies who issued rules and regulations and administrative orders. In 1946, the *Federal Register* printed only 2,355 pages. With interest in civil rights, consumer and environmental affairs, a deluge of federal laws were generated in the 1950s, 60s, and 70s. During 1975, the *Register* printed 60,221 pages. While no Code of Federal Regulations existed in 1946, 72,200 pages were printed in it during 1975. A horrendous proliferation of national regulations evolved, often at cross purposes, that few officials fully understood. State legislators followed the example of their federal cousins and passed an increasing number of laws every year to solve their problems. The new laws created more unproductive work and costs for businesses and the public.

The number of lawyers who work for government also increased. The greatest concentration of lawyers is in Washington D.C. where there is one lawyer in private practice for every 64 residents. This figure does not include the large number of government lawyers who work in the District. Thirteen percent of all attorneys are government lawyers.

Government laws and regulations increased at a tremendou

rate during the 1970s with the passage of the Environmental Protection Policy Act, Clean Water Act, Clean Air Act, and many others. More lawyers were needed to interpret and represent the agencies after the laws were passed.

Legal Systems in the Western World Today

Common law and civil law are the two basic systems practiced in the Western world today. As pointed out earlier, common law developed in England from decisions based on common sense and good conscience. Great Britain, and other English-speaking countries such as Canada, New Zealand, Australia, and the United States use the Common Law system. Places like South Africa use a mixture of Roman and Dutch law. Under the Common Law system, a judge has the power to create law based on his decisions. During later trials concerning similar subjects, his decisions serve as a guide and precedent for judges arriving at a decision.

Under Civil Law, laws are passed and made effective by the legislative bodies of the nation. France is a civil law country. Because Louisiana was first settled by the French, civil law is used as in the Province of Quebec in Canada. Most Latin American countries and Japan use a combination of civil and Common Law. Most of the communist countries use a system that permits government to control the affairs of the public more than in Western nations.

Private and Public Law

The United States, as in most Western nations, divides the law into two major branches: public and private law. Private law is concerned with the relationships between people and their rights and obligations. It is divided into six major legal divisions: 1) contracts, 2) property, 3) inheritance, 4) torts (accidental or intentional injury or wrongdoing by one party to another), 5) family law (involving marriage, divorce, and adoption), and 6) corporation law.

Public law regulates relationships between individuals and government. It is divided into four major divisions: 1) criminal law (criminal offenses and specific rules for arrest, trial, and punishment); 2) constitutional law (government's powers and people's rights based on federal and state constitutions); 3) administrative law (adminstratative or executive rules that regulate the activities of businesses, corporations, utilities, and businesses issued a license by the government); 4) international law (agreements and relations between nations).

Common Law has generally worked well in this country because it has changed as the needs of society have changed. In the United States and in most democracies laws can be changed by four different methods: 1) legislative bodies amend or repeal laws or pass new ones; 2) admininistrative agencies amend or repeal a regulation or adopt a new one; 3) courts declare a law unconstitutional; 4) the initiative is used by the public to propose and vote on new laws. The referendum can be used to vote on legislation passed or proposed by a legislative body.

The Adversary Process

In general the adversary process used in the United States works, but flaws exist in the system that need correction. The major characteristics of the process are based on court rules of conduct and remedies, rules of procedures, and rules of evidence; parties in disputes are provided opportunities to present evidence favorable to their case and to challenge evidence presented by their opposition; litigants have an opportunity to bring consultants and professional assistance to aid them in making their case presentation and challenging evidence; litigants have an opportunity to get information before the trial of the facts being presented by the opposite side; a trial administrator reduces the chance for bias or prejudice on the part of the judges or juries; and an opportunity exists within the system for review of decisions for error made in the judicial process.

Evolution of the Adversary and Grand Jury

During King Henry II's reign in England, 1154-1189, the jury system as we know it was developed. Jurors were first selected on the basis of their knowledge of a conflict or issue. Jurors served as witnesses and provided facts on disputes. The sheriff of the region, who was appointed by the king or his representatives, selected the jury. King Henry II wanted to control the jury members in order to consolidate his power and to transfer control of the justice system to himself from the barons and nobles.

The modern jury system evolved between the early thirteenth century and the end of the fourteenth century. The adversary system developed simultaneously with the jury system. Jurors were no longer expected to serve as witnesses to a conflict and the court appointed them in a non-witness role. It was the jury's duty to listen to evidence

214

and consider the facts and not speak out. Counselors asked witnesses to a crime to talk. Their testimony persuaded the jury to make a decision. Our present-day jury procedures, developed during the late medieval period, have changed little since then.

Litigants or their representatives had the right to challenge jurors for both 'cause' (prejudice) and preemptively, or without having to show cause. The British kept the jury selection process simple, and choose juries with great speed.

Just as today, juries made site visits and physically viewed property. Jurors were examined to determine their fitness to serve. Judges allowed counsels to make opening statements and to argue before the jury. The jury was instructed as to the law and reminded to make their decisions based on facts presented and on the law as outlined to them. Special rules of evidence, including the hearsay rule, insured that evidence presented was acceptable. The entire trial procedure resembles the present process.

Not all Englishmen qualified for an adversary trial by jury. Most of the trials during the sixteenth and seventeenth centuries were for criminal offenses. Most civil actions were not included or were handled by 'ad hoc' tribunals. The crown used the latter for treason trials. In these cases, members of the tribunal were selected carefully. In Sir Walter Raleigh's famous trial, the king was represented by the attorney general, but Raleigh represented himself without benefit of counsel. Raleigh could not face his accusers or question the state's witnesses, who never appeared in court. Raleigh made such an eloquent argument about his right to face his accusers that the hearsay rule of evidence was introduced soon afterwards.

The British adversary and jury system was transferred to the United States but changed drastically. Major changes occurred in the 1960s and 1970s when national interest peaked to provide more legal rights to low-income and minority people in the legal process.

After seeing the adversary system in practice many citizens don't like it. Larry Ray, the American Bar Association official who processes alternative dispute settlement research said recently that "A lot of people are just plain tired of the adversary system."

The Inquisitorial Process

Judges and lawyers play a different role in the inquisitorial system. In an adversary situation, the judge acts as a referee or court manager. In the inquisitorial process, the judge is the most active participant. The counsels represent their parties; but it's the judge who decides what witnesses should be called, what questions will be asked, and what documents and evidence will be considered. He also decides what pleadings should be heard and what legal theories can be used. Trials are also different. A series of several short-term trials can be held over a period of time, rather than one long continuing trial. A judge may hold a trial on one issue, find a need for additional information, and adjourn until a later date. The judge can also hold conferences with the disputants and their lawyers. The lawyer obtains evidence and analyzes its reliability for the case.

The judge in the inquisitorial process has a major role in arriving at the truth of the dispute. The lawyers are there essentially to aid him in finding the truth. The inquisitorial process is used by most of the Western European continental countries. Those countries claim that it is better adapted to obtain justice than the adversary process.

The inquisitorial system has many benefits if not abused by the government in power. Government intervention can be a problem to an accused when the salaries and appointments of judges, prosecutors and defense attorneys are made by the same government agency.

Should the Adversary Process Be Changed?

The adversary system obviously has some strong points in its favor, but relies too much on the quality of the counsels for both parties and that they will perform well. More emphasis is placed on winning than finding the truth in disputes. The restrictions of court-mandated rules, such as the exclusionary rules, further hamper a quest for truth. "Follow the rules or else" is the environment of the court.

To abandon our present system for the inquisitorial or another process would probably be a mistake. Much can be said for the inquisitorial process if government judges were consistently competent, fair and unbiased, and not influenced by an appointing authority's viewpoint. It seems better to keep our judges independent, but accountable to the law and a code of conduct. The world has seen countries such as Germany change laws to take away property and civil rights of specific groups to achieve state policies. German judges were informed by Nazi authorities that they were civil servants and to adhere to government policies. Judges were not considered independent of the state in arriving at decisions.

The British have utilized the adversary system wisely and managed to prevent abuses of it. Unlike the British, American courts have permitted irresponsible litigants, lawyers, and judges to abuse our adversary system and often turn it into a chaotic quagmire of technical legalese and an expensive courtroom debating society.

By making changes as suggested in other chapters of this book, the American adversary process could be kept, but improved and put back on the track toward providing restitution to victims and swift and fair justice for all.

LAWYERS AND CLIENTS—Lawyer–"The case is moving along."
Client–"You have been telling me that for four years. If it continues at this pace, I will no longer have boots to follow it."

CHAPTER TWELVE

SIGNS OF HOPE

Frustrated by the judiciary's inability to make changes and the legislators' slowness and stubbornness in passing court reform legislation, citizens complained, formed interest groups, and took action. Some action was heavy-handed due to lack of interest or support from bar associations and the judiciary. But groups passed initiatives, monitored judges, lobbied for new legislation, wrote legislators and judges, and campaigned vigorously for political candidates of their choice.

The public became more aware of activist judges who interpreted the Constitution along the lines of their biases and goals for society. Citizens became more aware of the chaos in the courts, and asked the legislatures of the country to do something about it. People were impatient for improvements. Legal assistance was too expensive and they knew it.

Direct Action By Citizens

The public's anger at a judge's light sentences of several rapists' forced him to increase the prison time of the offenders. In Dedham, Massachusetts in the Norfolk County Courthouse, five young men admitted to gang-raping a 38-year-old woman and pleaded guilty. The Superior Court Judge put the defendants on two years' probation, suspended their sentences to state prison of three to five years, and fined them $500 in court costs to be paid at the rate of $5 a week.[1] No restitution for the victim was considered.

An immediate outrage followed the announcement. The public, newspapers, radio, and TV stations blasted the judge. Hundreds of angry telephone callers attacked his decision. Elected officials quickly responded. The case was more complicated than the public realized; the District Attorney believed he had a weak case; but the public was not in a reasoning mood. After four days of intense pressure, the judge held a hearing in court. He revoked the suspended sentences, making the men serve three to five years in Walpole Prison unless they pleaded "not guilty" and stood trial. The judge's turnaround illustrates how sensitive the judiciary can be to negative public opinion. Individuals realized that they had more power to change judicial behavior than they realized.

Judge Beaten in Hawaii

In Honolulu, a crowd of 300 people outraged at a state judge for overturning a jury's murder verdict, physically attacked, and beat him so badly that emergency brain surgery was required.[2] While assaulting a judge is not proper, the act should serve as a message that the public takes the justice system seriously and will not tolerate indefinitely soft treatment of dangerous criminals.

Truth-in-Sentencing Legislation

In Boston Governor Dukakis campaigned to have the Massachusetts criminal code changed to provide tougher sentences for offenders. After seeing one sentencing plan defeated by the state legislature, he proposed a revised bill in January of 1985. The governor's bill would:

- Reclassify crimes against people, and specify a narrow range of years to be appropriate sentences for each.
- Require judges to state in writing why they hand out sentences that are higher or lower than those recommended in the law.
- Allow prosecutors, for the first time, to appeal sentences that are below the stated range.
- Require judges to sentence convicts to a specific number of years.
- Provide tougher sentences for repeat offenders.
- Abolish the 'Concord sentence,' which allows parole in one to two years on a 10-20-year sentence.

• Tighten parole and time-off guidelines and emphasize restitution.

The Chief Justice of the Massachusetts courts, Edward F. Hennesey endorsed the plan stating:

> The things that I support enthusiastically in the bill are the two great principles of the bill. First, truth in sentencing... and second, it tends to eliminate disparity.
> ...It does give a judge, in our courts, just as much discretion (over sentencing) as he has now. But it is a discretion controlled by standards and criteria.[3]

Rape Penalties

Under pressure from victim organizations and the public, the California Legislature increased penalties for rape. Sentences were increased to a maximum of eight years from five years for rape. With the use of weapons, the sentence was longer. As a result, two brothers who were convicted of several rapes, were sentenced to 118-year sentences. Others received prison terms of 38, 53, 83, and 100 years. To some the sentences seem harsh in relation to the average sentences given for voluntary manslaughter (five years) and for involuntary manslaughter (three years). Quite a gap!

A danger existed that these long sentences would encourage rapists to kill their victims, and not take a chance on being identified. The lengthy sentences could become counterproductive. Murderers in most states become eligible for parole after serving only four years.

While it's good news that the courts are getting tougher with rapists, the bad news is that rape witnesses may be harder to find. The backlash against rapists may have gone too far. A little moderation in the drive to punish is needed, or else rape victims will suffer greater harm.

Deputy Public Defender Katherine Houston of Santa Clara County, California, said,

> The word's pretty well out among the guys who do this sort of things is that you might as well kill your victim.... We've upped the ante for rape in this state. But I'm not

sure that such disparate treatment is going to result in what the Legislature intended.[4]

Mandatory Sentences

Some judges are not happy with mandatory sentencing. Gene Franchini, a New Mexico District Judge, resigned in protest at being forced to sentence a man to prison under a mandatory sentence law. The man with a clean record committed a minor crime. Judge Franchini gave him two years' probation and declared the mandatory law unconstitutional. Franchini saw the rush for mandatory sentencing laws as "nothing more than an attempt to apply a simple solution to a very complex problem."[5]

Public Protests Change Legislation

Primarily due to the effective lobbying by Stronger Legislation Against Child Molesters (SLAM), the California Legislature passed several bills sponsored by them. One bill, SB586, although not exactly what SLAM wanted, was an improvement. SB586 provided mandatory sentences of three, six and eight years for child sex offenders who:

- Held a position of trust, such as teachers, doctors, foster parents, and religious leaders.
- Had prior felony convictions.
- Kidnapped the victim.
- Used force or a weapon in the assault.
- Inflicted injury on the victim.
- Molested more than one child in the course of the crime.
- Had significant sexual contact—i.e., any kind of penetration or oral copulation for example—with the victim.

The bill provided that five years be tacked onto any sentence where the defendant had a prior felony sex conviction. It also called for a 15-years-to-life sentence for a defendant convicted a third time for a sex crime.

MADD Changes System

After 13-year-old Cari Lightner was killed by a drunk hit-and-run driver (who was free on bail from a previous arrest) her mother, Candy Lightner, started a movement to change the courts' treatment of drunk drivers. She organized MADD, Mothers Against Drunk Drivers, and brought about changes in drunk driving laws in California and the nation. By 1985, now headquartered in Texas, MADD had 340 chapters in 47 states, Canada, Great Britain, and Guam with over 75,000 members. On the attitude of the legal profession toward MADD, Lightner said: "Judges, public defenders, prosecutors and private defense lawyers don't like for us to be there. They feel we are intimidating them from exercising the unlimited power they felt they had."

In Hicksville, New York, Celia Stow's MADD chapter of 200 members believes they have been responsible for pushing the courts to give tougher sentences to drunk drivers. MADD works for stiffer drunk driving laws, public awareness, and victim advocacy. The national organization has indeed caught the attention of legislators and the public and has been responsible for changing federal and state laws on drunk driving and the treatment of offenders.

HALT Forms In Washington, D. C.

With intentions to reform the American legal system, HALT or Help Abolish Legal Tyranny was formed as a non-profit organizaion in Washington, D. C. HALT provides members with manuals on Shopping For a Lawyer, Small Claims Court, Probate, Real Estate and Using A Law Library, and a newsletter. In addition the organization also keeps members informed of legal reforms throughout the nation.

Vigilant Citizens Organize

To keep a watchful eye on judges, Citizens for Law and Order was formed by retired Army Colonel Earl Huntting from his base in Oakland, California. CLO claims to have over 8,000 members in more than eight counties. CLO was formed to publicize leniency by judges and push for legislation to get tough on crime. They monitor sentencing patterns of judges considered 'soft' on criminals. The CLO publishes a newsletter and they report that judges, prosecutors, and defense attorneys are uneasy about the groups' monitoring work. Huntting believes that "Our judges are much too lenient and they must be monitored."

Californians Organize To Change Legal System

For several years the California appellate courts and the Supreme Court had been under attack for being too sympathetic to criminals and writing decisions unfair to the public. Californians already unhappy with court actions, lost their patience and went into action to stop justice abuses by litigants, lawyers, and judges and bring a balance to the court and legal system. The citizens were not always successful, but they tried hard and made many inroads.

Formation of Criminal Justice Legal Foundation

To provide legal assistance to the people of the state in criminal cases and prevent courts from avoiding the laws of the state on the death penalty, the Criminal Justice Legal Foundation was formed by the California Chamber of Commerce. The Foundation is financed by private donations from businessmen and individuals to work against the interest of groups who oppose the death penalty and support criminal rights.

Reduction of Public Defender Budget

Objecting to the state public defender's lawyer's preoccupation with ideological and political concerns, Governor Deukmejian cut their budget in half in 1982. Partly in response to the budget reduction, Chief Justice Rose Bird announced in August of 1984 the formation of the California Appellate Project (CAP), a nonprofit corporation, to provide legal assistance to convicted criminals in cases of broad significance. CAP was funded by state funds, channeled through the Judicial Council and the state Supreme Court. It was believed that CAP was formed also in response to the creation of the Chamber of Commerce's Criminal Justice Legal Foundation (CJLF).

Initiative for Victim Bill of Rights

Unable to move the California Legislature to act on a 'bill of rights' for victims, Paul Gann, co-author of the famous Proposition 13 tax cut in California, sponsored a 'Victims' Bill of Rights'' initiative. He collected over 553,790 signatures and qualified the initiative for the ballot in 1982.

The victim 'Bill of Rights' required that: criminals make restitution to victims and pay damages; allow relevant evidence into criminal proceedings (weaken the exclusionary rule); permit use of criminal records in trials; abolish use of 'diminished capacity' as a defense in most criminal trials; ban plea bargaining in murder cases, voluntary manslaughter, rape and assault with deadly weapon cases; and permit school officials to ban undesirable or dangerous persons from school grounds. The initiative increased prison terms and gave relatives of victims the right to attend parole hearings.

The initiative was challenged by the American Civil Liberties Union and another group of lawyers. The Secretary of State ruled that Gann's initiative contained sufficient signatures to be put on the ballot. The decision was appealed to the state Supreme Court and, after protests by lawyers, the court upheld the Secretary of State's decision to put it on the June 1982 ballot.

In June of 1982, Californians voted 56% to 44% in support of Proposition 8, despite strong lobbying against the proposition by the legal profession. The public's action was a directive to the state Supreme Court to stop showing favoritism to criminal offenders, and to the Criminal Justice Committee of the California Assembly to stop preventing anti-crime and court improvement legislation from ever reaching the full legislature for a vote. The victim 'Bill of Rights' passed preliminary challenges; but defense lawyers and criminal rights supporters continued to snipe at it. The public's strong support of the law, however, served as a warning to legislators and the judiciary to improve the criminal court system or face more initiatives.

The California Supreme Court made its first ruling on it in September 1982, in a close four to three vote. They found that the amendment had been legally placed before the voters and did not violate any state constitutional requirements.

The then Attorney General George Deukmejian, a supporter of the bill, said that the court's decision reaffirmed the voters' "right to make essential changes in the law when the Legislature and the Supreme Court have lost sight of the people's wishes." He believed also that the voters were "weary of decisions favoring the rights of the accused and the convicted over the rights of victims and potential victims of crime and that the people have the right to make needed changes."

Changing 'Deep Pocket' Legislation

In many states, when an accident occurs, an injured party may sue a business or government agency where the event took place, and collect more in damages than occurred to a person even though the business was at fault only a small percent. Under current rules of 'joint and several liability' lawsuits are encouraged where defendants have assets or insurance; and not because they caused the accident.

To prevent this unfair legal action or 'deep pocket' suits, California State Senator John Foran introduced a bill (SB 75) to change the rules governing who pays for the damages. Under the bill, the 'damage pot' used to pay litigants and attorney's contingency fees will be reduced by limiting the amount paid for pain and suffering (non-economic loss) to the degree the defendant was at fault. Under SB 75, if a business owner is 5% responsible for an injury, he could not be found liable for anymore than 5% of the pain and suffering damage. The bill does not prevent an injured plaintiff from recovering all medical bills, lost wages, and property damage. The bill was opposed by the California Trial Lawyers Association.

Cities and counties faced by similar lawsuits met to discuss action to protect themselves from frivolous lawsuits from swimmers, surfers, and the like who were hurt while swimming in the ocean or using public facilities. In one coastal county an insurance company dropped its coverage of twelve cities. In Los Angeles County the Administrator concerned with losses of over $26 million in suits issued a report on solving their problems. The study proposed to share with the state local liability losses, and to reduce future costs by:

- Revising joint and several liability law to make damages proportionate to liability.
- Limiting the amount plaintiffs may receive for non-economic damages.
- Protecting public entities from persons hurt while using public facilities in direct violation of the law.

Bill to Review State Appellate Court Justice Appointments

State Senator Ed Davis, former Police Chief of Los Angeles, proposed a constitutional amendment that would require that the governor's appointment to an appellate court would be subject to the Senate's approval. Unfortunately the proposal made in 1982 did not receive a two-thirds vote from both houses and could not be placed on the general election ballot.

At present a three person Commission on Judicial Appointments (formed by the Attorney General, the Chief Justice of the Supreme Court, and a senior appellate court justice), approve appellate and Supreme Court justices. Another bill is likely to be submitted again.

Action To Remove Chief Justice Bird and Two Other Justices

Angry with the actions and decisions of the state Supreme Court, especially Chief Justice Rose Bird, and Associate Justice's Cruz Reynoso and Joseph Grodin, crime victims and other groups organized to defeat them when they come up for a public confirmation vote in November 1986. Some of the groups are the Californians to Defeat Rose Bird, Crime Victims for Court Reform, the Committee to Conserve the Courts, the California Birdwatchers Society, several police affiliates, and the California District Attorneys Association.

President of the California District Attorneys Association, Michael D. Bradbury, said the state Supreme Court has created "an unconscionable delay" in processing death penalty appeals. Speaking for the Association's case against Bird and the high court Bradbury said;

> The court must get moving. We have death penalty appeals that are six years old. Oral arguments have been heard in about 19 cases without a decision from this court. The delay has been almost three years from argument to decision.
>
> At least 100 cases have no oral arguments scheduled at all or briefs filed by the attorneys.
>
> During this time, what are the victims' families to do? What are the witnesses to do? Evidence must be held ready if retrials are ordered, as the court has done in 30 out of 33 death penalty cases. The lives of these people are in suspended animation while the Supreme Court drags out the appeals process. We've gone from 360 days to about 1,400 days for a decision in these cases.

The police have gathered evidence. Prosecutors have presented cases. Juries have rendered verdicts. Judges have sentenced. The Supreme Court meanwhile sits on the cases.

In 31 death penalties the court had reviewed, the District Attorney's Association indicated that 28 of them had been reversed.

Governor Deukmejian Criticizes State Court

On several occasions, Governor Deukmejian spoke out publicly against the state Supreme Court for its actions in favoring criminals over victims, undermining democracy by taking initiative measures off the statewide ballot, and being harmful to business by having a "negative impact upon the private sector's job-producing capabilities."

The Speedy Criminal Justice Initiative

Faced with increasing public expense in holding accused offenders in jail until trials were held and protecting victim/witnesses from dangerous offenders out on bail, a group of concerned Los Angeles County personnel, law enforcement, lawyers, and judges acted to better the congested courts. After watching futile attempts to get reforms through the lawyer-dominated Legislature, the group realized the public initiative was the only practical vehicle to improve the system. They formed the Criminal Justice Coordination Committee.

The group found that meaningful court changes must come from outside—not from within the courts. Those close to the problem (lawyers, judges, and court personnel) had vested interests and little motivation to change the organization. The group believed needed reforms could save taxpayers millions of dollars a year, and not infringe upon the constitutional rights of litigants.

The Los Angeles County Criminal Justice Coordination Committee, under a legislative subcommittee chaired by Assistant County Sheriff Robert A. Edmonds, proposed seven major recommendations for inclusion in a 'Speedy Criminal Justice Initiative,' later called 'Better Public Safety Through Court Reform,' to be put before the California voters. After long deliberations over these and other proposals for the initiative; and after hearing input from many professionals in the judiciary system, the subcommittee concluded that the proposed initiative should add new provisions and amend existing provisions of the State Constitution. They found that the existing Penal Code also should have new provisions added, others amended and/or repealed. The proposed law would add a new section to Article I of the State Constitution that reads:

> The People of the State of California find and declare that the achievement of swift criminal justice consistent with recognized constitutional safeguards is necessary for the preservation and promotion of public and personal welfare. Delays in the criminal justice system have denied justice to victims and defendants, have imposed hardships upon and disrupted the lives of victims, defendants, witnesses, and jurors, have caused the court to become congested with untried cases, and have increased the cost of court proceedings, all to the detriment of society in general.
>
> It is of the utmost importance, therefore, that delays in the criminal justice system be reduced to the greatest extent possible without infringing upon constitutional rights. To accomplish this goal, major reforms must be made in the procedures used to process criminal actions.

The initiative was printed and circulated to collect voter's signatures in order to put it on the ballot. The initiative recommended changes concerning the following: felony probable cause hearings; post-indictment preliminary hearings; parole and probation revocation hearings prior to trial; judicial voir dire or jury questioning by judges not case lawyers; voir dire in capital cases; reduction of continuances; and non-unanimous criminal jury verdicts.

The sincere and well-meaning group who drafted the Speedy Criminal Justice Initiative knew from their own experience how wasteful the criminal court system had become. The group wanted the voters of the State of California to have an opportunity to vote on reforming the courts, and decide if they wanted a swifter-moving criminal justice system without denying anyone's constitutional rights.

Only a few weeks after the Initiative was announced, the group was attacked by the American Civil Liberties Union (ACLU) and law professors, and sued to prevent the initiative from being put on the ballot. Trial lawyers, public defenders, and guardians of criminal rights, who had a vested interest in keeping the inefficient court system the way it is, fought tenaciously against the initiative.

Running out of time, the initiative group, backed by Sheriff Sherman R. Block, then Los Angeles District Attorney Robert H. Philibosian, and former state Attorney General Evelle J. Younger, announced that their petition drive had fallen 30,000 to 80,000 signatures short of the 630,136 required to place the initiative before the voters. By using volunteers to collect signatures, the group did not have the man-power to collect the names after the court delays. Many political analysts believed that if the initiative had been put on the ballot it would have passed on a close vote. The group vowed to try again; their supporters hope they will.

Comprehensive Crime Control Act of 1984

Among the provisions of Public Law 98-473, Title II, that Congress enacted in 1984, was the establishment of the Office of Justice Programs. This office is charged with developing justice information systems programs and assisting states and local governments in collecting, analyzing or disseminating justice data and statistics. This type of cooperation is greatly needed. The authors found it very difficult to obtain meaningful data on justice costs at the different levels of government.

Under the Comprehensive Crime Control Act, federal courts can require that offenders pay restitution to victims and prevent them from making money from books or movies about their crimes. If an offender commits a federal crime and restitution is required, a federal court can order that the defendant forfeit all or any part of proceeds from a contract relating to the crime from a movie, book, newspaper, magazine, radio, television, or live entertainment of any kind. These proceeds shall be retained in a Crime Victims Fund to satisfy any restitution required for victims, to pay any fines, or to pay the cost of legal counsel of defendants up to 20% of the total proceeds.

The Act is a major step in providing restitution to federal victims and to prevent criminals from gaining financially later from their crimes. Although the Comprehensive Crime control Act pertains to federal crimes, it represents positive recognition by congress that the criminal justice system is in need of clarification and simplification. It shows that pressure from constituents can result in positive action by elected representatives.

Signs of Hope From U. S. Supreme Court

In what could be an important change in direction by the United States Supreme Court, Justice Sandra Day O'Connor wrote two opinions limiting prisoner opportunities to file petitions for writs of habeas corpus challenging their conviction in state courts. Justice O'Connor wrote: "Writs of habeas corpus frequently cost society the right to punish admitted offenders. Passage of time, erosion of memory and dispersion of witnesses may render retrial difficult, even impossible." She wrote also that liberal use of writs of habeas corpus "undermines the usual principles of finality of litigation" and "degrades the prominence of the trial itself."

The two separate Supreme Court cases heard were from Ohio (Engle vs. Isaac) and the District of Columbia (U.S. vs. Frady). In the Ohio case, the United States 6th Circuit Court of Appeals had granted new trials to two men convicted of homicide and another found guilty of assault. All three convictions had been upheld in the state courts, but the convicted men later filed writs of habeas corpus in federal courts.

The other case involved a man convicted of murder in 1963. The United States Court of Appeals in the District of Columbia had thrown out the conviction of Joseph C. Frady, a Washington, D.C., resident. Prosecutors described Frady as a "brutal contract killer." O'Connor referred to his crime as one of "unspeakable brutality." The high court's ruling means that a prisoner generally cannot appeal on grounds of trial error years after he was found guilty unless he can prove "actual and substantial disadvantage" to his case defense because of some legal error.

O'Connor stated in her opinion that "the federal government, no less than the states, has an interest in the finality of its criminal judgments." Concerning constitutional rights of convicted criminals, she states, "We have long recognized... that the Constitution guarantees criminal defendants only a fair trial and a competent attorney. It does not ensure that defense counsel will recognize and raise every conceivable constitutional claim."

Supreme Court Acts on Miranda Warning

Hope exists that the United States Supreme Court may be relaxing its strict interpretation of what a policeman must say in advising a suspect of his rights before questioning him. Before interrogating a suspect, the Supreme Court ruled a policeman need not read the precise words of the "Miranda warning" as long as it is clear to the suspect that he has a right to a lawyer at some point.

In June of 1981, on a 6 to 3 decision the Supreme Court reversed a California Appeals Court ruling that required a new trial be held for Randall J. Prysock, 19 years of age. With another youth, Prysock had been convicted of murdering Iris Erickson, 47, in 1978. Iris Erickson had been beaten on the head, strangled, and stabbed several times with an ice pick.

After being informed of his right to be represented by a lawyer, Prysock confessed to a police officer on a tape-recorded statement. He was convicted. The state Court of Appeals overturned the conviction and ordered a new trial. They ruled that the officer had not clearly outlined Prysock's rights to him and his parents. The court held that Prysock had been told he could have a lawyer appointed to represent him in court and that he could hire a lawyer before being questioned, but not that he could obtain a lawyer at no cost before questioning. The Supreme Court believed that the California court had been too strict in its interpretation of the Miranda ruling. They found that the lower court decision unnecessarily required policemen to issue a "virtual incantation" of the precise language contained in the Miranda ruling.

The Supreme court stated:

> It is clear that the police in this case fully conveyed to [Prysock] his rights as required by Miranda. He was told of his right to have a lawyer present prior to and during interrogation and his right to have a lawyer appointed at no cost if he could not afford one. The Court of Appeals erred in holding that the warnings were inadequate simply because of the order in which they [the words] were given.

The Deputy California Attorney General who was in charge of the Prysock case, Carla Caruso, believed that the ruling would result in more criminal convictions.

Supreme Court Restrains Judiciary Activism

The Supreme Court of the United States apparently agreed with former Attorney General William French Smith's viewpoint that the federal judiciary should restrain its activism in court. In a case in which the Americans United for Separation of Church and State sued the federal government for releasing federal property to a college, the court ruled that Americans United had no direct interest in the transfer of the property to the college.

The Supreme Court decision issued January 12, 1982, written by Justice William H. Rehnquist, reminded federal judges that they are not to be involved in correcting errors or violations of the U.S. Constitution if there is no specific controversy at stake in a case. Rehnquist stated, "The federal courts were simply not constituted as ombudsmen for the general welfare." The opinion means that federal justices are to keep to a strictly limited role in reviewing government policies.

The court's ruling means that Americans United had no legal standing to sue the taxpayers because they did not have a specific, tangible, or personal stake in the sale of the property as would a nearby property owner. As a result of the ruling, individuals or groups will be limited from challenging government actions in the federal courts without having a specific or identified interest. In the future federal courts may not rule on a case unless one or more of the parties in a case are threatened with some financial or identifiable form of harm. Rehnquist said:

> There is no place in our constitutional scheme for the philosophy that the business of the federal courts is correcting constitutional errors and that 'cases and controversies' are at best merely convenient vehicles for doing so and, at worst, nuisances that may be dispensed with when they become obstacles to that transcendental endeavor.

Continuing, Rehnquist said that federal courts are to rule "not in the rarified atmosphere of a debating society, but in a concrete, factual context conducive to a realistic appreciation of the consequences of judicial action." He said also that the Supreme Court should not be considered as "a national classroom on the meaning of rights."

This decision should have a far-reaching effect on the activism of both federal judges and indirectly on actions of state court judges. Voting with Rehnquist in the 5 to 4 decision were Justices Burger, O'Connor, Powell, and White. With Justice O'Connor on the bench, the tenor of decisions made by the Supreme Court changed.

Federal Judges Prevented From Ruling On State Officials

The high court followed up its restrictions on federal judges in January 1984 with a ruling that federal courts have no authority to order state officials to obey state laws. While the case concerned the 3rd Circuit Court of Appeals in Philadelphia requiring state officials to provide care to mentally retarded residents, the decision was expected to have a far-reaching impact. The action would restrict federal judges from questioning state officials about their policies on criminal justice, corrections, hospitals, and other matters.

Restrictions on Right to Counsel

The Supreme Court made several decisions that indicated they were changing direction from the Warren Court. In July of 1983, the court ruled that a lawyer appointed to handle an appeal for an indigent criminal defendant was not required to raise every legal issue requested by his client. This decision could prevent irresponsible defendant lawyers from delaying trials by making numerous and unnecessary motions and frivolous challenges.

Writing for the Court, Chief Justice Burger stated that a defendant had the final say on whether to plead guilty, take the witness stand, or appeal a conviction; but it was up to the lawyer to use his "professional judgement" in presenting cases in court.

Restrictions on Death Penalty Appeals

The Supreme Court's ruling in July of 1983 on the appeal of Thomas A. Barefoot changed the manner in which federal courts reviewed death penalty inmate appeals. Barefoot had been convicted of murdering a policeman. Before the ruling, judges permitted Death Row inmates a full round of appeals in federal courts. This meant that appeals were heard by a federal district judge, a federal appeals court, and the Supreme Court after an inmate had exhausted appeals within the state court system.

As a result of the high court's action, federal judges may use special, speeded-up procedures to process appeals and stays of execution will not always be granted to hear the appeals.

Death Penalty Obstacles Removed

In January of 1984, the Supreme Court removed an obstacle to the resumption of capital punishment in the states, especially in California. The court ruled that the Constitution did not prevent one person from being executed while others convicted of crimes equally or more heinous are allowed to live. In other words, a 'proportionality review' was not necessary in capital punishment cases. The case involved the suit of Robert Alton Harris who had killed two 16-year-old boys in San Diego.

The court's action reversed a decision by the United States 9th Circuit Court of Appeals in San Francisco that had blocked the use of the death penalty in California. The Supreme Court's decision meant that executions could not be held up any longer in the states on the issue of proportionality review. During the following year, executions by injection started for condemned murderers in Texas, but not in California.

Use of Evidence in Courts Expanded

In three decisions during 1984, the Supreme court modified the controversial exclusionary rule, and made it easier to introduce evidence previously held to be illegal. In June of 1984, the court ruled that improperly obtained evidence may be used in criminal trials if its eventual discovery by legal means was "inevitable."

In an appeal of twice convicted Robert Anthony Williams, who murdered a 10-year old Iowa girl, the court found that even though he confessed to police as to the location of the girl's body, it was "inevitable" that her body would be found. Chief Justice Burger wrote that "...Exclusion of physical evidence that would inevitably have been discovered adds nothing to either the integrity or fairness of a criminal trial."

The power of police to search for drugs and use the evidence in court was strengthened when the court ruled that warrants are unnecessary when a package of drugs has been opened (by accident) by a private citizen or a mail delivery service.

In a major decision that further changed the exclusionary rule in July of 1984, the court found on a 6 to 3 vote that evidence obtained under a defective search warrant may still be used against a criminal defendant if police reasonably believed they were acting legally. Referred to as a 'good faith' exception to the 70-year-old rule, Justice Byron R. White writing for the majority found that the cost of allowing a guilty person to go free exceeds any benefits the exclusionary rule offers in such cases. He wrote:

> Penalizing the officer for the magistrate's error, rather than his own, cannot logically contribute to the deterrence of Fourth Amendment violations (right to be secure against unreasonable searches).

Changes to the Miranda Warning Rule

The high court made changes to the controversial Miranda rule in 1984 when it found that police officers do not need to read Miranda warnings advising suspects of their rights when "public safety" was at stake.

Although the above changes indicate a trend toward needed reform, much more needs to be accomplished. The public should not relax and abandon justice improvements to the legal profession.

Conclusion

Newspapers are clamoring for reform. An editorial in *The Washington Times* stated:

> The U.S. criminal justice system isn't working well... Experts agree that the greatest deterrent to crime is the certainty of being caught and punished. The nearest thing to certainty in the American criminal justice system is that the crook will not be caught and won't be punished.

Barney Brantingham of The *Santa Barbara News-Press* said: "Because of complaints... there is a rising cry for court reform, such as speedier juror selection. But so far the thrust is in the other direction."

The Wall Street Journal, Los Angeles Times, Time, and numerous other newspapers and magazines carry articles and editorials calling for reform. As previously mentioned prominent citizens like the President of Harvard University, Derek Bok, and Warren Burger, Chief Justice of the United States Supreme Court, called for reforms in the justice system.

In spite of all its defects, the American Justice System is a monument to the protection of individual liberty. Nowhere in the world, or for that matter in the history of the world, is there a structure like our courts. The judiciary, with all its faults, strives to provide protection to the accused and give fair treatment to all in court.

But the system has serious flaws. The current cumbersome and time-consuming criminal court processes, accepted as a judiciary norm, must be brought under control. The public is restless for changes to be made in our muddled and chaotic system. The public expects legislatures to do something, but they won't while lawyers are in control. The police, prosecutors, public defenders, trial lawyers, judges, probation, and corrections personnel are interrelated, yet uncoordinated and unsupervised by any one person or agency. No one is in charge. Actually, no justice 'system' really functions. A group of fiefdoms exist, accountable to a variety of elected and appointed officials, committees, and boards.

Improvements to the court process must be made; but only after careful consideration of their economic impact on related agencies and the public. A comprehensive approach must be taken or more problems may be generated. It will take time to bring about changes in the attitudes of litigants, public interest groups, legislators, prosecutors, trial lawyers, public defenders, trial and appellate judges because of their self interests. Many in the legal profession are working to make improvements, but they are in the minority. Only by the public's putting pressure on legislators and judicial appointing authorities will changes be made in the appointment of judges. The public must be alert, observant, active, and willing to speak out to obtain more objective, fair-minded trial, appellate, and supreme court justices. The courts are too important to be left solely to the lawyers.

A responsible and fair justice system is a fundamental cornerstone of the American way of life. To work well, the delicate and intangible process called a democracy, requires that all operating parts act in a responsible manner. The legislative, judicial, and executive branches of government must act responsibly or the democratic process breaks down. Loopholes do exist in our democracy, especially in our legal system. If too many litigants, legislators, lawyers, and judges abuse the courts, forget the intent of laws, and look for ways to take advantage of the system, or try to change the social structure of America to meet their goals, our democratic machinery can be damaged severely.

Too many public service lawyers acting selfishly for their defendant or 'causes' can cause great disharmony and discord, and de-

237

stroy the very freedom that gives activists the freedom to take advantage of the justice system. Unless our system is improved, citizens will attempt to take the law into their own hands. Responsible citizens will become lawless, and make drastic changes that may become counterproductive later.

Legislators, lawyers, judges, and correctional personnel may not like the public's ideas for change, but they are coming. Law schools, bar associations, and the judiciary should take the initiative (as some are doing), acknowledge past mistakes, and cooperate with justice consumers, in seeking a better court system. The courts can and will be improved!

CHAPTER FOOTNOTES

Chapter Two

1. *Wall Street Journal,* March 10, 1982.
2. "Administration of Civil Justice Position Paper," p. 60. Defense Research Institute, Milwaukee, Wisconsin, Vol. 1981, No. 1. Copyright 1981 by the Defense Research Institute, Inc. Reprinted with permission. All rights reserved.
3. United Press International, June 25, 1981.
4. Macklin Fleming, *The Price of Perfect Justice.* New York: Basic Books, Inc., 1974., p. 22.
5. Ibid., p. 23.
6. Ibid. p. 26.
7. George C. Doub, "The Case Against Modern Federal Habeas Corpus in a Court," *American Bar Association Journal* (1971, 57:323, p. 326.)
8. Judge Lumbard's report, (1970) appears in 25 Record, Assn. of Bar of New York, 516.
9. Harvey Krieger, "Junk Lawsuits," *Silver Circle,* 1984.
10. *Santa Barbara News-Press,* December 30, 1984.
11. J. S. Kakalik and R. L. Ross, *Costs of the Civil Justice System,* Institute for Civil Justice, The Rand Corporation, 1983.
12. "Malpractice Suits—a New Epidemic Faced by Doctors," *Los Angeles Times,* April 1, 1985.
13. Ibid.
14. "Administration of Civil Defense Paper," p. 70. Defense Research Institute, Milwaukee, Wisconsin, Vol. 1981, No. 1. Copyright 1981 by the Defense Research Institute, Inc. Reprinted with permission. All Rights Reserved.
15. Idem.
16. James S. Kakalik, Abby Eisenshtat Robyn, "Costs of the Civil Justice System; Court Expenditures for Processing Tort Cases," Institute for Civil Justice, Rand Corporation. p. 69. 1982.
17. Ibid, pp. 52-53.

Chapter Three

1. *Los Angeles Times,* June 1981.
2. Ventura *Star-Free Press,* February 21, 1981.
3. Ibid.

4. Manning Bayliss, "Hyperlexis: Our National Disease," 71Nw L. Rev. 67, 777 (1977).

5. David Adamany, "The Implementation of Court Improvements," *State Courts: A Blueprint for the Future,* 1978, Conference Monograph, National Center for State Courts.

6. Richard Neely, *Why Courts Don't Work,* NcGraw-Hill Book Co., 1983.

Chapter Four

1. Justice Byron R. White, American Bar Convention, August 1981.

2. Ibid.

3. Richard Neely, *Why Courts Don't Work,* New York: McGraw-Hill Book Co., 1982.

4. *Wall Street Journal,* November 27, 1973.

5. *New York Times,* August 7, 1973.

6. Derek C. Bok, "A Flawed System," *Harvard Magazine,* May-June 1983, p. 40.

7. Ibid., p. 40.

8. Delmar Karlen, *Judicial Administration—the American Experience,* Dobbs Ferry, New York: Oceana (1970), pp 76-77.

9. Macklin Fleming, *The Price of Perfect Justice,* New York: Basic books, Inc., 1974.

10. "Administration of Civil Justice," Position Paper, The Defense Research Institute Vol. 1981, No. 1. Copyright 1981 by the Defense Research Institute, Inc. Reprinted with permission. All rights reserved.

11. David H. Berg, "The FBI's Threat to Freedom," *Los Angeles Times,* February 27, 1981.

12. Idem.

13. "Suspensions Asked in Failed FBI 'Scam,'" United Press International, August 22, 1981.

14. "Won't End 'Stings', Justice Department Says, " *Los Angeles Times,* " August 18, 1984.

15. "Picking Targets: Antitrust Enforcement Will Be More Selective, Two Big Cases Indicate," *The Wall Street Journal,* January 11, 1982.

16. Idem.

17. "Wake of Disaster," *The Wall Street Journal,* " July 3, 1984.

18. Idem.

19. "Making Friends: Legal Profession Tops All Others in Financing Candidates for Congress," *The Wall Street Journal,* August 18, 1983.

20. *Cleveland State University Law Review,* January 1982.

21. Ibid.

22. Ibid.

23. Phyliss J. Hall, Letter to Editor, Ventura *Star-Free Press,* February 1, 1985.

24. Dereck C. Bok, "A Flawed System," *Harvard Magazine,* May-June 1983.

25. "Lawyer Disputes Chief Federal Judge's Sanity," *Los Angeles Times,* May 16, 1984.

Chapter Five

1. *The Wall Street Journal.*

2. Peter H. Metzger, Ph.D. and Richard A. Westfall, "Government Activits: How They Rip Off the Poor," Public service Co. of Colorado, Denver, Colorado, April 1, 1981.

3. Ibid., p. 25.

4. Idem.

5. "Lawyers for the Poor in Transition: Involvement, Reform and the Turnover Problem in the Legal Services Program," by Jack Katz, *Law and Society*, Winter 1978, p. 276.

6. Hearings before a Subcommittee of the Committee on Appropriations, U.S. House of Representatives, on 1980 appropriations for the Legal Services Corporation, March 27, 1980, p. 477.

7. Ibid., p. 478.

8. "Review of Legal Services Corporation's Activities Concerning Program Evaluation and Expansion," a report to the President of the Legal Services Corporation by the U.S. General Accounting Office, August 28, pp. 14-16.

9. West Texas Legal Services Community education Handbook (80-454-01) distributed by Taining Resource Center, Office of Program Support, Legal Services Corporation, 733 Fifteenth Street, N.W., Washington, D.C.

10. Legal Services Corporation Act. P.L. 93-355, 42 U.S.C., section 2996e(d) (4).

11. Op. Cit., ref. #8.

12. "If Agency Goes, the Need For Legal Services Remains," by James J. Kilpatrick, Universal Press, appearing in *The Sunday Boulder Camera*, March 22, 1981.

13. Metzger and Wesfall, "Government Activists,: How They Rip Off The Poor," Public Service Company of Colorado, Denver, Colorado, April 1, 1981.

14. Ibid., p. 2.

15. "A Sweetheart of a Lawsuit?," *The Wall Street Journal*, August 20, 1980.

16. "Memorandum Opinion," Elsie Simer, et, al. v. Graciela Olivarez et. al., in the U.S. District Court for the Northern District of Illinois, Eastern Division, by Judge John F. Grady, Civil Action No. 79.C3960, October 29, 1980.

17. Peter H. Metzger, Op. Cit., p. 13.

18. "A sweetheart of a Lawsuit?," *The Wall Journal*, August 20, 1980.

19. "Complaint and Request for Action Re: *Simer vs. Olivarez*, addressed to Richard Rios, Director, Community Services Administration, brought by the Capital Legal Foundation on behalf of Senators Paul Laxalt, Orrin G. Hatch, and Edward Zorinsky, September 29, 1980.

20. Op. Cit., "Government Activists:," p. 15.

21. "Fleecing the poor of $18 million," by Donald Lambro (United Feature Syndicate), Rocky Mountain News, October 10, 1980.

22. "Seventh Circuit to hear arguments in 'sweetheart case' this month," by Margaret Roberts, *Chicago Lawyer*, January 1981, p. 5.

23. Op. Cit., Simer.

24. Ibid.

Chapter Six

1. "Attorney Who Won Case Protests Court's Decision," *Los Angeles Times*, June 5, 1981.

2. "Lawyer Verdict," *Time* Magazine, June 22, 1981.

3. "Lawyer Faces Probe in Criticism of Court," *Los Angeles Times*, December 17, 1981.

4. Frank G. Carrington, *The Victims*, New Rochelle, NY: Arlington House Publishers, 1975, p. 101.

5. Miranda v. Arizona, 384 U.S. 437 (1966), p. 444.

6. Ibid., pp. 444-45.

7. 384 U.S. 539-40.

8. Excerpts from "Are Judges Abusing Our Rights?," By Rep. John Ashbrook, *Readers*

Digest, August 1981, p. 78. Reprinted with permission.

9. Ibid.

10. "Broad Impact Foreseen in Death Penalty Limitation," *Los Angeles Times,* December 14, 1983.

11. Macklin Fleming, *The Price of Perfect Justice,* New York: Basic Books, Inc., 1974, p 149.

12. "Biographies of the Lords of Appeal in Ordinary," in *Who's Who, 1971-1972,* (123rd ed.), St. Martin's Press, 1971.

13. *Los Angeles Times,* June 16, 1981.

14. Ibid.

15. Op. Cit., *Los Angeles Times* June 16, 1981.

16. "Governor Fields complaints in N.Y.: Business Leaders Take Aim at California's Legal Barriers," *Los Angeles Times,* 1984.

17. "Deukmejian Assails State Supreme Court," *Los Angeles Times,"* December 5, 1984.

18. Op. Cit., *Reader's Digest.*

19. Op. Cit., Macklin Fleming, p. 155.

20. Idem.

21. Charles Evans Hughes, *Addresses* (2d ed. 1916), New York: G. P. Putnam's Sons, p. 185.

22. Baldwin v. Missouri (1930), 281 U.S. 586, p. 595, dissenting opinion.

23. Op. cit., *Reader's Digest,* p. 80.

24. *The American Legion* magazine, January 1985.

25. William H. Rehnquist, Dissenting Opinion in Colman v. Balkcom (80-5980).

26. "Judge Censured for Misconduct Heads Judicial Unit," *Washington Post,* October 29, 1981.

27. "Reagan Judges Transforming Federal Bench," *Los Angeles Times,* February 24, 1985.

Chapter Seven

1. "We, The Jury Find the ...," *Time,* September 28, 1981.

2. "Report on the Judiciary," by Chief Justice Warren E. Burger, December 1984.

3. Ibid.

4. "Jury System Constitutes Waste of Citizen's Time," Letter to the Editor, by Sally Grodsky, *Los Angeles Times,* June 13, 1981.

5. "Justice Can be Served Despite Dissenting Votes," *Los Angeles Times,* 1981.

6. Ibid.

Chapter Eight

1. "Chaos In The Criminal Courts," By Joseph McNamara, *California Lawyer,* September 1981.

2. Macklin Fleming, *The Price of Perfect Justice,* New York: Basic Books, Inc., 1974, pp 151-152.

3. Ibid., pp. 152-153.

4. Ibid., p. 152.

5. Ibid., p. 153.

6. *Star-Free Press, June 7, 1981.*

7. *Ibid.*

8. *Automobile Injuries and Their compensation In The United States,* Insurance Industry

Studies by the All-Industry Research Advisory Committee, Volume I. March 1979, pp. 13-18.

9. "Belli: The 'King of Torts' on Law, Life," *Los Angeles Times,* December 18, 1981.

10. "More Firms Turn to Private Courts To Avoid Expensive Legal Fights," *The Wall Street Journal,* January 4, 1984.

11. "Chief Justice Calls for Out-of-Court Settlements," *The Sunday Star-Bulletin & Advertiser,* Honolulu, April 1, 1984.

12. Ibid.

13. "Administration of Civil Defense Position Paper," Defense Research Institute, Milwaukee, Wisconsin, Vol. 1981, No. 1, p. 25. Copyright 1981 by the Defense Research Institute, Inc. Reprinted with permission. All rights reserved.

14. "Soaring Costs of Civil Suits: The Lawyers' Answer," *U.S. News & World Report,* August 24, 1981.

15. Ibid., p. 52.

16. Idem.

17. "Judge Uses Computer to Speed Work, Cut Time," *United Press International,* November 8, 1984.

18. "Judge Putting His Fascination With Computers to Use," *Los Angeles Times,* 1984.

19. Idem.

20. "Civil Court Changes Urged by Rehnquist," *Los Angeles Times,* September 16, 1984.

21. Idem.

Chapter Nine

1. Speech by Chief Justice Warren Burger at University of Nebraska-Lincoln, December 16, 1981.

2. "Life Terms: Society Really Doesn't Mean It," *Los Angeles Times,* March 8, 1982.

3. "Survey: Serious Criminal Serves Smallest Part of Sentence," *Associated Press,* June 27, 1984.

4. "Prison Sentences Vary Extensively From State to State," *United Press International,* February 17, 1981.

5. *Time,* June 30. 1976.

6. *Los Angeles Times,* April 3, 1981.

7. *Los Angeles Herald-Examiner,* 1981.

8. "Social Security Pays $21,500 to Killer," *Los Angeles Times,* January 9, 1982.

9. "Restitution: Maybe They Have Something," *Los Angeles Times,* August 14, 1981.

10. Idem.

11. Idem.

12. Idem.

13. Idem.

14. Kathleen D. Smith, "Implementing Restitution Within a Penal Setting: The Case for the Self-determinate Sentence," Joe Hudson and Burt Galaway, *Restitution in Criminal Justice,* Lexington, Massachusetts, 1977, p. 134. Lexington Books. Quoted by permission of Social Development Associates, 155 Windson Court, New Brighton, MN 55122.

15. Ibid., pp. 134-135.

16. Ibid., p 135.

17. Idem.

18. Ibid., pp. 135-136.

19. Ibid., p. 136.
20. Idem.
21. Ibid., p. 139.
22. Idem.
23. Idem.
24. "Preliminary Analysis of Victim Loss Recovery—Analysis of MIS Data," Peter R Schneider, Ph.D., Ann L. Schneider, Ph.D. and William R. Griffith., Institute o Policy Analysis, May 1981.
25. "Victims Profit by Meeting Criminals," *News Chronicle,* Thousand Oaks, California June 20, 1979.

Chapter Ten

1. "Donations Help Defray Cost of Trial," *USA TODAY,* May 14, 1984.
2. "California Justice: Trouble in Paradise," *California Chamber of Commerce Alert,* Au gust 24, 1984.
3. "Woman in Affair With Psychiatrist Wins $4.6 Million," *Los Angeles Times,* Decem ber 4, 1981.

Chapter Eleven

1. Stephen Schafer, *The Victim and His Criminal;* Stephen Schafer, *Restitution to Victim. of Crime,* (Chicago: Quadranle Books, 1960). Joe Hudson and Burt Galaway, *Restitu tion in Criminal Justice,* 1977, Lexington Books. Quoted by permission of Social De velopment Associates, 155 Windsor Court, New Brighton, MN 55122.
2. Schafer, *The Victim and His Criminal,* pp. 11-12.
3. Schafer, *Restitution to Victims of Crime.*
4. Stephen Schafer, *Compensation and Restitution to Victims of Crime,* p. 6. Montclair: Pat terson Smith, 1970.
5. Joe Hudson and Burt Gallaway, *Considering the Victim,* p, xix; *Compensation and Resti tution to Victims of Crime,* p. 7. Comment, "Compensation to Victims," pp. 78-79 Quoted by permission of Social Development Associates, 155 Windsor Court, New Brigton, MN 55122.
6. Schafer, *The Victim and His Criminal,* p. 17.
7. Ibid. p. 18. Comment, "Compensation to Victims," p. 78.
8. Bruce Jacob, "The Concept of Restitution: An Historical Overview." Joe Hudson Bert Galaway, *Restitution in Criminal Justice,* Lexington Books, 1977. p. 51. Quotec by permission of Social Development Associates, 155 Windsor Court, New Bright on, MN 55122.
9. Ibid., p. 51.
10. Ibid., p. 47.

Chapter Twelve

1. *Los Angeles Times,* Nov. 27, 1981.
2. Idem.
3. "Dukakis Pushes Truth-in-Sentencing Plan," *Evening Gazette,* Worcester, Massachu setts, Jan. 26, 1985.
4. "Rape Penalties Getting Longer," *Los Angeles Times,* Oct. 12, 1981.
5. "Crime: We Are Afraid—Too Afraid," *Los Angeles Times,* Oct. 13,1981.

INDEX

INDEX

ORDER FORM

Pathfinder Publishing
458 Dorothy Ave.
Ventura, CA 93003
Telephone (805) 642-9278

Please send me the following books from Pathfinder Publishing by
Eugene Wheeler and Robert Kallman:

_____copies of Stop Justice Abuse @ $10.95 each. $_____

Coastal Crude: In a Sea of Conflict

_____copies of hardbound @ $12.95 each. $_____
_____copies of softbound @ $7.95 each. $_____
_____copies of Shipwrecks, Smugglers, and
        Maritime Mysteries @ $7.95 $_____

        Shipping & Handling $_____
        Californians: Please add 6% tax. $_____
                Grand Total $_____

I understand that I may return the book for a full refund if not
satisfied.

Name: _____

Company: _____

Address: _____

_____ Zip: _____

* Shipping: $1.50 for the first book and 25¢ for each additional
book.

ABOUT THE AUTHORS

EUGENE D. WHEELER: As a city planner, consultant, and expert witness, he is familiar with the legal process in the United States, Europe, and the Caribbean. He has drafted regulations and legislation on the east and west coast of the United States and in the Caribbean, while with the U.S. State Department. He has studied the planning legal process in Scandinavia and Great Britain while doing graduate work at the University of Stockholm and as a town planner for the Greater London Council. He has testified on urban planning matters in Maryland and California courts. While doing research on the civil court process for his first book, *The Taking*, he became interested in the problems of the criminal justice system. To gain knowledge of the system, he and co-author Kallman interviewed prosecutors, public defenders, lawyers, judges, law professors, court personnel, police, and correctional officials.

He holds a Master of City Planning degree from Harvard University, Bachelor of Science and Master of Arts degrees from the University of Southern California, and a diploma for graduate work at the University of Stockholm. He has been an instructor at Johns Hopkins University and the University of California at Santa Barbara.

ROBERT E. KALLMAN: As a Santa Barbara County Supervisor he has been involved with the funding, staffing, and housing of the courts and has an indepth knowledge of the problems and costs of the justice system. He has been on the California Regional Criminal Board, the California Coastal Commission, the County Grand Jury Justice Committee, the City Police Commission, and the County Supervisors Criminal Justice Cost Study Panel. His experiences on national, state, and local boards has made him aware of ill-conceived laws and legal procedures and their costly impact on the public.

Kallman has experienced the frustrations and complexities of civil court proceedings. A retired Navy captain, he graduated from the Military Justice Course and has served on General Courts Marial Boards. He holds a Bachelor of Arts Degree from the University of California.

Wheeler and Kallman co-authored *Coastal Crude: In a Sea of Conflict, Shipwrecks, Smugglers, and Maritime Mysteries,* and *Stop Justice Abuse.*